Sir Geoffrey Cox was born in Palmerston North in 1910. He attended Southland Boys High School and the University of Otago, graduating with an MA in History in 1931. Awarded a Rhodes Scholarship, he studied at Oriel College, Oxford, from 1932-35.

Securing a foothold in Fleet Street, he came through rapidly to success as a foreign correspondent in Europe for British newspapers, covering many of the main events leading to World War II. In 1940, he enlisted with the New Zealand Army and served with 2 NZ Division in Greece, Crete, North Africa and Italy, becoming Chief Intelligence Officer to General Freyberg. He also served for a period as first secretary of the New Zealand Legation in Washington.

After the war Geoffrey Cox returned to newspaper journalism in Britain. In 1956 he moved to television, becoming editor of the news service of the newly established commercial channel, Independent Television News (ITN). Under his editorship ITN pioneered the development of this new journalistic medium. In 1967 he founded *News at Ten*, the first half-hour news on British television. He was knighted in 1966 for services to journalism and later held a number of other top posts in television and radio. Since his retirement in 1976 he has lived in Gloucestershire.

By the same author

Defence of Madrid (1937)

The Red Army Moves (1941)

The Road to Trieste (1947)

The Race for Trieste (1977)

See it Happen – The Making of ITN (1983)

A Tale of Two Battles (1987)

Countdown to War (1988)

Pioneering Television News (1995)

Eyewitness

A Memoir of Europe in the 1930s

Geoffrey Cox

University of Otago Press

Published by the University of Otago Press
PO Box 56/56 Union Street, Dunedin, New Zealand
Fax: 64 3 479 8385
Email: university.press@stonebow.otago.ac.nz

First published 1999
ISBN 1 877133 70 1

Printed by GP Print Ltd, Wellington

Cover illustration features images of events witnessed by the author (pictured centre, as a Rhodes Scholar, 1932). Top left: German workers at a Nazi labour camp, (*Hamberg Illustriete*, September 1934); bottom right: Sir Oswald Mosley at a British facist rally, 1936 (Photobank NZ/Hulton Getty). Bottom left: Jarrow hunger marchers, 28 October 1936 (Photobank NZ/Hulton Getty).

Contents

PART I

1	*A Decisive Afternoon*	*11*
2	*Background*	*15*
3	*Outward Bound*	*25*
4	*Home*	*33*
5	*A Look at Russia*	*41*
6	*Moscow*	*49*
7	*Down the Volga*	*55*
8	*Berlin*	*65*
9	*Last Summer of Weimar*	*71*
10	*Two Pilgrimages*	*73*
11	*Summerhill*	*77*

PART II

12	*Oxford*	*87*
13	*Field Work*	*95*
14	*Viennese Summer*	*99*
15	*Mosley in Action*	*109*
16	*Oxford Revisited*	*117*
17	*Encounter with Storm Troops*	*127*
18	*A Nazi Labour Camp*	*135*
19	*Hitler at Nuremberg*	*139*

PART III

20	*Towards Journalism*	*147*
21	*Into Fleet Street*	*155*
22	*Learning on the Job*	*161*
23	*Two New Zealanders*	*171*

24	*An Editor is Sacked*	*177*
25	*The* News Chronicle	*181*
26	*Death of a King*	*185*
27	*Civil War in Spain*	*193*
28	*An Overseas Posting*	*197*
29	*War Correspondent*	*203*
30	*A City at Bay*	*211*
31	*The International Brigade*	*217*
32	*Grandstand View of War*	*221*

PART IV

33	*Crossing the Street*	*231*
34	*Posting to Vienna*	*241*
35	*Vienna Revisited*	*245*
36	*Foreign Correspondent*	*249*
37	*Balkan Newsbeat*	*255*
38	*Paris*	*263*
39	*Anschluss*	*267*

Postscript *277*
Index *284*

Acknowledgements

My sources include letters I wrote regularly to my parents, and intermittent diary notes. Except during my visit to Russia in 1932, I did not keep a regular diary. But from time to time I wrote an account of an incident or event which particularly interested me. I have drawn also on articles I contributed to New Zealand papers at the time.

After I became a professional journalist, my reports in the *News Chronicle* and the *Daily Express* have been available as a record.

Two men, whose friendship I greatly value, gave me particular help with this book. Bryce Harland, during his time as High Commissioner in London – and what a good High Commissioner he was – read the manuscript, and encouraged me to continue to seek its publication. Hugh Templeton, my fellow Southlander, gave me warm support in this venture, as he has done in other matters in recent years. To both I express my gratitude. I do so also to an even older friend, Sir John White, wartime ADC to General Freyberg, for permission to use his photograph of the General.

James McNeish, whose interest in this period of the nineteen thirties has been a further stimulus, gave me valuable advice, particularly about a title. Jackie Gumpert has once again shown her skill and patience in turning my typescript into word-processed copy. I offer her my warm thanks.

This is the first book I have published in New Zealand. I am proud that it has been published by the Press of the University of which I have the privilege of being a graduate. The book has gained much from the skills of Wendy Harrex and her team. It has been a pleasure to work with them.

Geoffrey Cox
March 1999

PART I

Setting Forth
1931–32

CHAPTER ONE

A Decisive Afternoon

The Governor-General was concerned about pigs. 'You say these are a Berkshire-Tamworth cross, and yet they are doing well simply on skim milk and the household left-overs?' He sounded disbelieving. 'They've all the skim they can drink,' I countered. 'We were milking sixteen cows, and there was no other use for the skim.'

The other six members of the Rhodes Scholarship selection committee gathered round the conference table in the Governor-General's study, its windows shaded against the bright New Zealand November sunshine, looked impatient. It was known that the Governor-General, Viscount Bledisloe, had been a keen pig breeder on his own farms in England, and was frequently photographed in his grey, long-tailed morning coat leaning over pig pens at New Zealand agricultural shows. But the relevance of this to my application for a Rhodes Scholarship must have seemed irritatingly tenuous. Yet I guessed what lay behind Lord Bledisloe's questioning. I had put into my application the fact that ever since I was fifteen I had worked during my school summer holidays, and then in my much longer university vacations, on sheep stations – in particular on a farm in the Waikato. He was probing as to whether I had held down real jobs or was merely dressing up farm holidays to look like a true working experience of the land – that land which was the reality and bedrock of New Zealand life.

I was able to answer with confidence. The seventeen-hundred-acre Waikato farm, still in the process of being broken in to grass from the scrub and fern of the pumice lands, was worked only by two men and a boy – a tiny staff in those pre-tractor days when all farm work depended upon living horse-power. They needed the labour I brought from each December to March, and I learnt in the process all the main summer farming skills, including the highly specialised task of shearing, for we sheared the forty or fifty stragglers which had escaped the main shearing muster.

My replies must have satisfied the Governor-General, because after an agonising wait – the selection had clearly been a matter of argument – his secretary told the eight of us waiting in the adjoining billiard room that the awards had gone to James Bertram of Auckland and Geoffrey Cox of Otago. One reason for the delay became apparent. Another candidate was called back into the committee room. This was John Mulgan, who within eight years was to win fame as the author of *Man Alone*, one of the first truly New Zealand novels. His academic, athletic and personal qualities seemed exactly what Cecil Rhodes had in mind, and I had regarded him as having one of the two scholarships in his pocket. But he was only nineteen, young enough to come forward again for at least two further years. The committee had, in passing him over this year, taken the unusual step of telling him that they were impressed by his qualifications and looked forward to seeing him in a year's time. This was a virtual guarantee of a scholarship in the next round. When Auckland University failed to renominate him in 1932, the committee were so incensed that they refused to appoint any of the alternative candidates, and the scholarships remained unawarded that year.

If my farming experience played a part in winning me in 1931 this chance which was so much to shape my life, it was fitting that it did so. For my summers at Ongaroto, five miles down the Waikato from Atiamuri in the heart of New Zealand's North Island, were a major formative influence in my life – certainly the main influence on my teens. I learnt there the satisfactions of hard physical work – and the monotony as well as searing fatigue which can be part of it. I tasted, too, the satisfaction of creativity, as year by year we turned these acres of virgin scrub, fern and bush into paddocks of ryegrass, cocksfoot and clover, or of turnips or oats. I had felt this most deeply when we worked on a rounded slope facing the homestead. It was covered with thick, tough manuka scrub which we hacked our way through with slashers and axes. The cut scrub was burnt, and then reburnt after, with our faces and arms blackened in the process, we had gathered into piles those branches and stumps which had escaped the first fire. It was a wet, windy summer, and the rain and wind stung my face as I drove the two horses pulling the harrows to break up the newly ploughed ground. The slope was too steep to sow with a drill, so we broadcast the fertiliser and grass seed by hand from bags of sacking which hung from our necks, bags so heavy that at the start of a row we could barely walk.

When I left at the end of the summer to return to the university, the hillside was still brown and ragged under this cultivation. But a year later, as the boss drove me up the valley from the railway siding in his T-model Ford, I noticed a change. The hillside now swelled a vivid green under its new grass, with only an occasional white pumice scar bearing witness to the way the wind had tossed around our thrown seed. A sense of fulfilment swept through me, though I was careful to disguise it with a non-committal 'the grass seems to be coming away on the Horse Paddock slope', and the boss hid his own pleasure under an equally non-committal grunt of approval.

This experience was gained amidst scenes of constant beauty. There may have been few reproductions then of great paintings to hang on our walls, and still fewer originals to look at in the Dominion's scanty art galleries, but we worked surrounded by scenes a Monet or Cézanne would have exulted in. The morning sunlight picked out the grey rocky outcrop on the great bluff which, like the prow of a battleship, guarded the western end of the valley; the midday haze lay like silk on the soft, grey-green native bush, so much truer to the New Zealand landscape than the dark, jagged alien shape of the later pervasive pine trees; at sunset the swift, opaque greenstone-coloured river was turned into a sheet of crimson. In every mood this remote valley – for there was no through road, and we were twenty miles from the nearest township – was a living personality, company enough in itself when one was working alone all day in a distant paddock. As life unfolded, the experience of those farming summers was to influence and buttress my thinking more deeply than any theories or faiths.

Ongaroto also brought home to me the reality of that event which was to affect deeply the lives and attitudes of my generation – the slump. When wool prices fell from over twenty pence per pound to five pence, when butterfat came down by two-thirds, these were not just statistics in the papers. They were the life blood of Ongaroto and thousands of other farms draining away. They were the harsh facts reflected in the set, bitter faces of men working on municipal relief schemes, chipping away at weeds along park roadways in Dunedin, their eyes following me as I carried my books down to the economics lectures which sought to explain this. In January 1933 Ongaroto had to be sold because it could not withstand the combined pressure of low prices and of bush sickness, that mysterious ailment which afflicted stock in the pumice lands, and for which a cure was not found until late in the thirties. I was at Oxford when I learnt of the sale and I felt as if a staunch, close friend had died. It was a shock that reinforced powerfully in me the instinct which stirs in each generation to find a better way of organising things than their elders have done.

I had paid a final visit to Ongaroto in January 1932. For the last time I forked hay onto a stack in the Bluff Paddock, with the broad, swift blue-green river sweeping through the manuka below. For the last time I galloped through the fern, chasing maverick steers that had broken through the boundary fence at the back of the bush. I was waiting for the train at the siding when the local Maori chief, Watene, walked across from the pa, with its half-dozen unpainted, weatherboard houses, and its meeting house fronted by red carved lintels, to the railway siding. In crumpled tweed trousers and collarless shirt, he was nevertheless a figure of remarkable dignity, with a tui feather as a badge of authority in the band of his old felt hat. Grave and erect, he spoke a few sentences in Maori, shook my hand, and stood alongside the boss on the small wooden platform until the train, with its trucks of fresh sawn timber and its one passenger carriage, made its slow way up from the wide valley floor. It carried me on the first stage of a journey which – though I had no inkling of this at the time – was to give me a first-hand view of many of the main events of the turbulent thirties.

CHAPTER TWO

Background

My parents were both first generation New Zealanders, representative of the two main streams of organised colonisation of New Zealand's South Island: the very English and Anglican settlement of Canterbury, and the very Scottish and Presbyterian one of Otago. My grandfather on my father's side, Charles Percy Cox, had emigrated to Canterbury in 1853 when he was only eighteen. He came of a military family, whose sons had for some generations gone out from their home – a small, beautiful Georgian country house in the Oxfordshire village of Sandford St Martin – to hold commissions in the British or the East India Company armies. Charles's father had fought at the age of nineteen as a cornet in the 1st Life Guards at the battle of Waterloo, and his portrait in scarlet tunic, wearing the Waterloo medal and with a high braid collar and heavy epaulettes hung on the wall of my grandfather's home in Christchurch. Cornet Samuel Fortnum Cox had married Emily Sheffield. Her great-grandfather had been the only, though illegitimate, son of the Duke of Buckingham who, as the Marquess of Normanby, had been a favourite courtier of Queen Anne. Though he could not inherit the dukedom, he did inherit the family property, which included Buckingham House in London. This he sold to George III, who enlarged it into the present palace. Emily Sheffield had a reputation as a beauty, and was portrayed as the bride in Sir David Wilkie's painting *The Penny Wedding* which hangs in Buckingham Palace. Early in the 1960s I made an appointment to see it, but at the last moment the plans were cancelled. No doubt the Surveyor of the Queen's Pictures, Sir Anthony Blunt, soon to be exposed as a Soviet spy, had other things on his mind at the time.

My grandfather took rapidly to farming on the wide, tussock-covered plains and hillsides of Canterbury, and was soon an expert stockman. He drove herds of cattle southwards to feed the goldminers who had rushed to the gullies of Central Otago, and became skilled at breaking in and training young horses. Seven years after his arrival in New Zealand he married Sarah Harper, a daughter of the first Bishop of the Canterbury settlement. She is portrayed – a grave, round-faced young girl clasping her mother's sleeve – in an alabaster panel on the side of the pulpit in Christchurch Cathedral, depicting the arrival of the Bishop.

My grandfather had capital enough to secure in time the lease of a stretch of hill country at Mount Somers, in the foothills of the Southern Alps. The owner of a neighbouring run was Samuel Butler, and the wide, gravel-strewn river valleys of the area, stretching back towards abrupt alpine mountainsides, form the setting for the opening chapter of Butler's *Erewhon*. After fifteen years at Mount Somers my grandfather was caught, as were so many early pioneers, by a shortage of cash during one of the depressions of the time – this was before refrigeration had given New Zealand a stable English market for its mutton and lamb. He had to sell out and move to Christchurch, where he made a precarious living in a variety of occupations, ranging from land valuing to invigilating at university examinations.

My father had been born at Mount Somers, and was given the name of Sandford as a link with Sandford Park in Oxfordshire then – but only for a few more years – the family home. The second son in a family of six boys and four girls, he had to abandon early his hopes of becoming a farmer, and took on a job in a bank in order to bring some ready cash into the family coffers. He remained in the Bank of New South Wales for the rest of his life, becoming ultimately manager of one of their main branches, in Dunedin. Of good judgement, quiet, firm and courteous, he lacked the ruthlessness and ambition necessary for supreme success in business. *Processe Quam Conspici* – which might be translated as 'Be judged by your work, rather than by your acclaim' – had been the motto on the Cox family arms, and it fitted well my father's character.

If my father was very English in origin, my mother, Mary, was fiercely Scottish, a MacGregor claiming (even if the proof was somewhat tenuous) descent from Rob Roy. On the wall of her bedroom hung a picture of the MacGregor tartan and the clan badge of an uprooted pine tree crossed by a claymore. Certainly she held within her slight, eager person the vitality, forthrightness and strength of will which had made the troublesome MacGregors a proscribed clan for over two centuries. Her father was the son of a stonemason in Aberfeldy, the Perthshire town where General Wade's fine bridge spans the River Tay. Duncan MacGregor had made his way along the path which was to bring so many Scots to the fore in British life in the nineteenth century – that of the village school and, in his case, of Bredalbane Academy. He won scholarships to Aberdeen University, where he took a First in Classics and Philosophy, and then went on to study medicine at Edinburgh. After graduating there he was appointed, at the age of twenty-seven, to the Chair of Mental and Moral Philosophy at the University of Otago, becoming one of the first four professors brought out to Dunedin to establish this, the first university in New Zealand.

Duncan MacGregor held this post for fifteen years, until his independence of mind brought him into conflict with the Synod of the Presbyterian Church, who sponsored the Chair which he held. Among other heresies it seemed that the professor even showed himself prepared to listen to what Charles Darwin had to say. He fought off these critics, and in 1886 one of his former pupils, Robert Stout, who had by then become a Cabinet minister, extricated him from this arid conflict by offering him the post of Inspector-General of Lunatic Asylums, Hospitals and Charitable Institutions for the Dominion. This post Dr MacGregor executed with a success New Zealand social historians have readily acknowledged. He gave New Zealand not only a firmly based hospital service with high professional standards of nursing and midwifery, but also pioneered new ways of treating mental illness, a development symbolised by his insisting, as one of his first actions, that the name 'lunatic asylum' be changed to 'mental hospital'. (New Zealand was the first country to do this.)

Over six feet in height, a formidable athlete with a splendid full beard, Dr MacGregor campaigned for money and for modern methods, particularly in the structure of relief for the unemployed and the sick and the aged. His campaigns brought him into constant conflict with the politicians. This intensified after his friend Sir Robert Stout was ousted as leader of the Liberal Party by the less scrupulous Richard John Seddon, with whose support for Fabianism my grandfather, very much an individualist, had little sympathy. This led Sidney and Beatrice Webb, who visited New Zealand in 1898, to a waspish denuniciation of Dr MacGregor's annual reports as 'tirades against socialism and democracy', though they showed no hesitation in basing their own views on New Zealand social affairs largely on the contents of those reports. Had he been of their generation I would like to have heard what this 'voluble Highlander' (to quote Sidney Webb again) would have made of their bland endorsement of Stalinism thirty years later.

Duncan MacGregor was a good public speaker in that pre-microphone era when oratory was still a major art. He faced an early test when in 1871 Anthony Trollope, then on a tour of New Zealand, failed to arrive in Dunedin in time to speak at a conversazione to mark Sir Walter Scott's birthday. Professor MacGregor was called upon to speak in the novelist's place. His speech went well, particularly after he had put himself onside with his audience by quoting from the letter he had received from the committee. 'If Mr Trollope comes to make a speech we will hold you excused. If he does not, you must make a speech, and if you don't make a speech we will advertise you as the ruin of the affair.'

I never knew my grandfather – he died in 1906, four years before I was born – except through the recollections of my parents, and his writings.

My mother, until she married, had worked as her father's assistant. This brought her close to the heart of power in the compact socicty of New Zealand's capital, Wellington. After church on Sunday mornings, ministers and other public leaders often gathered at the MacGregor home in Hill Street (on one occasion an informal Cabinet meeting was held around the dining-room table), or would join the doctor and his family – he had four daughters and one son – for walks on the Tinakori Hills. This gave my mother not only a taste for the excitement of power, but for the satisfaction of publicly recognised achievement which the rest of her life was cruelly to deny her. When she married my father – and they were a deeply devoted couple – his banking career required him to serve his turn as manager in small country townships, in which she found life suffocatingly narrow. Even the relatively important post of manager in Invercargill meant living in the smallest of New Zealand cities, a long way from the fuller life of Wellington and Auckland. This left my mother with a longing to be at the heart of events which conveyed itself to me, and which may have helped to carry me into journalism, particularly as it went hand in hand with another belief she had inherited from her father: that you should try to play some part in shaping the events of your times, and not merely see life in terms of making your own way in it.

One of the first actions of my great-grandfather, Bishop Harper, had been to found in Christchurch the equivalent of an English public school, Christ's College. With its grey stone buildings and creeper-covered walls, its chapel and quadrangle and wide playing fields, it quickly became the Eton of New Zealand. My two older brothers and our many male cousins (my grandfather had twenty-eight grandchildren) all went to Christ's College as a matter of course. But when my time came, we were into the post-war slump, and my father's salary, as manager of the Invercargill branch of the Bank of New South Wales, could not run to boarding school fees. So I was sent to Southland Boys High School in Invercargill.

This was for me a fortunate development. For one thing Christ's College in those days did not set much store by getting its pupils into the university, which I knew was my best way forward. Most of their boys were destined to work on the family sheep station or in the family business. But, more importantly, at Southland Boys High School I found myself in the mainstream of New Zealand life. Each morning, as I cycled off to school with my schoolbag strapped over the bar of my bicycle, and my sports togs slung from the handle-bars, I faced the same opportunities and grappled with the same difficulties as most of my contemporaries. This was better than being educated in an enclave which, however sincere its aims, tended to perpetuate in this new land the social stratifications of Britain. Little if any such differentiation between private and state schools in New Zealand has persisted into more recent times. But in the 1920s the line was sharply drawn.

Invercargill brought too the boon of growing up in a region with a strong local patriotism, quite as strong as, for instance, animates the Geordies of Northumberland. (This is perhaps why I felt at home the first day, two-thirds of a lifetime later, on which I went to work in Newcastle-upon-Tyne.) It is a characteristic of places which feel themselves geographically set apart. Invercargill in the 1920s seemed very much on the edge of the world. Large tracts of its hinterland, which draining and artificial fertilisers have since transformed into lush pastures, were still sour, unproductive marshlands. The wide streets of the city, laid out by the far-seeing pioneers and broad enough for boulevards, carried little traffic then, and the fine trees which today dignify its parks and offset its flatness were only saplings. It seemed to lie wide open to every wind from the Antarctic, a staging post for gales reaching us across miles of wild, icy seas. Yet its inhabitants met this relative isolation with a vigorous, self-contained lifestyle which I found fulfilling. Though I spent more of my childhood and youth in other parts of New Zealand, it never entered my mind, when I enlisted in 1940, to put myself down for any other battalion than one drawn from Southland and Otago.

I did not set out to be a journalist. I wanted to be a lawyer, attracted by the cut and thrust of court work, and it was to study law that I entered Otago University in February 1928. It was the custom then for those seeking the degree of Bachelor of Laws, the qualification necessary for legal practice, to study part time. They worked as clerks in law offices during the day, and attended lectures placed to meet their needs in the early morning or the evening. This provided both practical experience and made some contribution towards the cost of study. I found myself in a position to depart from this norm. I had won not only a state scholarship, which met all my university fees, but also one of the few other scholarships to Otago – one for history, established by a pioneer settler called Lizzie Rathbone. This brought me in £50 a year. A generous uncle who was also my godfather matched this with a further £50, which, with my vacation earnings, freed me to study full time. Such was the value of money then that board and lodging in a student residential hall cost only £1 10s a week.

I used this chance to give myself a wider education than the law course provided. When, in the Invercargill Public Library, I used to mull over, in the university calendar, the requirements for an LL B, my eye would be constantly drawn to the tantalising fare offered to those who studied for a Bachelor of Arts degree. Ever since my childhood I had had an ardent interest in history, aroused perhaps by the dramas of World War I which filled the newspapers and magazines as I learnt to read. Anyone who made history their main subject for a BA would not be confined to studying English history from 1715 to 1900, the period upon which New Zealand schools then concentrated, but could range over European history, that of the United States and even, glory be (if one continued into a fourth year for an MA) over New Zealand history, a subject known to me only from my private reading. Other mouthwatering subjects could be studied as part of a history degree – English literature, economics, anthropology, even one defined as 'Greek history, art and literature (no knowledge of Greek required)'. This definition was apt to raise sardonic eyebrows when I told classicists in Oxford later of it, yet it did at least open our eyes and minds to Greek civilisation, largely due to the infectious passion for her subject of the lecturer, Miss Jessie Mackay. It was also to have a practical value for me. In Athens in 1941, on my way to the front, I used such spare time as I had to seek out some of the places about which we had learned, including the road from Marathon along which Philippides had carried his despatch. A fortnight later this saved me vital time when I was sent out to reconnoitre the route by which the New Zealand Fifth Brigade would retreat towards that port, for evacuation to Crete.

But that was thirteen years in the future. My problem now was how to enjoy the delights offered in these wider academic fields without abandoning the practical advantages of a law degree. Lizzie Rathbone's generosity provided an interim solution. I could postpone for a year securing a job in a law firm, and in the meantime study the first section of subjects for an LL B with a year of the BA courses for history and English.

This I did – only to find myself at the end of that year facing a dilemma. I had emerged as the head of my class in history, and the professor, Dr J.R. Elder, had been so welcoming and enthusiastic, treating me more as someone who shared a common interest than as a pupil, that it seemed like treason to abandon this course in midstream. I very much wanted to complete my BA, yet it opened the way to only two careers, teaching or journalism, neither of which in the conditions of the day appealed to me. But if I postponed qualifying in law I could find myself a dangerously late entrant into an already crowded profession.

I resolved this dilemma by deciding to study for both a BA and an LL B simultaneously. I would work for an arts degree within its normal three-year span, but spread the law degree over five years – something many of the part-timers did. This worked out well. I took my BA on schedule, and went on to take an MA with first class honours in history in a fourth year. By this time I had qualified in all but three subjects for my law degree, which I could complete within a further six months. Though there had been a slight overlap in my first year, with Latin and constitutional history counting for both degrees, the achievement was considerable enough to be a major argument for my Rhodes Scholarship.

Nor had pressure of work ruled me out of other aspects of university life. These had been four marvellous years. Lord Reith in his *Diaries* exulted in the times when he was 'at full stretch'. This was such a time for me, not only in my work, but in the games which were an important part of our lives – rugby football in the winter, cricket and tennis and fives in the summer – and in student activities, the chief of which for me was editing the fortnightly student paper, the *Critic*, and, ultimately, the annual and more highbrow *Review*. During my shorter spring vacations we went deer and pig shooting in the hills and mountains where Southland's plains gave way to Fiordland, often moving by compass and by the lie of the land through thick bush and along ridges where almost certainly no human being had ever been before. During term time I lived in Selwyn College, a residential hall with its own vigorous life. Tiwha Bennett, a son of the Maori bishop and a dentistry student, was a naturally gifted jazz pianist who could pick up any tune simply from hearing it played over on a gramophone, and 'Tea for Two' and 'The Birth of the Blues' provided a background theme music for our lives. As I walked to lectures I would pass the four red brick houses which had been built for the first professors of the university, and in one of which my mother had lived as a girl.

In these years too I first began to write for publication, contributing feature articles on travel, or on farming activities like mustering or shearing, as I had known them on mountain sheep stations of back-blocks Otago and Southland. I made, too, occasional forays into history, writing stories based on the diaries of early settlers in Dunedin's Hocken Library. The first of these, I grandly entitled 'Rabbiting: A Great Winter Trade' (as those were the days when rabbit fur was much in demand for the felt hats most men wore until the young bareheaded President Kennedy changed the fashion at a stroke in 1960), I sent it off to the *Otago Witness*, the local weekly magazine-cum-newspaper. I heard nothing of its fate and assumed it had found its way into the wastepaper basket, until one morning, glancing through the *Witness* in the Selwyn College commonroom, I came upon the article with 'By G.S. Cox' at its head. The stab of joy which went through me I can feel to this day, and the ten shillings it brought was a valuable contribution to my finances.

In my descriptions of mountains and the bush and the tussock-covered hills, and of the hard but fulfilling life lived amongst them, I tried to express some of the emotion the New Zealand landscape aroused in me. It is possible, as my Ongaroto experience confirmed, to love places quite as deeply as one loves people. This is particularly true when you are young, and such places are the setting for events which challenge and shape you. New Zealand is, for the most part, a very positive country, its sharp ridges rising steeply from deep blue and deep green seas, its features kept clear over long distances by the almost constant winds. The landscape enters your life like a strong human personality: not just a scenic backdrop, but very much part of the cast. Had I had the capacity to write fiction, I would have tried to express these feelings through novels or short stories, the best way in prose of expressing the truth. I did win a literary prize for a short story in my first year at Otago, but I came to realise that I had neither the skill to create characters afresh, nor the ruthlessness to carry into my writings people whom I knew. So I did what I could in the exercise of this lesser art.

For the first three of these four years, until the slump overturned New Zealand life, we could, at the university's annual capping concert, sing 'Gaudeamus igitur' with sincerity, for life ahead seemed full of promise – and security. Continued world peace we took for granted. Though ours was the generation fated to fight the next war, no such possibility entered our minds. At parades at the Invercargill War Memorial on Anzac Day we in the school cadets would study the lined, often prematurely aged faces of the veterans of Messines and Gallipoli and Hill 60 as those of men who had experienced something which we, and those who came after us, would never know. This impression was strengthened when in 1930 the government did away with the part-time military training which, since 1909, had been compulsory for all young New Zealand men. This for us had included a fortnight's annual camp on a sun-browned plain to the north of Dunedin. Since war was so clearly not on the cards, we cursed this as a waste of time. Yet many of us, I suspect, enjoyed the physical fitness and the camaraderie, particularly when the full battalion was drawn up on parade, with the sun flashing on our bayonets as we presented arms, and with the sea gleaming behind our tent lines.

Only in my final year did the shuddering decline in the prices for butter, cheese, wool and meat make the ground under our feet suddenly unstable, calling into question much we had until then taken for granted. Politics had played no part in the student life of Otago in my previous years, and indeed were to play none until in 1932 riots by the unemployed in Dunedin and Auckland abruptly sharpened student attitudes, not least because many students were called upon to act as special constables. Otago University in my time had no political societies: political issues received cursory or bantering treatment in student debates. My own practical contact with elections had been confined to acting as a polling clerk in a nearby school hall for the 1931 General Election. As with all elections since 1918, the vigorous Temperance Movement ensured that, in parallel with the parliamentary poll, the electorate was asked to vote on whether liquor should or should not be sold within their locality. (Invercargill had been a dry town: Dunedin had a plenitude of pubs.) As the hour to close our polling booth approached, a last-minute voter, a lorry driver, drove up to the doorway, jumped out of his cab, and enquired anxiously if he was in time. Impressed by this evidence of the public exercising its fundamental democratic right, I offered him a voting paper with the list of parliamentary candidates, and began the ritual of explaining how he should express his choice. 'Never mind that,' he said with impatience, 'just tell me how I vote for the booze.'

But as 1931 unfolded it became clear to me not only that the future of Ongaroto but of a multitude of other farms was at stake. When men I had known as proud shepherds or stockmen on sheep stations now queued for relief, and graduates who had left us confidently six months before were still out of a job, my mind turned to what could be done to check and change this. The answer I hit upon would not, I realised, have commended itself to my individualistic Scottish grandfather. For it seemed to me that one way out which ought to be tried was state intervention – indeed if need be state ownership, if not of the land itself, then certainly of the institutions that financed the farmers and sold, or failed to sell, their produce. No Marxist tracts or political oratory brought me to this view. Marx was to me merely one more name in the books of European theory I had glanced at for my studies, one of a dozen or so nineteenth-century theorists whose ideas had flared up, causing perhaps riot and revolution, and then died away. The view that socialism might be the answer had for me a more empirical origin. State intervention had been the means adopted by New Zealand's Liberal Government to deal with the depression of the 1890s. Under R.J. Seddon it had not only put a number of welfare and factory acts onto the statute books, which had social reformers hurrying from all over the world to study this experiment in Fabianism, but it had introduced compulsory arbitration as a way of sharing out the product of industry. It seemed no great step from that to the state holding a stake in the organisations which produced that product. In the railways New Zealand had long had an efficient publicly owned industry. Its Public Trustee and State Insurance offices had provided services which, in other countries, were in private hands. From England, newspapers and periodicals proclaimed the success of the new device of the public corporation as a method of public ownership which was not direct state control, holding up the BBC and the newly formed London Transport as proof. Surely such experiments in public ownership were preferable to the widespread bankruptcy of farmers and of the multitude of other industries dependent upon them.

When I first tried out these ideas on colleagues and on some of my teachers, I was surprised at the hostility they aroused. One and all saw such thinking either as anathema or nonsense. This tended to harden my own defence of them, until I found myself at times taking up positions a good deal more doctrinaire than I in fact believed to be true, often merely for the sake of argument. But the process at least set me thinking about what was to become a central issue for the decade ahead.

CHAPTER THREE

Outward Bound

On a day of warm, strong summer rain in February 1932 I sailed from Wellington for Sydney, on the first stage of my journey to England. As we moved out towards the harbour entrance the clouds were low on the bush-covered hills that rose steeply above the beaches whose beauty in Edwardian days has been caught for all time in Katherine Mansfield's 'At the Bay'. In Cook Strait, the sea was grey and the mountains of the South Island were hard and black against a sunset which slowly turned Golden Bay the colour of its name.

To travel abroad, particularly to Britain, was the ambition of almost every New Zealander I knew. This derived not only from the natural instinct of people in a distant country to explore the world beyond the oceans whose great breakers rolled ceaselessly against our coasts. It was fuelled also by a desire to see the reality of the Britain which was the setting for so much of what we read and which was depicted in photographs, and in the line drawings still common in periodicals of the time. This was still the heyday of the written word. Radio in New Zealand was in its infancy. Film was already a powerful influence, but predominately a source of entertainment rather than information. Yet New Zealand had two written cultures, its own and that derived from Britain. Most of the books on the shelves of our excellent public libraries were of British origin. This applied particularly in the case of fiction. The only New Zealand novel of any significance was published overseas. There were few New Zealand periodicals, apart from the weekly editions put out by the main New Zealand newspapers, editions designed to give a week's news for farmers who lived too far away and were too busy to read a daily paper, and which contained a certain amount of feature material, chiefly on sport, fashion and the home. This left the way open for the weekly and monthly magazines from Britain. *The Illustrated London News*, the *Sphere*, the *Tatler* and the *Sporting and Dramatic* were read as regularly in New Zealand libraries, and in some homes, as in the Home Counties of Britain. So too were the flourishing monthly magazines of the day, the *Strand*, *Pearson's* and *Newnes*, offering short stories and serials by writers like H.G. Wells, P.G. Wodehouse, Edgar Wallace, and Dornford Yates. For the higher-minded there were the *Spectator* and the grey-covered *Round Table*, which strove to develop a mystique of Commonwealth and Empire.

It took at least a month for these to reach New Zealand by the fastest route, by sea through the Panama Canal, but we grew accustomed to throwing our minds back four weeks for events to be assessed and illustrated. All of this made the contemporary Britain scene familiar. It was natural, therefore, that we should wish to see for ourselves the streets and buildings and countryside we had come to know so well at one remove. Moreover, given that this was the land from which our forebears had emigrated, as well as the land of Shakespeare, Dickens, Thackeray and Tennyson and the other writers in whose works we had been strenuously schooled, the urge to see Britain at first hand was considerable.

It was not an easy urge to satisfy. For students overseas scholarships were rare. Besides the two annual Rhodes Scholarships, only one other scholarship was available for study at a British university. None was available for study in the United States or in any of our fellow Dominions. For the ordinary young New Zealander seeking what was not yet termed 'Overseas Experience' the chances were scant indeed, unless their parents could find the money for their fares and keep when abroad. Travel by sea was the only route, and the chances of working your passage, perhaps as a steward or deckhand or fireman, were few and far between. Even if you were able to make your way to Britain, you arrived in the depths of the depression, with jobs virtually impossible to find, and with no form of social security or support available for outsiders – and mighty little for the Britons themselves.

This meant that a journey abroad was very much a privilege of the reasonably well-to-do or of the truly adventurous who were prepared to risk genuine hardship. With cars still relatively scarce in New Zealand, people tended to stay put even within the country itself. This state of affairs lasted right up to the outbreak of war. In September 1939, when a survey was made on a train taking the first volunteers for the Army from Otago and Southland northwards to Burnham Camp, it was found that more than 80 per cent of the men had never been out of South Island, and well over half had never before been beyond their home province.

My generation still used the parlance of our parents, and spoke of a trip to Britain as 'going home'. But time had worn away much of the phrase's emotional undertones, and by 1932 'home' was largely a convenient shorthand for 'the British Isles'. Yet in one respect it was significant: we felt ourselves to be not only New Zealanders, but British – members of a world-wide community whose heartland was in the British Isles and above all in London. This did not diminish in any way our sense of independence and individuality as New Zealanders, as citizens of a country whose destiny was in our own hands. It did not derive, either, from the fact that Britain was our main market and the Royal Navy, with its apparently impregnable base at Singapore, our main protector. It reflected rather the intangible but powerful sense of being British we shared with the people of the British Isles and with those other parts of the Commonwealth which had been settled by people of British descent. This was not a political concept, stemming from membership of the British Commonwealth. It was an instinctive sharing of common origins, common traditions and common types of institution. We travelled on British, not New Zealand, passports – these had yet to come into being – and we saw in this no whit of diminution of our national independence. Were we not as much entitled to call ourselves British as anyone born in England, or in any other part of the British Isles? It was a good concept, rising above the constraints of a narrow nationalism, and its erosion in the stresses of the past forty years has been a retrograde step.

New Zealanders of the time were prepared, too, to accept a share of the responsibilities – and of the opportunities – offered by the Commonwealth and Empire. Both the Rhodes Scholars who had gone to Oxford two years ahead of me – James Dakin of Otago and Percy Minns of Auckland – entered the British Colonial Service, and had distinguished careers as administrators in East Africa. Another Otago graduate, Ralph Stephenson, was in the same service in the Far East and Africa. And Ralph Grey of Auckland gave up law in New Zealand for a career in the Colonial Service, which led on to his becoming the Governor of Northern Ireland and a life peer. For most of us in those days the British Commonwealth and Empire seemed not only to be a good thing, but also a durable one, worthy of our loyalty.

I landed in a Sydney gripped with excitement about the New Guard. This was a paramilitary organisation headed by a Great War veteran, Colonel Campbell, its aims being to save New South Wales from the Red Menace and the Yellow Peril. The Red Menace took the immediate form of the Labour Government of Premier John Lang, which threatened to repudiate the state debts. Members of the New Guard drove out into the bush to drill at night, and mounted a round-the-clock guard over Colonel Campbell's suburban home. Fashionable Sydney queued at Government House to strike their names out of the visitors' book in protest against the Governor's action in fulfilling his constitutional duty to approve the appointment of a number of Labour nominees to the state's upper chamber.

Both Campbell and Lang addressed mass meetings when I was in Sydney, and both meetings were broadcast live on what we then termed the wireless. The Australian authorities were clearly untroubled by the constraints which guided British broadcasting at this stage, when Winston Churchill was being rigorously denied access to the microphone. Campbell came across as truculent and emotional, and with a gift for vituperation. 'Lang has called me a bald-headed sabre rattler,' he thundered against the excited shouts of his supporters. 'Yes, I am bald – and why? Because I lost my hair wearing a steel helmet in the war to protect Conchies like Lang who were skulking here at home.'

Campbell was better at stating his case than arguing it. Two years later, when he came to Britain for talks with Mosley, I heard him speak at a Fascist meeting in Oxford. When an undergraduate asked him, in languid upper-class tones which Campbell no doubt expected to guarantee a right-wing orthodoxy, why he regarded the Japanese as inferiors, the Australian replied in surprise, 'Why, everyone knows that a yellow man is inferior to a white man.'

'But why,' the leisurely confident voice continued, 'but why do you think so yourself?' Campbell seemed to swell with rage. 'Because I don't like the way he brushes his hair – see?' he thundered, and his audience rose to their feet in an ecstasy of applause.

Though the New Guard forged formal links with Mosley's British Union of Fascists, it had no body of theory, and merited more the term Fascistic than Fascist. It belonged to that wave of right-wing private armies of the 1930s which stood for a simple patriotism and support for private property. In Germany this found expression in the Stalhelm movement, in Austria in Dollfuss's Catholic Heimwehr, and in France in Colonel de la Roque's Croix de Feu. The New Guard got itself into the world headlines when one of its sympathisers, an ADC on the Governor's staff, determined to prevent the Lang government from having the credit for opening the Sydney harbour bridge, and galloped forward at the opening ceremony to slash the ribbon with his sword before the ceremonial scissors could be used. But in 1934 the ground was cut from under the New Guard's feet when the Governor interpreted his constitutional duty widely enough to dismiss Lang, even though he commanded a majority in Parliament. In the subsequent election Labour was swept from power. The New Guard shrivelled away, to become a seldom recalled footnote to Australian history – even though its other warning, of the dangers of Japanese invasion, was within a decade to prove more real than, I suspect, even Colonel Campbell had believed.

But these political rumblings were only part of life in those brilliant summer days in Sydney. We surfed at Coogee in the early morning, watched Japan play Australia in the Davis Cup, and drove along reddish earthen roads, through the blue-grey primeval bush, to Bulli. There we gazed along the wide beach where D.H. Lawrence had lived during the three months that gave birth to *Kangaroo*, in which he had predicted ten years previously just such a movement as the New Guard, though he had made its leader markedly more intellectual than Campbell.

The *Moldavia*, the P&O liner on which I was to continue my journey, sailed from Sydney's Circular Quay on a morning of gleaming sunshine. I am glad I began my journeying in the days of steamship and railways, for they made a departure an occasion. The wharf was crowded: the half-completed harbour bridge loomed behind us while a band played the hit tunes of the day, 'The More We Are Together' and 'Goodnight Sweetheart'. The rainbow of streamers from ship to shore lengthened till it broke, strand by strand, and we moved out into the harbour and on through the heads to begin our voyage along the southern coast of Australia and then into the Indian Ocean.

Colombo provided my first sight of the world beyond Australasia. We smelt the East before we saw it. On the evening before we made landfall a wind sprang up from the still unseen shore, bringing an unmistakable, haunting smell of sandalwood. A rusty tramp steamer which passed us, southward bound, was right out of a Conrad novel. Colombo city the next morning, under a blazing blue sky, was vivid, dirty like the bedraggled motley of a clown in a travelling circus, and yet swarmingly alive. Children wearing only loin cloths ran alongside our car, chanting 'Tipperary' and shouting for pennies. A rotund yellow Buddha gazed benignly across a temple courtyard thronged with beggars and with priests in dirty saffron robes offering souvenirs for sale. A small Mohammedan mosque nearby was cool, and worshippers washed their feet and rinsed out their mouths before midday prayers. In the bazaar a meat seller thrust forward a skinned rabbit in his grimy hand. Two white oxen, preceded by a herald with cymbals, drew a gilded and betasselled wagon. I took it for a bridal car, until a placard at the back proved it to be an advertisement for *Dancing Daughters* at a cinema.

Bombay offered in part wide, Europeanised business streets, and suburbs of big houses in big gardens, and in part narrow, noisy, winding streets crowded with white-clad Indians, where mattresses were slung to air over balcony rails in the sunlight, and where craftsmen hammered and stitched and shouted in the shaded caverns of small open workshops. As the ship drew out, the white domes and towers of the city sank gradually between sea and sky, whilst three RAF biplanes circled overhead, farewelling friends sailing with us. From Bombay onwards ship life was dominated by the confident, assertive Britons who had come aboard – army officers and civil servants, planters and engineers going home on leave, their voices ringing loud on the decks and in the bars. The handful of English who had been with us since Australia, mostly immigrants who had failed to make it, were revealed now as being of a lower caste and withdrew from the limelight they had briefly held. For the first time I watched the sharply defined class structure of inter-war Britain reflected in subtle mannerisms and clothing and accents. More from instinct than from knowledge, I argued the case for Indian Home Rule with a young officer of the Gordon Highlanders going home on leave. He pointed to three Indians playing deck quoits and said with scorn, 'Imagine those governing a country.' When I pointed out that one was an Oxford tennis blue he snorted, 'Tennis. Yes, it would be tennis.'

Another passenger, Edmund Thompson, poet and lecturer on Oriental languages, who had been an adviser at the recent Round Table conference on India's future, was on his way back from a visit to Gandhi in prison. He feared that the Mahatma's idealism was now being obscured by politics. To Thompson, Home Rule for India was inevitable, and by delaying it we were repeating the mistakes of Ireland.

Aden we saw only at night. We drove out in the moonlight through the desert, with jagged peaks ahead and camels crouched by the roadside and bundles of rags which were men sleeping under every wall. A garage proprietor slept in a wide, brass knobbed double bed (alone) under the open sky beside his petrol pump. The Red Sea the next day was blue-grey satin, unbroken except for the folds of our wake. Far ahead a wide dark line was pencilled in the sky, coming up out of Africa and curving away into the sheer mountains of Sinai. It was made up of a column of huge birds – cranes I think– flying five or six abreast, hour after hour, migrating back to Europe: an omen that we were moving towards spring. At Suez we got our first mail from England. A man from Newbury, returning after ten bitter and bankrupted years growing tomatoes and sugarcane in Queensland, found a letter waiting for him from the girl he was coming back to marry, to say she was marrying a doctor instead. Port Said, in the cool morning, had herds of goats being driven through the streets to be milked in response to orders shouted down from behind latticed balconies. Merchants in white or grey gabardines drank black coffee in little cafés beside open, dusty markets.

Then we were out into the Mediterranean. A day or two later the tangerine-coloured cliffs of the Riviera were in sight, and we were drawing into Marseilles, with quay after quay of ocean-going vessels, and its cathedral on the skyline. Marseilles gave me my first intoxicating glimpse of Europe.

In the old port quarter great tenement houses, their plaster decayed and cracking, faced each other across narrow, winding streets. Drab old women, dark-eyed ragged children and sveltely dressed girls in high-heeled shoes passed in and out of the high, arched doorways. It was easy to realise that from these same streets had surged the revolutionary mob which gave France its national anthem.

Beyond this *quartier* modern Marseilles was urbane, chic, assured. After the outward uniformity and the public reserve of people in new countries, the rich variety of human types, and their easy, unselfconscious self-expression were exhilarating. In a large cafe on the Cannebière, small, suave men gesticulated and argued over glasses of quinquina and vermouth cassis. Two men at a corner table leant in intent silence over a chessboard, watched by talkative neighbours at the next table; there was even a pair of bearded artists, portfolios stacked against the side of their table. On the pavements beyond the big plate-glass window workmen in the loose blue or khaki smocks which they wore like uniforms, businessmen in black jackets and grey bowler hats, and schoolgirls and boys in short grey overalls surged animatedly along. But it was the women who were most strikingly different. In their furs and sleek costumes, eyelids darkened and lips crimsoned, they seemed, even when sitting silent, to express and luxuriate in an arrogant femininity enhanced by an air of holding themselves apart.

An Australian who knew Marseilles well from his days as a wartime interpreter took us to dine at a restaurant which had been in the same family *de père en fils* since 1820. It had bare walls and coarse white tablecloths, and we went into the kitchen to select our own fish for the bouillabaisse, and drank white wine from long-necked bottles. As we drove back afterwards to the quayside, I knew this would be a continent which could quickly become hard to leave.

Then a raging Gulf of Lyons; Easter Sunday in rich sunshine off the Spanish coast; Gibraltar crouching dark against the dawn sky; and, at last, the stone walls and green fields and square houses of the Isle of Wight, and the long line of the mainland with its white piers, the greyish-white cliffs of Dover, and the afternoon boat drawing in from Ostend, under Dover Castle on its headland.

CHAPTER FOUR

Home

In those days voyagers from Australasia entered London by the back door. Our first sight of England, after the dockside of Tilbury on an overcast April morning, was the discouraging one of mile upon mile of nondescript suburban housing as the train made its way through Dagenham and Hornchurch, followed by mile upon mile of drab grey brick back-to-back terraces of the East End. Then came the cavern of St Pancras Station, red buses and squat fussy taxis, and grey pigeons whirling round the barrel organ in the street outside my room in Maidavale, that haven of bedsitters then much favoured by Antipodeans.

Much of the spring which followed I spent fitting the reality of England to the picture which years of reading had built up in my mind. London was then an easy city in which to get about. The Underground was clean; the buses were frequent, and on some routes the upper deck was open – an aid to sightseeing. There was joy in adventuring down the tiled catacombs of the Tube, and emerging in Trafalgar Square to see Nelson's column spiring towards the clouds and Whitehall sweeping away in front towards the towers of Parliament. There was a sharp pleasure in seeing the first white-gloved London policeman, in glimpsing the scarlet of sentries outside Buckingham Palace, in hearing the thud of horses hooves in Rotten Row – not because they were new, but because they were familiar. There was a thrill in seeing the words 'Downing Street' or 'Whitehall' or 'Piccadilly' placarded on a street corner like any other street sign.

There was enough too of an older London still extant to fill out the background to fiction as well as to fact. The squares of South Kensington, the high stuccoed terraces of Bayswater were, one felt, very much as the Forsytes would have known them; there were still enough bow-windowed mansions in Park Lane, enough privately occupied houses in Mayfair, with striped awnings over doorways and maids in white aprons and caps to be glimpsed in basements, to illustrate Trollope and Thackeray, Michael Arden and P.G. Wodehouse. Baker Street, with the Abbey National's office block occupying the site of 221b, was at first sight a disappointment. But lower down, towards Portman Square, its long façades were still intact. An occasional hansom cab still stood on a rank outside Baker Street Station, and it required no great feat of the imagination to envisage Holmes and Watson hurrying off to one further case. To the north of Regent's Park, Acacia Road was just as it was when Katherine Mansfield resolved there to write 'Prelude' and 'At the Bay'. The big Victorian house in Beauchamp Place, her first London home, could readily be identified near the canal basin in Little Venice, where indeed it still stands today, the lone survivor of the terrace of which it was a part, stranded by the swirling traffic of the Harrow Road.

What matter that there were patches of disappointment? Piccadilly Circus was smaller, more garish, more cluttered than befitted what we had come to think of as the hub of the world. The grandeur of Westminster Abbey was diminished by the museum-like jostle of busts and monuments in Poet's Corner, and by obdurate beadles demanding sixpence before they would unlock the gates in the iron railings which barred off Henry VIII's Chapel as if it were a prison cell. Nor had anything I had read – though no doubt H.G. Wells had described it – prepared me for the wide, drab monotony of South London suburbia, and the new, constrained districts of timorous identical post-war houses staring at each other through their lace-curtained windows. But beyond this was the countryside – not yet invaded by the mass-owned motor car and the tar-macadamed side road, yet readily accessible to the walker prepared to travel out by the frequent, efficient and low-priced trains. Here the imagined scene and the reality fitted perfectly.

In the Chilterns the beeches, still leafless in April, stood iron-dark alongside wide muddy rides. In Kent the bluebells were plentiful around farms with plump red-brick oast houses and stackyards still holding the remains of last season's hay. Little, musty-smelling country churches provided a reminder that this was still the heartland of an empire. Brass plates on the walls recorded '… of this parish, killed in action … died in Malaya … in Melbourne, Australia … in British Guyana … in Natal'. By the tomb of an Elizabethan sailor – a ruff-collared figure in marble, its surface worn smooth by the hands of centuries – a donation box sought help for 'this magnificent Norman Tower, now menaced by the Death Watch Beetle'. Across the years images from my first glimpses of the English countryside remain freshly minted – a fair-haired girl taking five spaniels for a walk in a leafy damp lane near Oxted; the yellow splendour of a field of mustard in bloom; a church bell ringing out in the evening stillness as we strode up a village street towards the railway station to take the train home after a day on the North Downs.

At weekends I was certainly not alone in exploring this countryside. The bicycle and low railway fares had opened the regions around the big cities to the young of the working class and the lower middle class. Long columns of swift cyclists, often several hundred strong, wearing dark brown corduroy shorts and jackets, and displaying an extraordinary range of physiques from the very skinny to the very plump, would sweep suddenly around the corner of a quiet country road, or assert themselves amidst the cars and charabancs on a crowded highway. At Victoria or Waterloo the hikers would gather on a Sunday morning – men in khaki shorts with rucksacks, girls in shorts or tweed skirts – carrying maps or the excellent small handbooks of country walks published by London Transport. Poster art flourished in those pre-television days, and Paul Nash and Jacob Epstein were amongst the artists who contributed to the brightly coloured pictures displayed outside tube and railway stations preaching the virtues of hiking, and supported by a Spanish proverb: 'Man must smell the earth or perish'.

But this was the England not only of the novelists and the historians, but also of the Great Depression. You did not have to look far for signs of it. Stunted men in cloth caps with white mufflers around their necks, their faces gaunt and peaked or flabby with malnutrition, stood idle in Trafalgar Square, or moved in small groups, forming a brass band with three or four instruments, or singing together as they begged their slow way through the shoppers in Oxford Street or Regent Street. These bands would wear their World War I medals as they held out a battered cap for pennies. From the windows of suburban trains running into Liverpool Street or Waterloo or London Bridge, swathes of slum land were readily visible – a mass of grey slate roofs and smoking chimneys above backyards hung with washing. Men and women stared out of the houses, enjoying the evening sun, while the streets teemed with grubby, noisy children.

In Poplar and Bethnal Green, Whitechapel and Stepney mile upon mile of yellowish-grey, two-storeyed brick houses faced each other, in one monotonous terrace, across street after street. The dry smell of dust and rotting straw, characteristic of London in those days when horse vans were common in the streets, was strong in these East End areas. Around the newsagent's shop on the corner, and the eating house with steamed windows where untidy white lettering advertised 'Tripe and Mash', or 'Jellied Eels', would be more groups of men in flat-topped caps and white mufflers, often standing silent and idle. It was not the dilapidation of these areas which caught the eye. The shabby unpainted wooden houses of Auckland's few slums in Greys Avenue, or of Sydney's Surrey Hills were more manifestly sordid. What marked London's East End was the sullen hopeless monotony of the scene, and the vastness of the area over which it stretched. Yet many of these drab houses had their doorsteps scrubbed white, and their curtains – even when tattered – were usually scrupulously clean. Through an occasional open doorway you could glimpse the bare, oil-clothed hallway and rooms crowded with beds, washing, and cooking gear, and meet the reek of cooking and of unwashed people. But these were glimpses only, for you were obviously a stranger, conspicuous in the grey flannels and sports jacket of the middle class, and the East End wanted no truck with outsiders who came slumming, however sympathetic their attitude might be.

Late one afternoon in early June I walked through the streets of Bermondsey. There were scatterings of horse dung in the street, where grubby children played. Women in drab clothes, wearing sackcloth aprons, coarse black cotton stockings, and downtrodden shapeless shoes, leaned out of windows or stood in doorways, talking. Many would have been handsome but for their indifferent, grimy look, and hair straying in wisps across their foreheads. At one corner, set into brickwork scrawled with initials and a chalked assertion that 'Jerry loves Molly Peak', was a small tablet with the wording 'Thirty men from this street served their country in its hour of need, 1914–18'. Half a mile further and I was on London Bridge, across which poured the full homegoing tide of city workers, bowler-hatted and carrying rolled umbrellas and folded newspapers.

I had been prepared for Britain to be a land of distinct class stratifications. New Zealand had, for all its assertive democracy, its own subtle gradations of class, and the books of Sinclair Lewis had dissected the same phenomena in Middle America. Dress provided one immediate clue to such differences in London. Corduroy trousers and coarse woollen jackets were as much the uniform of the working man as were the blue smocks of his French counterpart. Shop assistants and junior clerks wore dark suits, their seniors striped trousers with black coats and bowler hats. Top hats were still everyday wear for politicians, for wealthy shoppers in Burlington Arcade or Bond Street, and for leading figures in the City – though there the unskilled eye could confuse them with the toppers worn by bank messengers in green uniform coats. Pork-pie felt hats, perhaps with a jaunty feather in the brim, and plus-fours were a regulation middle-class garb for young men. Grey spats were a common addition to the dress of the middle class as well as the rich. Women's fashions in dress, set by the rich, were slavishly copied, in gradations of quality of material and workmanship, down to the High Street level.

Physique, too, marked off the classes as sharply as did dress. At Epsom on Derby Day the grey-hatted men and the silk-clad women who walked down from the stands to view the horses in the paddock towered literally head and shoulders above the mass of other racegoers. Bad teeth, causing misshapen mouths, were common amongst the working class, and poor diets and a shortage of protein made faces with regular features, which we take for granted today, a rarity amongst the mass of people – something which gives the films of that era a character quite distinct from those of the sixties onward. The shop girls and typists seemed to have had so little chance for exercise, or so inadequate a diet, that their complexions often had a faintly greenish, silken pallor, making their skin look so fragile that you felt it would shred if a thumb were pressed hard against it.

It was in accent and bearing, however, that class most markedly asserted itself. Each grade in this caste structure spoke in its own particular manner, and each could be cuttingly and unhesitatingly rude to the groups below it – and indeed ingratiatingly polite to those higher up the scale. Within the broad mass of the working class, these differences of tone could be as sharp as those between the classes, as any private soldier on the receiving end of a sergeant major's sardonic abuse could testify. But such interchanges were seldom resented, for they were expressed in a shared accent, and were based upon gradations of authority within the same class, not on assumptions of superiority as human beings. But the bearing and speech of the upper classes conveyed, whether intentionally or not, the assumption that those socially inferior were also inferior human beings, something which could hurt deeply – as J.B. Priestley's novels of the period so skilfully convey.

I first became aware of this on the crowded upper deck of a bus in Regent Street. Two ladies, whose thick furs, gleaming hats and expensive perfumes marked them out as unmistakably upper middle class, talked to one another throughout their journey in loud ringing tones which carried about the deck. They discussed the difficulty of getting gardeners, the inadequacy of a friend's cook, the movements of their children, in a way which made clear they were indifferent not only as to whether the other passengers heard, but whether they even existed. The bus might have been empty so far as they were concerned – and so indeed it was of anyone with whom they were likely to be concerned. There was an unintentional but unmistakable discourtesy in this arrogant disregard of the presence, indeed of the existence, of others. They conveyed an air of being not so much of another class as almost of another segment of humanity, and glances of resentment followed them as, unconcerned to the last, they swept towards the stairway.

Over the years I was to observe a multitude of such behaviours, varying from unconscious arrogance to calculated rudeness, as each caste asserted itself against its neighbours. As a New Zealander, whose accent and schooling could not easily be placed, I was largely exempt from this process and could study it with my own feelings unhurt. But I often had occasion to agree with Lord Wavell, who, commenting on the British attitude to the Indians, said once that if we lost the Empire, we would be the first imperial people to do so largely through bad manners. Other arrogances, combined with bad language and verbal aggression, have subsequently emerged as new evils in people's public conduct. But today, by and large, we behave towards each other in Britain as human beings rather than as members of a social class.

My first sight of Oxford could not have been bettered, even if it had been staged for a film. It was not of my own college, Oriel, but of its grander neighbour, Christ Church. A don from Christ Church, who had been touring New Zealand at the time my scholarship was awarded, had invited me to stay overnight in the college, and to dine at the High Table. We came into the great hall of Christ Church out of a misty April evening. On either side big open log-fires sent red flames leaping, lighting up the faces of the nearest undergraduates and of scouts hurrying past with piles of plates, and catching the crimson of Cardinal Wolsey's gown and of the pale face of Gladstone, amid the portraits of famous former members of the college which covered much of the walls.

At the long wooden tables, lit by green-shaded table lamps, the undergraduates, gowns over the sports jackets which most of them wore, sat on backless forms, laughing and talking amongst themselves with an assurance I envied. The bustle and the informality of it all were a surprise. I had expected rows of undergraduates sitting rather formally – as if at a banquet, I suppose – at tables covered with white cloths. Yet here they strolled in late, took any place free, and once the closing grace had been said strolled out as they wished, or stayed on to talk over tankards of beer and cider.

At the High Table, on a dais above the dim depths of the hall, we wore dinner jackets and the stiff shirt fronts of the time. The main guest was Albert Einstein, not yet a refugee from what was not yet Hitlerian Germany. With a great shock of grey hair above a wide forehead, sharp eager eyes, and a Lloyd Georgian moustache, he sat on the right hand of the Master, flanked on the other side by his host, a bald man with an expression both good humoured and sardonic. This was Professor Lindemann, in time to be 'the Prof' of Churchill's wartime entourage, and already celebrated for having, in World War I, worked out mathematically the way to take an aeroplane out of a spin – and having himself taken up a plane and put his theory to the test.

In the senior common room after dinner, as the port circulated around the deeply polished table, I found myself in the midst of an argument between two dons, a young Frank Pakenham and a young Patrick Gordon Walker, both to be ministers in the Labour Government of 1945. The evening papers had reported a proposal that the gangster Al Capone would be released from gaol to search for the missing baby son of the American aviator Colonel Charles Lindbergh. The boy had been kidnapped and was, some days after this discussion, found dead. Was it ethically justifiable to free Capone? Could a man who had done wrong be exempted from the consequences just because he might right another wrong? This issue they debated deftly but thoroughly, trading arguments from Aristotle and Plato, Descartes and Kant in a bantering yet fundamentally serious way. On my other side the Master was dealing with a less immediate problem. 'The port which those three-bottle-a-night men of the eighteenth century drank must surely have been lighter than this?' he queried of the senior history don. 'Yes, it was more like an ordinary red wine. And the bottles were much smaller – more of a pint size', came the ready reply.

I was drawn into a discussion about the future of another guest, an undergraduate from Corpus called Denis Clarke. He was the son of Tom Clarke, the hard-driving news editor of Northcliffe's *Daily Mail* in its early great days. Denis Clarke had been offered a post on the *Daily Express* by Lord Beaverbrook, and was planning to leave Oxford without completing his degree. Was this wise? The common room thought not, and I thought not, too – though I could understand why Clarke was tempted, for jobs for graduates were rare in those slump-ridden days. He accepted the offer, becoming in time the Vienna correspondent of the *Daily Express* – a post in which I was to succeed him almost exactly five years after that April evening.

The port, the talk, the atmosphere, were all stimulating. This indeed was the Oxford I had dreamed of. I was therefore astonished when, as my host and I settled down for a final drink in his sitting room, he asked me, after some tense clearing of his throat, if I was aware of the physical actions by which children were procreated. His manner becoming increasingly strained, he went on to explain that many students came up to Oxford unaware of such matters, and he felt it his duty to explain to them just what happened.

Sexual eccentricity was something which had not been encompassed by my New Zealand experience. I cut the conversation short and took myself off to the guest room allocated to me. It was a jarring note on which to end what had been for me an exhilarating introduction to Oxford. A chilly restraint hung over the breakfast table in the morning, and I was glad when the time came for me to leave for my train. After I had gone up to Oriel that autumn

I occasionally passed my host of that night in the street. He gave no sign of recognising me, nor I of him. No doubt he as was as disappointed in me as I was in him.

CHAPTER FIVE

A Look at Russia

Shortly before I left New Zealand I had gone to the lodgings of a lecturer at the university to return some books I had borrowed. On the table was a copy of a periodical I had not seen before, the Soviet propaganda monthly *Russia Today*. Its cover photograph showed a phalanx of tractors pulling ploughs across a wide plain, opening up black swathes of what was described as virgin Siberian steppe. It was, on a grand scale, what we had been doing at Ongaroto, and I felt an instinctive sympathy for people whose aim was also, in Swift's words, to make two blades of grass grow where only one had grown before. (My reaction was indeed an example of the force of the visual image even in those pre-television days.)

I was not ignorant of the political methods which lay behind the Soviet experiment. The bloodshed, famine and terror of life in Russia during the past fifteen years had had their full place in the columns of New Zealand newspapers. But this image of Russia as a savage land had been somewhat overlaid in more recent times by reports of industrialisation and the collectivisation of agriculture under the First Five Year Plan. This social experiment had been vividly described – and ardently supported – in two books, *Humanity Uprooted* and *Red Bread*, by Maurice Hindus, the American son of a Jewish family who had emigrated to the States from the Ukraine. Hindus had gone back to his former homeland to find everything there – well, virtually everything – illuminated by the glow of a marvellous new dawn. Though I suspected the gloss he put on the human cost of all this, and on the brutal repression of the new order, his writings made me want to see the Russian scene and this gigantic experiment myself. When, in the window of the Intourist offices in Haymarket, I saw a twenty-one day tour of the Soviet Union on offer for £28, I decided this would be a good way to utilise some of my time before I went up to Oxford. So one Saturday afternoon late that June I found myself at Hay's Wharf in the Pool of London ready to board the Soviet steamer *Jan Rudjutak* for her five-day journey to Leningrad.

On the dockside a group of soberly dressed Soviet officials and their wives, stationed in London, had come down to see their children off on a month's holiday in a Communist Young Pioneer camp in Russia. The children, all wearing red ties and under the leadership of a tall dark girl in a red beret, sang from the ship's rail, in unison with their parents on the dockside, the *Internationale* and other revolutionary songs. As the ship drew slowly away from the wharf they began a plaintive Russian peasant song, which mingled with the sound of traffic as the cars and buses moved across London Bridge. A glimpse of scarlet where the guard's sentry stood before a sentry box at the Tower, white gloves of a policeman on Tower Bridge, primrose-gold of the summer evening sky, dusky wharves and cranes – and swiftly we slipped downstream towards the North Sea.

Leaning over the steerage rail beside me was a stocky man with a pitted, lined face. He told me that he was an American communist on his way back to his birthplace, the Ukraine. 'I got out of the States,' he said in the strongly nasal tones of the Bronx. 'They made it too hot for me.' He had eyed with particular care an Australian girl who had come down to see me off. Tall, dark, very good looking and wearing a wine-red coat and skirt, she had looked elegantly out of place on that earnest quayside. 'That dame that saw you off,' he continued challengingly. I braced myself to meet a denunciation of the bourgeoisie. Instead he looked at me warmly. 'Swell dame,' he said. 'Now that's a real swell dame. I wish I had had someone like that to see me off.' We talked a lot during the days of the voyage. He stressed again and again his confidence that a good life, even if a hard one, lay ahead for him in Russia, as if anxious to assure himself as much as to convince me, as if he sensed that not only Russia but the yet uncharted Gulag Archipelago lay ahead. If he escaped from a prison camp over the years ahead, he would have been one of the very few returning exiles to do so.

The ship brought us our first glimpse of Russian life. At its stern was a red-panelled Lenin Corner, a crew's clubroom where meetings and concerts were held. It had a bronze bust of Lenin – the first of the thousands that would meet our eyes in the coming weeks. The high forehead, stub nose, full lips and sharp chin radiated determination, neatness, cleverness, perhaps cruelty, certainly relentlessness. On the wall was the ship's wall newspaper, with news and self-criticism. One handwritten article criticised the ship's carpenter, who, because his duties were light, thought himself free to lounge in the sun instead of fulfilling his comradely duty of helping others. 'He could clean the lavatories for the stewardesses' was the final suggestion. We had a concert, with peasant songs – sometimes haunting, sometimes ebullient – sung by one of the good-looking but sallow stewardesses with untidy hair. But she would sing only after the first officer had pleaded with her for almost five minutes. We had, too, our first taste of Russian food – soup with a halved hard-boiled egg floating in it; black bread, which was really dark brown and full of salty taste; cucumbers and cheese and a pale butter; and tea, hot with a slice of lemon floating in it, served in glasses after every meal. Even in the steerage (most of the other tourists had paid a bit extra and were travelling first class), it was plentiful and good – far better than anything which awaited us in the Soviet Union itself.

I found there were three other Rhodes Scholars on board – two from Rhodesia, and one from the Orange Free State. The South African was Bram Fischer, who was to lead the defence of Nelson Mandela when he was charged with treason in 1963. Fischer was later to die in prison, sentenced for being a Communist. A short, cheerful, self-possessed man, who had for me the additional virtue of having played scrum half for the Orange Free State against the All Blacks, he was at this stage no Communist – or at least gave no sign of it in our many discussions then – or, for that matter, over the years ahead at Oxford. Fischer's attitude in 1932 was essentially that of a liberal, testing systems by the degree of freedom and equality they offered.

Another member of the group was a young don from New College, Tom Jarman. He had great charm as well as a sharp intelligence, and was to bring an invaluable bantering, sceptical candour to bear on what we saw and heard in the weeks ahead. My earnestness was at times angered by Jarman's apparent refusal to take anything too seriously, but when I came to think over the tour at the end I found it was Jarman's quiet, good-humoured questioning both of Soviet attitudes – and of our often naive assumptions about what we saw – that stayed in my mind. He was later, too, as a professor at Bristol, to take a courageous lead in trying to get Fischer released from gaol in South Africa. There was one female undergraduate in the party – Jane Rendel from Lady Margaret Hall at Oxford, thoughtful and scholarly, anxious to test her intellectual left-wing convictions against the Soviet reality.

The Soviet Union had not yet become a place of pilgrimage for fellow travellers – that process only really got underway from 1933 onwards – and our group was made up chiefly of the genuinely curious or of the avowedly communist. There were three Quakers – an elderly couple and their grown-up daughter – who addressed one another as 'thou' and 'thee'; an earnest young factory clerk whose convictions were forcing him reluctantly, but it seemed inescapably, towards communism; a level-headed member of the ILP who was a Nottingham councillor; a tense young London communist in khaki shorts; and two girls in their early twenties, given to quoting Virginia Woolf and the *New Statesman*. I fear they retained the illusion that Russia was still the country of free love. Once we were into the sunshine of the

Baltic they found a quiet spot in the stern of the ship and stripped off to the waist. Unfortunately their faces were far from being as attractive as their figures, and they remained throughout the afternoon in a somewhat embarrassed isolation, left to themselves except for the reproached ship's carpenter, who suddenly decided that the railings near their sunbathing spot urgently needed a coat of paint.

There was too a sturdy old socialist from the Clyde, who had saved for years for this trip, and his white-haired, quiet wife; a doctor from Bolton with a large working-class panel of patients; the assistant city librarian from Cork; and a Scottish schoolteacher who made great play of the fact that he had already been on an Intourist trip to Russia. He was, he assured us, a figure of influence there. He called a meeting in the saloon to tell us what to expect, and promised to get the Society for Cultural Relations with the USSR to organise a banquet for us. In Leningrad he proved to be completely unknown and ineffectual. But he had had his hour of glory, and retired for the rest of the trip to press his attentions on the two would-be Bloomsbury girls.

Leningrad, in the pale grey light of an early Northern morning, was a magnificent slum. The high stucco buildings lining the banks of the Neva were drab, their plaster peeling, their paint faded. Yet this could not destroy their grand Palladian outlines, with, towering above, the dome of St Isaac's Cathedral, like a gilded St Paul's. Ashore we drove through wide, rough cobbled streets marked with potholes to an hotel on the October Square, the wide expanse in front of the Finland Station which had been the setting for the riots and demonstrations of the March Revolution of 1917 – the photographs of those events had reached even the remote townships of New Zealand. On a stone plinth at its centre a bronze horse reared up, ridden by a bronze Czar Alexander. 'One beast riding on another,' quoted our guide. From the square the Nevsky Prospekt stretched its wide, roughly paved surface, lined with plaster-fronted buildings of uniform height, some crumbling and peeling, others newly painted in pink or pale green or mustard yellow. Along it moved crowded tram cars, battered dhroskies drawn by horses with high wooden arches above their collars, wagons piled high with hay, and an occasional motor car.

The pavements were thronged with men in drab, threadbare clothes and cloth caps, or in high-necked Russian blouses, belted at the waist; with older women in short skirts, coarse cotton stockings and heavy shoes, their heads covered with white or red kerchiefs; with young women in cotton dresses, bare headed, often with a red kerchief around their necks; and peasants in straw shoes, their trousers bound round with strips of bast. All were hurrying,

hurrying, their sheer numbers and sense of being constantly under pressure off-setting the atmosphere of decay which surrounded the buildings.

In places the roadway was being repaired. Piles of stones were heaped by the roadside, and sturdy peasant women wearing sacking aprons carted cement in crude wooden barrows. Many shop windows were empty except for a few red paper hangings. In others a few packets of tea, a single set of shoes, or a wireless set would be all the dusty wooden shelves carried, whilst flies buzzed up against the inside of the grubby panes. On one broken window were the remains of the gold lettering of what had once been the sign of a fashionable jeweller. And everywhere the crowds hurried and pressed, intent and silent.

The cashier in the hotel used an abacus for her calculations, swiftly moving its round wooden counters along their wires. It was an instrument we would find in use everywhere. In the dining room many of the men diners were collarless and unshaven, their hair cropped, their shirts grimy. The proletariat in power were not making – or, at any rate, not yet making – any concession to bourgeois customs or fashions.

They took us first to see the Hermitage, but I had not the knowledge to appreciate fully the Rembrandts and the Tintorettos – and anyway I had not come to Russia to see Western art. I was thankful when we moved on to the wide square in front of the white and gilt Winter Palace, virtually unchanged since the workers' demonstration had been fired on there in 1905, precipitating the abortive rising of that year, and since the Bolshevik cadres had streamed across it in the decisive battle of the October 1917 revolution. History was written across the face of Leningrad.

The hotel in which we were housed had been, only twelve years or so ago, a prison for bourgeois suspects, and people had been woken in these same rooms at night by the light of the torches of the guards taking them to their death. At the far end of the Nevsky Prospekt, the great yellow buildings curving round Admiralty Square had been the administrative centre of the government until 1917. The cathedral nearby had been erected over the spot where Czar Alexander was assassinated by a nihilist bomb in 1886. In the Smolney Institute, in the northern suburbs, were the two bare, whitewashed, sparsely furnished rooms in which Lenin and his wife, Krupskaya, had lived and from which he had directed the onslaught on the Winter Palace. Nearby, in a palace built by Catherine the Great for her favourite, Potemkin, Lenin had addressed the Congress of Peasants' deputies, and in a speech which lasted only ten minutes had won over this previously antagonistic gathering to the support of the Bolsheviks.

Our guide, a slim, dark-haired girl in her late twenties with neat features and a soft clear complexion – a rare thing in those days of inadequate food – had heard Lenin speak from the top of an armoured car in 1917. He spoke, she said, always quietly, simply 'so that you felt this is the truth. He was not afraid to admit his mistakes. His speeches often contained the words "We were wrong there, but this is what we intended to do to remedy the wrong." When he died people said, "At all events, he never lied to us."' He was, in our guide's recollection, a rare type of orator, someone who moved crowds not by an impassioned appeal to the emotions, but by the simple force of his arguments.

Interwoven with these historical scenes was the strident propaganda of the present. The Cathedral of St Isaac had been turned into an anti-religious museum, with a huge pendulum hanging from under its dome, re-enacting Gallileo's way of proving that the earth went round the sun, the heresy which brought his conviction by the Inquisition. A Park of Rest and Culture just off the Nevsky Prospekt had not only an outdoor theatre, a band, an orchestra and reading rooms, but was liberally decorated with big cut-out figures ridiculing and attacking Kulaks for resisting collectivisation, as well as the routine figures of a blood-thirsty John Bull and Uncle Sam. In the park an unshaven young man in a worn blue suit, stained cloth cap and downtrodden shoes, spoke to our guide. I took him for a factory worker curious about these foreign visitors, but she explained that he was her fiancé, a law student.

The new workers' Leningrad was on the outskirts – steel and glass and concrete factories and workers' clubs and restaurants, a theatre, baths, and block after block of flats rising five or six storeys high, usually above unmade dusty, rutted roads. In an engineering works we met the workers' committee, heavily built men in their overalls sitting on the platform of a red-bannered hall. Indifferent to our better clothes, to our university degrees, they gave back their answers swiftly and confidently through an interpreter. One of them entered into an eager argument on economic theory with an Irish professor of economics in our group. Suddenly one could sense the fulfilment this new system was bringing to those who had gained power and responsibility under it. Here were men who might in the past never have risen above foreman, speaking with the assurance not only of those who have become the bosses, but who have pride in their work, in what they are making and achieving. Their faces were not yet clamped into the uniform, deadpan wariness which was to mark Soviet officialdom once the Stalinist terror got fully into its stride. These were working men who had, apparently, within their grasp that self-fulfilment of which self-educated but frustrated workers whom I had known on New Zealand farms had dreamed. I warmed to them, even whilst my mind noted how narrow and dogmatic were their arguments.

Further out from the main city were other reminders of the days of revolution, then still fresh in the minds of the people amongst whom we moved. Tsarkeyselo, the Czar's village ten miles from Leningrad, could have changed little in the intervening fifteen years. It was still a place of dusty, tree-lined streets of wooden houses with shingle roofs and wide wooden shutters, each in its small plot of poorly grassed ground behind a wooden picket fence. The royal summer residences were here. One was the Catherine Palace, the great white and red palace built by Catherine the Great, the Versailles or Potsdam of Russia, with miles of gilt rooms, a glittering chapel, fountained gardens where now the grass was lank and where workers and their families picnicked or strolled, singing to their banjos. In front of the buildings red banners proclaimed their slogans, a radio crackled and orated, and a brass band played to the holidaymakers.

The other, the Alexander Palace, had no grandeur but was merely a big, low comfortable late nineteenth-century villa, like an exaggerated version of the homestead of some wealthy New Zealand or Australian sheep farmer. It was from here that the Czar Nicholas had been taken by the Bolsheviks to his last prison in the Urals. The Czarina's sitting room had pink wallpaper festooned with white roses, and the corners were hung with fretwork cabinets. There were many family photographs, including one from Queen Alexandra and another from the Kaiser, and the many icons to which the Czarina had prayed for the health of her haemophilic son. Most poignant was a painting of a little German town, its baroque church-tower grey above close-packed red roofs, set amid the green fields of peasant farms – the safe home in Germany from which the young princess had come to be the last Empress of All the Russias.

The whole building was redolent – as the guides took care to point out – of softness, indolence, pettiness, of the lack of any deep culture behind the 'Little Father' of the nation. In the billiard room the table was still covered with maps of the Eastern Front, just as the Czar had left them, and a yellowing calendar on the wall showed 'July 1917'. At one end was a gallery where the Czarina used to stand, listening to the deliberations of the Czar and his advisers in the room below.

Back in the main city the Nevsky Prospekt that evening was a mixture of squalor and beauty. Near the pavement edge a burly man, dead drunk with vodka, lay inert, ignored by passers-by as if he were a pile of rubble. On the steps of a disused church a mass of people in ragged peasant garb were shouting and bargaining, selling the return half of their railway tickets. Yet on the park benches in a little garden beside the Neva Canal couples were locked in each other's arms; a women's rowing eight paddled home in the dusk; there was still sunlight enough to show the golden spire on the Admiralty building slim and alert against the sky, and to make plain the turquoise colouring on the minaret of a Mohammedan mosque. From a dingy beer cellar came the sound of an accordion. Further up the wide street what looked like a riot was in progress, but it proved to be only mounted police breaking up a crowd trying to get into a vodka shop. In October Square two armoured cars drove swiftly across, and the trams still jangled their way late in the half-light which passed for darkness in Leningrad in July.

CHAPTER SIX

Moscow

We travelled overnight to Moscow, approaching it in the morning sunlight across wide, rolling farmland with forests of silver birch, and unpainted wooden villages, and an occasional big wooden villa right out of Tolstoi or Chekhov. Moscow was a city of red banners and white buildings, with a wide blue sky arched overhead and a midday heat that reminded us we were back east of Suez. It was brighter and marginally more prosperous than Leningrad. There were more cars and lorries in the streets and more goods in the shop windows, though these too were at times cracked, and often dirty. People drank kvass from street booths, and sunned themselves alongside the Moscow River. In a garden near the opera a band played in the evenings. At five o'clock the pavements were as crowded and busy as in any other big city at rush hour. The people exuding the same air of effort and doggedness as in Leningrad, but with an added touch of hope. There was a sense of enjoyment as well as of activity – of some gilt on the socialist gingerbread.

Inside the Kremlin the gold and white Czarist state rooms had been carefully preserved, or carefully restored; in the Museum of the Revolution, Tom Jarman stung the guides to anger by pointing out that all traces of Trotsky had been removed; in a splendid villa facing the Moskva River was the collection of French Impressionists gathered by the former merchants Shehukins and Moroyov before the Revolution, and I got my first rewarding sight of Monet and Renoir and Matisse, and my first disappointing sight of Gauguin. Great artist he may have been, but he never captured the exultant, sweeping beauty of the Pacific. We trudged around the new post office, a new newspaper building and new factories, the first fruits of the Five Year Plan, each with its own restaurants, hospitals, apartment blocks and schools. Our guide excused as the hasty workmanship of a newly trained workforce the cracked concrete and peeling plaster which was often already apparent. One factory's infant school, in a big wooden house set among pine trees, was full of plump, sun-browned children wearing red shorts and large white hats as they ate their dinners at small tables. Slogans decorated the walls, alongside portraits of Stalin and Lenin, and a photograph of a podgy-faced infant in white clothes who was Lenin as a child. But the kindergarten teachers were big calm peasant girls whose instinctive affection and simplicity offset all this.

Red Square was unmarred by modernity. The long brick walls of the Kremlin were a warm rose red, Lenin's tomb a square-cut mass of crimson and brown, and the many turban-like towers of St Basil's Cathedral showed all the colours of the rainbow. In the afternoon heat a queue stretched back from the tomb, made up of workers, peasants, children, off-duty soldiers in khaki. In the warm, brightly lit interior Lenin's body lay under a glass museum-style casing, his khaki-clad arms crossed on his chest. His embalmed face with its neat features and its small reddish beard looked more like that of a small tradesman than of a revolutionary. In the calmness of death his countenance showed little sense of force or domination. It was difficult to believe that this was the man who had unleashed such stupendous forces on the world.

The full impact of Stalin's terror had not then reached the cities, and people showed little anxiety about contact with foreigners. When I got separated from the rest of the party in one of Moscow's unbelievably overcrowded trams and was carried past our stop, plenty of people were cheerfully ready to set me on the route back to our hotel. When in a People's Court, where we were taken to see the legal process in action, one of our party sat himself on the prisoners' bench, where a pale youth accused of theft sat between two soldiers with fixed bayonets. Even the stern-faced woman judge broke into a smile, and suggested he would be better placed elsewhere.

One of our guides, a girl of nineteen, did not hesitate, when Bram Fischer and I argued that we had not been shown the inside of an ordinary Russian home, to take us back to the apartment she and her husband, an economist in the State Planning Commission, occupied. It consisted of a single room – looking overcrowded with bed, samovar, wardrobe and small cooking stove – in a new apartment block overlooking a dusty, unpaved square. She conceded it was small, but at least it had enabled them to marry young, a rare enough thing then in the middle class in Western countries. When I asked her about the promiscuous lovemaking then assumed to be part of Russian life, she flared with anger: 'It is not true. In the early chaos of the revolution, perhaps. But not now. And what of your society? Have you no prostitutes, no marriages of convenience, no free love?'

At the opera, during the intermissions of *Boris Godonuv*, the audience promenaded in a wide circle, round and round in the foyer. When we joined this parade, people with some knowledge of English moved up alongside us, eager to try their skills. In the final entr'acte a lithe, brown-skinned, black-haired Georgian girl attached herself to the London communist, who for this occasion had changed his khaki shorts into khaki longs. It seemed, however, that her aim was more than friendship, for when he turned up at the hotel with her the night porter chased her angrily away, and wagged his finger in admonition at the now highly embarrassed Party stalwart.

The Soviet Union at this time competed in no international sport. Yet at a workers' sportsground on the outskirts of Moscow there were signs of what was to come. A cinder running track encircled a green football pitch, and the physique of the men and women training on it was superb, their heavy peasant strength refined and made more supple by gymnastics. A dozen sun-tanned Joan Hunter Duns paced one another in the evening sunlight. There was a swimming pool, and handball and tennis courts, and an open-air dance floor where a band of Ukrainian dancers swirled and turned and stamped to the music of a small balalaika orchestra. The facilities may not have been much better than those British banks, or the BBC, or other big companies had begun to offer their employees. But they were rich indeed compared with hiking or cycling, or swimming in a drab municipal pool, which were the main sporting opportunities available to most city workers in Britain or France. Sport had played such a key – and fulfilling – role in our lives in New Zealand that this seemed to me one product of Soviet communism which must surely be good. That it might in time be twisted into an instrument of national propaganda was a possibility too far off in the misty future to flaw this spectacle that July evening.

This workers' stadium, like the many Parks of Rest and Culture, had its full share of the propaganda which was everywhere apparent. Banners strung across the entrance proclaimed 'Sport Means Healthy Soviet Citizens' and 'Train Yourselves for Athletics: Soviet Banners Need Strong Arms to Carry Them'. At one end of the ground the committee was meeting on a red-draped open air platform to decide what action it would take to celebrate Constitution Day. Every time it passed a resolution the band would play a few bars of the *Internationale*. There were fourteen resolutions.

Radios – at street corners, in factory courtyards, in restaurants – clacked out speeches, talks, revolutionary songs. In the parks shooting booths and cock shies offered as targets a figure of a blood-stained John Bull, or the Pope brandishing a bomb, or a monocled Austen Chamberlain, and a wide range of shaggy haired, grotesquely ugly and fat kulaks. Drunkenness was another favourite topic assailed in posters – at one factory we were shown a special booth, decorated with red-nosed, wet-lipped drunkards, from which slack employees had to draw their pay. That inert figure in the Leningrad gutter had clearly been in no way exceptional.

Propaganda also impregnated every official statement made to us, ranging from the patient explanations of our assiduous guides to the declarations of a sub-Commissar for Education, a heavy, dark-jowelled man in a high-necked blue peasant blouse, who met us in his office. He snorted with astonishment when we asked if corporal punishment was permitted in Russian schools. 'We are industrially backward, but our civilisation has passed that stage, at least,' he replied.

Two themes dominated the arguments constantly put to us: socialism alone provided an answer to the economic problems plaguing the western world, and socialism could be attained only by revolution. There was no hope of advance through parliamentary democracy. The defection of Ramsay MacDonald – an event then not a year old – was cited as proof positive of this. The propagandists' voices rang with indignation when they denounced the sins of capitalism but rose to a new peak of fury when they spoke of the British Labour Party, or the French Socialists, or the German Social Democrats.

This second point worried deeply one of the few members of our group who was genuinely caught up in politics, the young ILP councillor in Nottingham. He had been an active supporter of the Labour Party since his teens. On our last night in Moscow we walked around the old Chinese city where merchants from the east had once stabled their caravans, and whose white-walled, narrow streets lay just off Red Square, discussing the Russian assertion that Labour in Britain could never achieve socialism. Did this mean he must turn communist? 'But that means I would lose my job, and many of my friends. And frankly the communists in my city are some of the sorriest specimens you could meet. I haven't any confidence in the British Communist Party as a revolutionary body. And at any rate the winning of communism is a long way off. Yet I want to get on and achieve something worthwhile. To try to be a successful capitalist businessman would be just to support a system I believe to be rotten. Yet to replace it seems an impossible task.' I could see no easy answer, and we walked back in silence along the side of Red Square, where the beam of a searchlight picked out the red flag flying on the white government buildings within the Kremlin walls.

One fact no propaganda could gainsay was that our own direct experience of Russia had been of frequent inefficiency. Trains started late and ran late. In the hotel dining room waiters stood immobile by the door, murmuring '*Sechasse, sechasse* – just a minute' for ten, twenty minutes – perhaps even half an hour – in response to our entreaties for service. The bus due to take us on an excursion would invariably be late. Once it arrived we would stand in the heat – or drift away, ensuring more delays until the group was rounded up – whilst the guides, the bus driver and, it seemed, any stray passers-by would argue the details of our next move. Long queues waited in the shops for the few goods on sale. Handles on hotel doors jammed or pulled away in your hand. An English engineer we encountered, who had been seven years in the country, admitted there was the same inefficiency among his workers. 'But until twelve years ago they never made a decision for themselves,' he said. 'Now they have to do it all. Do you wonder we spend a lot of time parleying?'

Another phenomenon owed more to fifteen years of war and revolution than to any system. This was the stench of unwashed human beings which pervaded every public building, every tramcar, every hallway – a cloying, sweetish, repulsive smell, such as might come from an unventilated storeroom filled with unwashed socks. It must have been the outcome of year upon year of people being short of soap, short of opportunities to wash, let alone to bathe, short too of the means to wash their clothes. A much milder form of this same smell could be detected in some of the big London department stores towards the end of the war. I have since come across it in full bouquet on only one occasion. In 1937 I was reporting events in Danzig and took a boat trip out into the bay from nearby Gydinia. On the excursion were twenty or thirty boys from a Polish orphanage, whose bodies and clothes gave off this same unmistakable odour. So pungent was it that, even though we were in the midst of a wide inlet, on the open deck, it was advisable to get well to the windward of them. In this first week in Leningrad and Moscow we encountered the smell everywhere – something which one came to endure, but never to be unaware of. No reporting from Russia, no photographs or films had mentioned this fact of life. Amidst the pencilled notes I kept of the journey I find that I had written, 'The camera cannot lie, but neither can it capture smells.'

Food, too, had been poor – even in our privileged hotel. For breakfast we had dark bread, a sliver of cheese, pale butter and coffee; for lunch, soup, meat, spaghetti and sometimes a watery ice cream, or fruit – once even some small strawberries. Supper was liable to be boiled fish and bread and butter. So often did we get this same soft tasteless fish that we used to argue that a shoal of whales must have been washed up on the banks of the Moscow River. In the workers' restaurants we saw at times lettuces and other fresh vegetables and meat being served, but we had no means of knowing how widely available they were. What in fact we were experiencing

– though we had no knowledge of it at the time – was the impact on the cities of the collapse of agricultural production as farming was collectivised, a process which was then underway, particularly in the Ukraine. The next stage of our journey was to provide us with first-hand evidence of this profound event.

CHAPTER SEVEN

Down the Volga

Nizhni Novgorod – its historic name not yet degraded into Gorkigrad – half a day's journey to the east, was part old provincial city, part new industrial metropolis. Its central streets were wide and cobbled, pitted with muddy puddles and piles of refuse. On many of the ochre-coloured buildings the plaster was peeling and faded, with bricks and untidy mortar showing beneath. Most of the people wore coarse, patched peasant blouses and bast leggings, and many had straw shoes. The dhrosky drivers had long greasy capes, like the robes of monks. Goats searched the refuse in the streets, above which hung huge red banners with hand-painted slogans in white or black. The best thing was the horses, great raking bays and Arabs, their coats sleek. Above the Volga the high brick walls of the Kremlin, which had guarded this approach to the Russian heartland, were overgrown with moss and grasses. I climbed to them with our guide. She allowed herself a moment of instinctive patriotism as we looked across the wide plain stretching eastwards towards the Urals and said, 'I love to think of the old Tartars and the Eastern horsemen riding round these walls, challenging the Russian garrisons in the Middle Ages.'

From the barracks across the street came the sound of soldiers singing. It was, she explained, a revolutionary tune, a workers' fighting song. 'Always revolution, always communism, always the Five Year Plan. Do you never tire of it?' I asked. She turned, indignant. 'You do not understand. It is the thing nearest to our hearts. And one does not tire of that. You do not think it wrong of a person to give up everything for an ideal. Well, that is what we are doing. What right have you to scoff, you who have everything? We have given up a great deal, but we are happy in our work. Why should we not sing of it?' Words of the skilled propagandist, or of the sincere believer? Perhaps a blend of both.

The reality of that dream lay in the new areas of the city – four colossal factories producing machine tools, wireless sets, diesel engines, and Ford cars and tanks; block upon block of workers' flats; kitchens where thirty thousand meals were cooked a day; a circus building; a workers' club; a technical school and theatre and library. Many of the buildings were rough and poorly finished, with broken windows and with plaster and rubble lying in the unpaved dusty streets. But food seemed more plentiful here. In the old town was an open-air market with booths of dark bread and milk, fruit and meat. And at the hotel we had for supper a tranche of rich, golden omelette filled with mushrooms – by far the best meal we were to have in Russia.

Four days travelling by paddle steamer down the Volga brought us a haunting, puzzling picture not just of peasant Russia but of peasant Russia on the move, in a massive, unexplained migration. Between decks the third-class quarters of the steamship were packed with peasants – backward, dirty, semi-Asiatic – men with beards, women with sun-browned faces, eager children, all crammed in with their bundles, sacks and carved wooden boxes, chewing cucumbers and sunflower seeds as they lay waiting, for the most part silent, in a stench which seemed even more unendurable than ever. Every hour or two we would put in to some riverside town or village. On every wharf similar crowds would be waiting, weighed down by huge bundles, ready to stampede for the gangplank as soon as the disembarking passengers were clear. There was never room enough for all, and as soon as the decks of the steamer were crammed, sailors stationed at the gangplank would elbow and herd and bully away like animals those for whom there was no space, apparently indifferent to the cries and expostulations as families were separated. In one place a husband became separated from his wife, who was left sobbing and shrieking on the quayside. In another case a boy in tattered coat and trousers, like a figure out of Dickens, was left, dumb with anguish, as his frantic parents were carried off in the vessel. As stampede followed stampede, one of the Rhodesian Rhodes Scholars said, 'They are just like kaffirs.' When I asked the guide why these crowds were so docile, accepting this treatment with anguish but – it seemed – without anger, she retorted quickly, 'Docile? You should have seen them in 1917, when they took the land from the landlords!'

But this was not 1917. It was fifteen years later, and now the Communist Party was in turn taking the land from the individual peasants in the drive for collective farming. We were witnessing – though we had no idea of it then – the shock waves of that process, as dispossessed peasants and their families sought refuge in other parts of the country. It was a process even more apparent once we got to the Ukraine. There every railway station was a solid mass of people and bundles – cramming every inch of the platforms, crowding every corner of the trains, riding not only on the carriage doorways, but on rails and pipes under the carriages and trucks. At each wayside halt the conductors would hustle off these extra passengers, but, mysteriously, they would be back again when we reached the next stop.

But there were other scenes to study as we sailed on down the huge, swift, mud-coloured Volga. Beyond wide, unfenced fields of wheat and sunflowers and maize, the small wooden-roofed villages were grouped round the white tower of a church. There were windmills, and herds of cattle standing at the water's edge, flicking at white moths with their tails.

As we moved past one riverside village our senior woman guide watched intently from the ship's rail. 'I was born there,' she said. 'And lived there till the revolution. My parents are still there, and cannot read or write.' She herself was fluent in English, French and German. We passed other paddle steamers and fishing vessels and long lines of barges with oil from Baku, as our wake unfolded behind us in sweeping, shiny waves. From white dusty roads tall Cossacks in high black astrakhan caps watched us. At one wharf a girl with an innocent virginal face, a black shawl over her head, a huge knotted bundle by her side, could have been Katusha in Tolstoi's *Resurrection*, as he described her coming from church on Easter morning.

There were reminders, too, that we were now in the east, already east of Aden. On the deck of one fishing boat three men dipped their hands into a common dish to eat, and our peasant passengers had the Oriental capacity to sleep anywhere. I noted down 'a pamphlet on the boats refers to "the celebrated Volga cuisine". Scene: twenty hungry tourists, having waited half an hour for dinner, watch the third-class passengers being woken from their sleep on the dining table so that the meal may be laid.'

At Samara, where we made an excursion ashore, the plate-glass windows of the new seven-storeyed headquarters of the Red Army gleamed in the intense sunlight. The headquarters had been set here, well away from both western and eastern frontiers, with reason. A decade later, renamed Kuybyshev, this was to become Russia's seat of government when the Germans reached the outskirts of Moscow. In its dusty main street we came suddenly upon a long column of peasants, old big-bearded men in patched clothes and straw gaiters, being marched towards the landing stage, guarded by Red Army soldiers wearing high-peaked cloth caps with a red star on the front and carrying rifles with long sword bayonets. It was a scene I had often seen depicted in drawings in magazines like the *Illustrated London News* from the days of the civil war. Reluctantly the guides agreed that these were peasants being taken off to prison camps 'for sabotaging the communal property of the new co-operatives in their village'. It was a rare glimpse of the realities of collectivisation.

Stalingrad, where our boat journey ended, was a grey city on a grey day, with a dust storm blowing in from the steppes. Like Nizhni Novgorod, at its centre it was an old provincial town, with its main buildings in peeling plaster, and with wooden houses with ornamented gables and shutters. Beyond this were the new factories and new dwelling areas – mile upon mile of grey concrete walls rising from flat, open countryside. The tractor factory – much publicised as proof of the success of the Five Year Plan – was closed to visitors, leading the more sceptical members of our group to mutter, 'They don't want us to see that it is really turning out tanks.' But there were workers' clubs, sportsgrounds, crèches and apartment houses in abundance, including a huge workers' canteen that looked as large as a factory itself. Even by the low standards of hygiene we had come to expect, it was particularly dirty. The flooring around the long service hatches was springy underfoot. I wondered if they had invented a new, more supple type of linoleum, only to find that it was nearly an inch deep in crushed, downtrodden food scraps.

Elsewhere Stalingrad offered a rich array of contrasts. In the dusty open marketplace a meat seller offered pieces of meat on a wooden tray. A peasant woman weighed each piece in her hand before selecting one, with which she went off, clutching it unwrapped. At the next stall a young woman selling raspberries had plucked eyebrows and reddened lips. Through the market a column of young pioneers in clean khaki uniforms with red scarves marched off to a month's holiday in camp. The local Intourist agent, whom the two Irishmen in our midst declared to be the twin of de Valera, entertained us on a grand piano which had somehow found its way into the hotel dining room. An excellent pianist, he played peasant dances, waltzes, airs from ballet and opera, revolutionary marches, the *Internationale*, and finally 'Yes, we have no bananas'. By ear he picked up from one of the Irishmen, who proved to be an equally good pianist, 'The Birth of the Blues' and a couple of Noel Coward tunes, listening to them as hungrily as the Soviet youth who would later seek tapes of the Beatles and the Rolling Stones. And to counter the heat of the afternoon we swam in the Volga, stripping off at the foot of the low clay cliffs which marked the western edge – the same cliffs into which would be built the dugouts of the final Soviet bridgehead during the Battle of Stalingrad.

Then on to Rostov, in the basin of the Don, where we were to visit Camel, the most prestigious of the large-scale state farms, much praised in Hindus' *Red Bread*. The road to it, a narrow dusty track, wound across steppes thick with fields of wheat, beans, maize and sunflowers, mustard and tobacco – unfenced acre after unfenced acre. At intervals were villages of wooden houses with carved gables, set in small dusty gardens, each village with a white-towered, gilt-domed church in its midst. The road was rough, the sun very hot, and in the morning's drive we managed seventeen punctures between our bus and the two accompanying cars. The bus driver, it seemed, was in love with one of the guides and determined to show his prowess. Talking hard, gesticulating with his left arm, he would take a bend in the rutted road at high speed, and *crack* another of our tyres would be gone.

Camel, when we got there, was a town of ten thousand people housed in blocks of flats, but in the open steppe, with an agricultural university, machine shops, a library, and schools. Disused and damaged farm machinery lay about, uncared for. An American engineer working there on contract said that little by little the workers on the farm were learning to use machinery, but it was a slow process. 'After all,' he said, 'it's only ten years ago that they were still grinding their corn in Siberia between two stones – and now they have to use combines.'

Camel presented the harassed Intourist guides with an unexpected problem. No one had warned us that its water possessed the qualities of Epsom salts. When the results became apparent, a queue formed outside the one lavatory, a small corrugated-iron structure prominently placed in the centre of an open space. Our group, all travelling third class, had been joined by a well-dressed American family of father, mother and grown-up son, who as first-class tourists had travelled separately in a large black limousine. When the water proved no respecter of such distinctions, the woman of the party, clad in a flowing purple dress, strode to the head of the queue and demanded priority. 'I am travelling first,' she cried indignantly, 'and I should go first!' But democracy prevailed, and she had to take her place as number seven in the rapidly lengthening queue.

All of this made it difficult to concentrate on the statistics the camp manager poured out to us later about crop yields and average incomes. But no figures were available about the yields on the holdings of the kulaks who had been dispossessed to make way for this vast enterprise covering five hundred thousand acres. Nor could statistics offset the sense of disarray and inefficiency conveyed by this gaunt, untidy settlement, where getting workers to and from distant fields could take up to half the working day. The same gigantism was apparent on the nearby state dairy farm, with two thousand cows housed in a series of barns which formed a small town in themselves. The cows, pedigree Holsteins, looked in good condition but the cost of their maintenance must have been high as they were kept indoors and stall-fed for much of the year. To get a herd of this size to and from outdoor pastures had proved too time-consuming to be practical. The milking machines were excellent modern models but many were out of action, and the manager told me at least a third of the herd was being milked by hand. He agreed that ten smaller units would be more economic. It was a wasteful use of this rich black soil, the fertility of which was apparent at every wayside railway station. There peasant women sold the produce of the small individual plots they were allowed to retain: strawberries, raspberries, cherries, cucumbers, sunflower seeds, apple turnovers, bottles of home-brewed kvass, even an occasional small roast pig.

We went back to Rostov by train. As we waited on a grassy bank by the little village station one of the Irishmen in our party gently teased a guide who had joined us especially for this outing, a dark-haired, vivid-lipped Southern Russian. 'Why should a good-looking girl like you be a Communist?'

She laughed with her reply. 'Good-looking, perhaps. But I have a black heart.'

The Irishman laughed in turn. 'Nonsense. You are too good-looking to have a black heart.'

Suddenly her eyes flashed and she replied, 'Right, I will tell you. When I was a child in Kiev, the Whites captured the town. Russians, Poles, some French. A White officer comes to live with us. At first he is friendly. Then he finds my father has served under the Soviets. They take him away to prison, where he is beaten so terribly he loses the sight of one eye. Now do you wonder I am a Communist?'

Kiev, further west in the Ukraine, offered long, tree-shaded streets, the most comfortable hotel we were to encounter, and a wealth of more orthodox sightseeing. In the great cathedral the gilt altar screen rose superbly against the background of the eleventh-century mosaics, and incense lingered in the dark interior of the church. Only a handful of people were in the congregation, all standing as is the Orthodox practice. Many were young, drawn there, it seemed, more out of curiosity than reverence. One old woman guided a child's hand in the sign of the cross. But the priest, a white-bearded man in gold robes, retained an impressive dignity, and when one of our party accidentally stood between him and the altar as he moved in procession round the church, he waved her aside with a gesture which sent her hurrying into the shadows. We came out into the square, past the beggars crowding the doorway, to see two huge monoplanes with a Soviet star on their wings flying overhead whilst in the roadway three girl consomols in uniform pointed up, excitedly.

From Kiev we embarked on a train journey northwards to Leningrad, which was to take in all fifty-four hours and was interrupted repeatedly by unexplained stops, often in open countryside and once, at night, illuminated by a huge red glow on the horizon ahead, apparently from a crashed train.

We filled the time by arguing about what we had seen, debating whether Soviet communism offered an answer to the slump then blighting life throughout the rest of the world. In that summer of 1932 the Great Depression reached its deepest point. Unemployment was soaring in Germany, providing the conditions which were to bring Hitler to power within six months. In the United States Herbert Hoover, still in the White House, had no solution to the widespread waves of bankruptcy and business collapse. The long, hopeless queues of unemployed shuffled their way past soup kitchens in every town and city across America. This was the summer of Steinbeck's *Grapes of Wrath*, of unsold coffee being used as fuel for Brazilian locomotives. Capitalism seemed unable to engender an answer to all this, and to the sense of hopelessness which went with it.

We had had only a glimpse of communism in action, so that our judgements were going to be based more on impressions than on firm evidence. Some of my impressions were certainly good. The sense of fulfilment of the factory committee in Leningrad, the athletes in the Moscow park, the children in the carefully tended kindergartens, and the multi-lingual guide gazing at the primitive village of her forebears were all heart warming. So too was the sense of common striving towards a common goal in the Five Year Plan.

It was too early to say whether the system would work. Large-scale farming seemed no way to deal with the problems of livestock raising, even if it might be suitable for arable crops. Yet the massive industrialisation, however slapdash much of it was, had been impressive. And it was possible to shrug off some of the manifest inefficiency as being due more to Russian backwardness than to some basic flaw in communism. There was no doubt that the Soviet Union was building for the future on a vast scale.

Against this had, however, to be set another impression – the feeling that these achievements were vitiated by a sense of constant strain, of wary uneasiness, indeed of fear. It was something I came to know later in Nazi Germany and in Fascist Italy, but was new and strange to me in that hot summer in Russia. It arose partly from particular events such as the cowed but determined crowds struggling to board the Volga steamer; the resigned yet upright bearing of the peasants being marched off in Samara; the bewildered masses, mostly women and children and the old, filling with their bundles every inch of every railway platform in the Ukraine; the mounted police riding into the vodka queue in Leningrad; and the drunk, lying neglected in the gutter. There was, too, the constant awareness that only one point of view was allowed expression, and the wary, guarded manner in which the Russians with whom we came into contact dealt not with us, but with each other. This could be no more than a generalised feeling on my part, as I had no knowledge of the Russian language with which to put these feelings to the test. But it added up to a sense that somehow the place did not feel right, and certainly did not feel happy. I was forced inescapably to the view that the Soviet system we had seen in those July days of 1932 did not offer an acceptable answer to the problems which the slump had thrust upon us. But, acceptable or not, the fact that communism was a major force in Europe was equally inescapable.

A further impression I carried away from the trip was quite unexpected. This was the possibility of another European war – and in the near future. In the Soviet Union the danger of a further European war was everywhere proclaimed. Warnings of war, training for war, signs of preparations for war had been with us since our first day in Leningrad. In the streets of every town and city the khaki-clad Red Army men, well clothed, shod in heavy boots, often slovenly in appearance but bearing themselves with self-reliance, stood out from the drab, hurrying crowds. When our Volga steamer went under a bridge, or our train over one, all the passengers were commanded to stay in the cabin or the carriage, and the blinds were drawn. Every factory was ringed with barbed wire and guarded by sentries. At the main gateway of the Stalingrad tractor factory a machine gun was mounted. In Leningrad there were armoured cars in the streets, and even the workers acting as guards in the parks had been armed with rifles. On the walls of workers' clubrooms, in theatre foyers and in university halls were diagrams of the mechanism of a rifle or a hand grenade or a light machine gun. The sports fields had sections for musketry and for hand-grenade practice. Posters showed the capitalist, with cigar and spats, backed by an unctuous Pope, training guns on a Red soldier; a Sir Austen Chamberlain, a favourite figure with his monocle and top hat, being married by the Pope to a cannon dressed as a bride. Banners called on workers to train as soldiers to defend the Soviet Union.

In every discussion with factory committees or groups of workers one question was sure: 'Will Britain make war on the Soviet Union?' When we answered 'No', a common reply was 'You may not want it personally. But circumstances can prove stronger than men.' This was understandable, because the wars of intervention had stopped only a decade earlier. But the assumption that a future war was probable and must be prepared for was a shock, so sharply did it contrast with the belief in which we had grown up:

that the War to End Wars had been fought – and won. It was perhaps the dominant thought in my mind when I stood again at the rail of the *Jan Rudjutak*, this time London bound, and watched the Russian coast dwindle to a thin wooded line against the cloudless evening sky.

CHAPTER EIGHT

Berlin

More immediate conflict was in the air when, thirty-six hours later, I landed at Kiel. The narrow streets of the central city were hung with party flags, often long banners stretching down the two or three storeys – the red, white and black of the monarchist Nationalists; the triple arrows on a red ground of the Social Democrats; an occasional Communist hammer and sickle; many Nazi swastikas, black in a white circle, set on red banners. Green-jacketed, black-helmeted police packed crowded patrol wagons which hurtled through the streets, sirens wailing. Half the people on the pavements seemed to be in uniform of one kind or another, the Nazis with their swastika armbands again prominent. The evening papers screamed, in thick black headlines two inches deep, of political murders and of fights between the private armies of the parties. I had arrived on an evening fateful for Germany. In Berlin von Papen, the ex-cavalry officer who was then Chancellor of Germany, had dismissed from office the democratically elected Social Democratic government of Prussia, and had taken over the government of that heartland of Germany himself. The Socialist Defence Corps, the storm troops of the Socialist Party had gathered at their barracks, ready to resist this illegal usurpation. But their leaders caved in, and Germany moved one step nearer to a dictatorial system, smoothing the way for Hitler.

I was in Kiel en route to Denmark, a country I wanted to see because its farmers were the main rivals on the British market to the hard-pressed farmers of New Zealand. In Esbjerg the next morning breakfast, after three weeks of Russian fare, was a feast – rolls, croissants, coffee, butter, cream, even a slice of cake. The same contrast was apparent on the ferry which the next afternoon – a Sunday – took us from Odense to Zetland. Even at four o'clock in the afternoon the ship's restaurant was busy serving up schnitzels and potatoes, stews, sauerkraut, spaghetti, pastries, cakes, and stein after stein of lager to people who looked heavy, overfed, bulging out of their Sunday clothes.

In the sunshine of the next seven days – the summer of 1932 was outstandingly fine throughout Europe – Denmark unfolded itself as a neat, clean, level land of white-walled, red-tiled farmhouses, set against the reddish bronze of ripening wheat, the yellow-green of newly cut hay fields, and the blue of the lakes and estuaries with which the land is shot through. The little towns with their castles, inns, half-timbered old houses and platoons of dark red-brick modern houses looked more like film sets than real places. Their farming methods were manifestly more disciplined than the slapdash style of an Australian or New Zealand dairy farm. Cows were tethered in lines so that they could eat their way evenly across a field, cropping it like a mower. No halved benzine tins, their rims hammered flat, served as milk buckets here. Dairies had electrically driven separators and their floors were tiled rather than made of rough concrete or of trodden earth holding the stale smell of spilt milk. Most farms were like fortresses, with whitewashed buildings round a square, with perhaps a walnut tree in its centre.

At Elsinore the castle, with its elegant towers and greenish steep copper roof, was more of a chateau than the stern fortress I had always envisaged as the setting for Hamlet's meeting with his father's ghost. Young Danes in red and blue beach pyjamas, high fashion in that year, cycled past its walls. On the outskirts of the town was its Folk High School, a celebrated place of the adult education in which the Danes were pioneers. Here I encountered for the first time the pacifist movement which, through bodies like the Peace Pledge Union, was soon to prove a potent, if shortlived, force in British politics. Some months earlier, at the opening of the League of Nations Disarmament Conference, petitions signed by four million people had been presented by women from many parts of the world. This ceremony was re-enacted at the college, and one of the delegates who had been in Geneva spoke fervently of the need to avoid another war. But for all the sincerity of those involved, it seemed to me no answer to the dangers ahead. With the sententiousness of youth I noted at the time 'there is something pallid, thin gruel, in the negativism of the pacifist's appeal. Disarmament, no more war. Yes, they are essential. But this sort of pacifism, with its refusal to acknowledge the lusty, animal side of human nature, is never going to achieve it.'

There was nothing pallid about Berlin when I arrived there on Sunday 31 July. It was polling day in a general election (the first of the two to be held in Germany that year) out of which the Nazis were to emerge as the strongest party in the Reichstag, providing them with the base from which Hitler was to clamber to power six months later. In New Zealand all hotels had been closed on election day. Here the polling booths were often in beer halls and cafes, outside which stood the uniformed representatives of the parties – Nazis, Social Democrats, Catholics, Communists, Conservatives

– holding placards and saluting their supporters as they arrived to vote. Bands of brownshirted Nazis – loud voiced, assertive – clattered along the pavements in their heavy, shin-high boots, or rushed past on bicycles, bells insistent. Every cyclist carried his party flag on his handlebars. The pavements were littered with discarded political pamphlets and newspapers, and with tiny paper swastikas or hammer-and-sickle badges.

But it was Imperial Berlin I most wanted to see, the Berlin depicted in the photographs of August 1914, as the columns of German troops in pointed helmets marched off to war, the Berlin that had loomed up like the bull's-eye on the maps of Western Europe which, studded with flags, had recorded on our walls in Geraldine the long years of war. Unter den Linden was much as it had appeared in those photographs, with the Brandenburg Gate strong and proud at one end; with the lime trees, their leaves white with dust, shading the central avenue; and with police guards, armed with rifles, guarding the Reich Chancellor's residence. The cafés were crowded and, in the evening dusk, brilliant with lights. Grubby beggars thronged the street corners. To the east the avenue opened out into the huge square where stood the gilt ornamented baroque palace of the Kaiser. Here Wilhelm II, the Kaiser Bill of wartime propaganda, had looked down on the crowds as war was declared. An American tourist with me was moved to eloquence: 'Just think of the old devil standing there saying "we will not sheath the sword till we have the lot" and the crowd cheering fit to burst.' Five hundred yards further back on Unter den Linden a yellow flame burned unceasingly in the dim interior of the Unknown Soldier's tomb, guarded by two immobile soldiers in steel helmets and Reichswehr grey.

But Berlin in that summer of 1932 was not just a city of past history and present tension. It was also, I was surprised to find, a city of freshness and freedom. In the pine woods on its western outskirts a big exhibition proclaimed Weimar Germany's new love for sport and for the open air. Camping, canoeing, hiking, sailing, mountaineering and skiing were portrayed in films and demonstrations, with a few discreetly filmed sequences of nudist camps to please the avant-garde. Small wooden chalets with big windows and wide porches were on display as weekend homes, the German equivalent of the seaside 'bach' of New Zealand families. The crowds who thronged the exhibition were lithe, sunburnt, glowing with health – a very different Germany from that of the portly, thick-necked men and women, or the arrogant young men with sabre scars on their cheeks whom I had expected to find – and had indeed found – in the streets of central Berlin. But even there this other Germany was much in evidence. The bank clerk who cashed my travellers cheque in the Wilhelmstrasse wore shorts and a short-sleeved bright blue shirt, something inconceivable in a New Zealand or Australian bank, where even in midsummer a blue serge suit and collar and tie was the unvarying garb. In cafés and theatres shorts and red, yellow, green or blue shirts were regular wear for men, and on the pavements of the Kurfurstendam not only girls but middle-aged women wore bright, light dresses and had bare, sunburnt legs. This healthy aspect of pre-Hitler Germany has been obscured by the obsession of the histories of the period with the decadence of its art and literature, and by the sexual ambiguities of its night life. Yet these were phenomena confined mainly to Berlin, Munich and Hamburg.

Nevertheless amidst the sunshine this was a land of three million unemployed, a land facing a brutal choice. *Germany: Nazi or Communist?* was the title of a new best-seller by the leading American correspondent of the day, H.R. Knickerbocker. The German edition was on sale in the window of every Berlin bookshop, its cover split diagonally between the swastika and the hammer and sickle, under the title *Deutschland – So – Oder So?* I sought for signs of this crisis in the working-class districts of North Berlin. The big stuccoed apartment blocks gave little outward sign of the poverty endured within, though the people in the streets were often gaunt and thin under their sunburn, and the small corner cafés and bier halls were half deserted. There were some fine municipal housing estates in red brick and white concrete, the balconies hung with flags, mostly the triple-arrowed banners of the Social Democrats. Near them were acre upon acre of allotments, green with vegetable crops, and studded with small wooden hutments and occasional tents. Outside one cabin a gramophone was playing the *Internationale*, and a man with close-cropped grey hair was teaching a little girl to sing it.

This was the period captured by Christopher Isherwood's camera-pen, and some of the flavour of Sally Bowles' Berlin was apparent even in my brief stay. From midday onwards the Freiderichstrasse, especially where it crossed the Unter den Linden, had prostitutes at every corner, sauntering on every pavement, seated, alert, their eyes constantly on the move, in every café, flashily dressed as the sign of their trade. Their presence was not in itself unusual. The centre of every European city then accepted the outward display of prostitution as normal, as commonplace as the presence of newspaper sellers or flower vendors or bootblacks. But in this part of Berlin the prostitutes were present in their hundreds. One afternoon a thunderstorm brought a rush of them, for shelter, into a pavement café where I was sitting. Suddenly the whole café was filled with vividly made-up girls in summer dresses and large hats, laughing and chattering and shrieking as the rain poured down on the awning, and shrugging off the efforts of the waiters to get them to leave – like a cage full of tropical birds in a rather tatty pet shop. Of the more arcane pleasures sought by Isherwood's Mr Norris there were signs only after dark. Then the lamplight in side streets would reveal a gleam of long black high-heeled boots, or of the pigtails and white handbags of what purported to be a group of schoolgirls.

My third morning in Berlin was not only very hot but very humid. The tar was melting on the roadway outside the small café in Wilhelmstrasse where I drank my breakfast coffee. I thought longingly of Taupo, with a light wind coming off the fern hills, and the lake, sheer blue. The cover of the *Berlin Illustriete* on the next table showed a holidaying couple looking up from a river towards the old castle at Heidelberg. That, I decided on impulse, would be my next destination.

Whilst I waited for the overnight train, I saw in a cinema Pabst's *1914*. The programme gave a synopsis of the film in English and underlined its anti-war theme. The cry of the wounded soldier staggering about a casualty station – '*Ich bin blind ... blind ... blind*' – was still in my ears as I came out into the street. A siren sounded behind me, and a lorry loaded with steel helmeted troops carrying rifles raced past, pursued by cars and cyclists, as if they were following a fire engine. I was with an American who spoke German, and who asked a bystander what was happening. He got a vehement reply: 'They're off to deal with the Communists. And the Communists deserve everything they get. Why? Because they betrayed Germany in 1918, and they would betray her again. But wait until Hitler rules Germany. Then you will see.'

In the distance the police sirens could be heard, fading but still insistent, picking up the note of the soldier's cry, '*Ich bin blind ... blind.*'

CHAPTER NINE

Last Summer of Weimar

Heidelberg proved to be a quiet, red-sandstone town under pine hills by the brown River Neckar. I found lodgings in the house of a war widow, where my bedroom looked across a cherry orchard to the red, broken tower of the castle. All day long there was the sound of music: the voices of housemaids singing in the morning as they spread mattresses to air over wooden balconies; gramophones in canoes on the river; bands of hikers, mandolins strumming, marching through the streets towards the hills; the jazz band in the café in the castle gardens in the evening; strollers singing in deep German voices far into the night. Upstream, where the village of Heilbron stood red roofed and white walled on a green hilltop, approached by a white dusty road alongside which the hay was neatly scythed under the apple trees, a little orchestra in the village café played a tune from the stage hit of the day, *The Congress Dances*:

Das gibt nur einmal, es kommt nicht wieder,
Morgen ist es schon vorbei.

It was the university vacation, and only occasionally did I see students in the shiny peaked caps, each in its distinctive colours, which marked the different fencing clubs. They swaggered cheerfully through the narrow streets, swinging their small canes, and many had sabre scars on their cheeks. Political banners were much fewer here than in Prussia; most were Nationalists but there were many swastikas and Nazis in uniform, and 'Deutschland Erwache' and 'Wahlt Hitler' were splashed in huge white letters on the side of the new bridge.

Here I settled down to learn German. It was a wise decision. Though I never became a perfect German speaker, I learnt the language well enough over the next three years for it to provide me with a valuable lever when I sought a job as a foreign correspondent, and to open up to me in the war the fascinating field of military intelligence. I worked from Hugo's German course (as Christopher Isherwood records he too had done) aided by lessons from the other lodger, a retired teacher. I gained a lot by making my first contact with the language in Germany itself, rather than in a British schoolroom, for from the outset my ear was attuned to its rhythms and cadences, and I picked up its slang at the same time as grappling with its classics.

My landlady dressed always in black, and I never saw her smile. Her husband and her three sons had all been killed in the first war and she had, she explained, lost all her money during the inflation years. To help me practise my German, she would sit and talk to me as I ate the supper of brown bread and slices of different, and delicious, types of sausages. At times I would catch her gazing at me with a sudden intentness. Was she, I wondered, asking herself if my father or my uncles had killed her men folk as, had they been a few years younger, they might well have done? When I left she clutched my hand in an abrupt handshake and said very quietly, '*Gibt's nie wieder krieg*.' But the Herr Professor from whom I took my formal lessons had no such worries. 'When Hitler comes, all will be well,' he would say, swallowing his kirchenwasser with one gulp.

But Hitler had missed his moment, I was assured by a young economics lecturer to whom I had a letter of introduction, and who invited me to his modern flat overlooking the old stone bridge, over the Neckar – the most beautiful bridge in the world, according to Goethe. 'Hitler will never succeed now. Von Papen and Schleicher have matters too firmly in control.'

He listened eagerly to all I had to say of Russia, quoting from Marx's letters about Russian backwardness. 'Marx stated some great truths, but the whole of Marxism needs rewriting in the terms of modern research and modern experience. The Communist Party here is entangling itself in Marxist phrases.'

'Are you then a Communist?' I asked.

'One does not say so in Germany now, if one is a lecturer. But …'

His wife, a luscious figure with black hair and a very white skin, swinging her silken blue-trousered legs over the arm of her chair, listened closely.

'Will there be a Communist revolution in Germany?'

'Not for many years now. The Right are too strong. And first there will be another war.'

They were almost certainly Jewish. What lay ahead for them? A professorship at Harvard? Auschwitz? Either would have seemed equally inconceivable on that hazy August afternoon, as the pleasure steamers on the Neckar made their stately way downstream, and the holidaymakers on their decks, with traditional Gemutlichkeit, waved to the people strolling on the grassy riverbanks.

CHAPTER TEN

Two Pilgrimages

Before I began my first term at Oxford in October I had two pilgrimages to make. The first, to the battlefields of the Western Front, I made on my way back from Heidelberg. By the roadside a few kilometres south of Ostend a milestone, carved on the top to represent a French steel helmet, recorded that 'Here the German advance was checked by the French, August 1914'. At this spot the French troops had linked up with the retreating Belgians and had exchanged shots with the Germans across a narrow canal which flanked the road. On the wall of our kitchen at home we had throughout much of the war a drawing of French outposts along this canal firing on the unsuspecting Uhlans of the German advance guard.

One of the main New Zealand battlefields had been in the salient east of Ypres, at Messines Ridge and Hill 60. It proved to be an area of disappointing ordinariness, where fields of grass and an occasional wheat crop sloped up in unremarkable contours. It differed from the parts of the Belgian countryside unaffected by the war only in the newness of the brick farmhouses, the smallness of the recently planted poplars, and the sight of an occasional concrete pillbox or machine gun emplacement, crouching like a grey beast in the corn. It was my first indication that few battlefields, viewed later, have an appearance worthy of the effort, suffering, heroism, fear and death which events have poured out on them. Only occasionally, as at Cassino, with its operatic backdrop of sheer mountains and high walled monastery, is the setting as grand as the event. Certainly these Flanders fields fourteen years after the Great War offered no sense of grandeur, or indeed of much dignity.

A segment of the Hindenburg Line had been fenced off by some local entrepreneur, and you paid five francs to pass through a turnstile, as if into a side-show at a fun fair, to see the concrete trench walls with grass and weeds growing in their cracks, and a line of rusted barbed wire, scattered bullet cases, and an old machine gun pointing out towards the British trenches. This gun must have killed hundreds of British troops, spilling their blood into the earth of the far bank of the canal where two old men now stood, fishing. Guides importuned you to buy booklets and souvenirs. These, including cartridge cases shaped as inkstands, enabled you no doubt to have on your desk an inkstand which might once have held the death charge of a friend, or a brother.

At Hill 60, where fierce hand-to-hand fighting had ranged round the perimeter caused by the explosion of a huge underground mine, you had to buy a ticket before you could pass down a narrow fenced pathway to view a patch of muddy, dilapidated trenches. A new café offered coffee and teas and postcards, and a large placard proclaimed the virtues of a new aperitif. The scene sickened a burly ex-soldier, still only in his mid-thirties, who was with our party: 'I lost two good friends right here. Every inch of this ground cost at least one man's life. You would think they would at least let it go back into fields, instead of making a trippers' paradise out of it.'

But the small cemetery outside Ypres' Menin Gate was dignified and quiet. Two of the white headstones marked the graves of Maoris – one of a boy of eighteen – and the streets of the town, rebuilt in a new raw brick, were a reassuring sign of life reasserting itself.

My other pilgrimage was to the land of my Highland forebears. I started from a youth hostel on the western side of Loch Lomond, just north of Glenfruin, the scene of the battle which had, in 1603, led to the MacGregor clan being proscribed. They had not only slaughtered a great number of their traditional foes, the Colquhouns, but for good measure had killed a party of theological students from Glasgow who had been rash enough to come out to watch the fight. James VI of Scotland, soon to be James I of England, was sufficiently angered by this to forbid the MacGregors thenceforth to use their own name (Rob Roy was, formally, Rob Roy Campbell) or to gather together in groups of more than four – a proscription which was to last for some two centuries.

The more obdurate MacGregors established a sort of guerrilla fastness to the east of Loch Lomond, from which Rob Roy in the early eighteenth century exacted his own tolls from the cattle farmers on the plains around Callender and Stirling in return for protecting them from raids by his fellow Highlanders, or – if the farmer did not pay – from his own followers. I got a lift by boat across the Loch, and on a grey September morning climbed over the shoulder of Ben Lomond and down into the glens around Aberfoyle and the Trossachs, and then over a further mountain range to the braes of Balquidder, Rob Roy's main base. These heather-clad hills were very like the tussock-covered slopes of Otago and Southland, and for the next four days I made my daily twenty or thirty miles across them alone, which in retrospect was rash. Had I broken a leg no one would have known of my whereabouts, for no other hikers would have come along the tracks until the weekend. But the clan ghosts shepherded me well and I came safely through to Balquidder, where Rob Roy is buried under a high gravestone. From there I took a bus to Aberfeldy, where I tracked down a very old man who, in brief bursts of lucidity between long periods of staring silently into a peat fire, identified for me my grandfather's home – a sturdy granite-built house by the Tay – and recalled my grandfather at eighteen swimming, for a dare, the Tay when it was running bank high in a spate.

My last stop was the Border country around Sir Walter Scott's Abbotsford. My solitude ended abruptly when, at the weekend, a column of cyclists from the Gorbals took over the youth hostel. They at first made clear that they resented an apparently middle-class figure like myself taking up space in what they saw as their domain, but relented when my accent revealed that I was no Sassenach and provided no guide to my class status. I was admitted to their circle around the large open fireplace where their leader, a sturdy youth with jet black hair, who radiated a remarkable natural authority (I am sure a decade later he and his like, sergeants' stripes on their sleeves, led the Highland Division's attack at El Alamein), held out to the flames a large frying pan filled with sizzling kippers, whilst with the other hand he fondled the breasts of his adoring girlfriend, who cuddled up to him in her white shirt and corduroy shorts. The air was thick with the fumes of kippers and half-burnt toast and Woodbine cigarettes, and with banter exchanged in incomprehensible Glaswegian accents. Outside the stars were sharp points in the early autumn dark as I walked my five miles to the station to take the night train back to London.

CHAPTER ELEVEN

Summerhill

Before I left England for Russia I had visited another place seeking to change society – though in a very different manner, through the individual. This was Summerhill, the uninhibited school in Suffolk run by A.S. Neill, then the foremost pioneer in new and freer methods of education.

I had read Neill's book *The Problem Child*, which set out his view that troubled – and troublesome – children (the term 'maladjusted' belonged to a later age) could become adjusted to normal life and normal society if they were given complete freedom within a loving environment. His further book, *The Problem Parent*, had just been published. Its opening two sentences summed up his philosophy: 'There is never a problem child: there is only a problem parent. That may not be the whole truth, but it's nearly the whole truth.' One of my fellow passengers on the *Moldavia* had been a friend of Neill, and gave me an introduction to him. So on a superb day early in June 1932 I travelled in a slow local train across the wide plains of Suffolk, where the fields were aglow with ripening wheat and barley and vivid yellow mustard, to the small town of Leiston, on the outskirts of which Neill had set up his school. It was an isolated part of Britain then, some two miles inland from a lonely stretch of North Sea coast, as yet undisturbed by today's atomic power station at nearby Sizewell.

Summerhill proved to be a big brick house standing amidst trees and lawns. On window ledges near the open front door a group of children, mostly dressed only in shorts, basked in the sun, waiting for lunch. One tiny boy, his sun-browned body completely naked, stood watching absorbedly two older boys fixing the brake on a motor cycle. Inside, in a large bare hall, other children waited in a tumultuous queue to draw their weekly pocket money, which was set at half their age in pennies. Under the trees outside an older boy had set up a stall, where he sold chocolate and ice creams.

Neill came out to meet me, shirtless in the heat, wearing sandals and old flannel trousers. He was a tall, white-haired Scot, with features which would have been gaunt but for the brightness in his eyes, and a quiet, whimsical reserve of a kind I had encountered in shepherds and back-country farmers in New Zealand. Indeed there was a good deal of a back-country homestead about Summerhill, with its battered, well lived-in appearance and the noise, frankness and old clothes of its inhabitants. I took to it – and to Neill – immediately.

We lunched in a dining room filled with small crowded tables at which children talked and argued loudly or read the journal of their choice – the *Autocar*, *Popular Wireless*, the *Daily Worker*, the *Daily Telegraph*, *Comic Cuts*, whilst a loud speaker relayed gramophone records from Neill's sitting room. For much of the afternoon I talked with Neill, and with his wife – a short, neat, middle-aged Australian with shingled brown hair, called by everyone Mrs Lins, an abbreviation of her maiden name of Lindesay Richardson. She was the younger sister of Ethel Richardson, the Australian novelist who had gained fame under the name of Henry Handel Richardson, and who lived and wrote in Leipzig. I met her later when she visited Summerhill, a quiet, watchful figure with enigmatic, heavily lidded eyes.

As the afternoon wore on I played tennis with one of the senior boys, who had been runner-up in the Suffolk junior championships, until the shadows of the aspens and laburnum trees stretched across the grass court and a band of younger boys in feathers and war paint straggled back from their game of Indians amidst the long grass on the edge of the nearby playing field. Mrs Lins called to a girl reading under a tree in the garden: 'Ann, you really need another lesson on those English set books. Are you free now?'

'Yes – let's go in the sun by the hedge. I'll call the other two. You remember, they want to come too.'

By contrast with the rigid disciplinarianism which was the norm in schools of all kinds at that time, it was a captivating atmosphere, and I was captivated by it. For the next two years Summerhill was to become for me a second home, and I loved it as one loves one's home, at first uncritically, and then critically, but no less deeply.

Neill's aim was to give children an attitude to life which would be creative, courageous, loving. He believed that this was best attained by leaving the child free to develop his, or her, own personality in a free environment, where the only rules were those made by the whole school – children and teachers alike – in an open meeting. Neill had arrived at this view by instinct as well as by intellect, as an alternative to the rigid, oppressive, tawse-dominated regime of sterile book learning he had experienced in the Scottish school of his youth. Over the years he had found theoretical support for it in the ideas of Freud, which in the twenties were beginning to exercise a grip on European and American thinking. If children were allowed to live out and express their childish desires as these occurred (however unpleasant such manifestations might appear to adults) they would not, as Freud believed, become the prisoners in later life of the subconscious mind – of the more primitive Id which could hamper and distort the conscious mind, the Ego. Summerhill's methods were based on the view that if you free the child from internal conflicts with his or her repressed desires, you leave that child free to go on studying and doing. Young children, in Neill's experience, adapted themselves quickly to Summerhill, and soon – however deep the problems they had had before – joined in with the class work as well as the play of the others. Older children tended to lapse into idleness for a spell of weeks, even months, before getting underway. One boy who had come to Summerhill from a big traditional public school spent his first six weeks in old clothes helping the local coalman deliver coal. He then persuaded his father to buy him an old second-hand car, which he spent most of his time overhauling and repairing. Eventually he resumed his former neatness of dress and set about studying for entrance to an engineering college. Another boy of sixteen learnt enough Latin in a year to secure the 'O' level pass he needed for university entrance. And proudly the school would point out that Diana Fishwick, the English Ladies Amateur Golf Champion, had been amongst its earliest pupils.

There were plenty of rules – set bedtime hours, nobody under seven to go into the town alone, younger children not to use the front stairs. But all these (in theory at least) had been made by vote of the school. School meetings were held in the big, bare-walled lounge on the ground floor. The staff and all the children except the very tiny ones would gather, sitting on the stairs, on the chairs or on cushions, or leaning against the walls. At the first I attended the chairman, one of the older boys, leant against the mantelpiece. He kept order briskly: 'Shut up, you kids over there. All right, that's the second time, Virginia. You're fined a halfpenny. Now Humphrey has got a charge against Vos, a charge of bullying. What's your story, Humphrey?'

Humphrey, curly haired, in his fringed Red Indian trousers and with warpaint still on his face, begins: 'Well, I was playing out by the big beech tree, and Vos …'

Witnesses are called, and Vos gives his version. A jury of six, nominated by the chairman and containing no more than one member of staff, retires to consider its verdict: 'We find Vos guilty, and fine him two weeks' pocket money.'

There was one celebrated mutiny against such methods. A group of children complained: 'This is supposed to be a free school, and yet there are rules everywhere.' Neill countered at once by proposing there be no rules at all. The meeting carried the proposal enthusiastically and rushed out to climb all the forbidden trees, ride each other's bicycles, use each other's wireless sets. By lunch time enthusiasm had diminished a bit, and slumped further when they found there was no lunch. 'Oh, no,' said Mrs Lins. 'There's no rule that there should be lunch, so I let the maids go home.' The more defiant laughed and went off to buy chocolate and biscuits with their pocket money. But by supper time a hastily summoned special meeting had voted back all the rules, 'especially the one that there should be supper'.

Summerhill was capable of laughing at itself. Amongst the plays staged in the gymnasium, which was also fitted with a stage to serve as a theatre, was one in which Neill had portrayed what would happen if his ideas were carried to absurdity. In it the Prime Minister was a boy of nine, the headmaster of Eton was seven, the Home Secretary fifteen. The result was a revolution by old men, who finally fell under the domination of old women.

Neill's pawky sense of humour helped greatly to sell his books – and his ideas. It lasted into his old age. In a letter to me in 1965, when he was eighty-two, he wrote:

> School full, sixty, thirty-six of them Americans. Place changed; central heating in house and carriages … had to install it cos the Yanks couldn't stand our Spartan cold. But life is too full now. Loads of visitors whom the kids get fed up with. My fan mail from the USA is almost of Beatle size … without Beatle income. I'll give you fame, laddie; its price is too high, and it has come too late. As Barrie put it, 'They give you nuts to chew when your teeth are gone.'
>
> Speaking of ITV I had a man here in summer thinking of sending his son. We got on to talking about TV. Said I 'I seldom switch on ITV for I can't stand the lying ads … Daz washes whiter.'
>
> 'It does,' he said. 'I'm a traveller for Daz.'

Sometimes there would be an evening of impromptu acting: 'You are lost on a railway station in Germany, and speak no German' or 'You are a dictator, and the mother of a man you have condemned to death comes to see you.' At one stage the school went through an intense Communist period, with speakers invited to tell them of the joys of Russia. But soon the children had too much of it, and when some of the older boys put on a play on the Five Year Plan the audience rose and countered with 'Rule Britannia'.

There were more orthodox moments. On winter evenings Mrs Lins would read to a group of the older children in Neill's big study, the walls of which were lined with untidy bookshelves, and which had a comfortable sofa and armchairs, and a gramophone and piles of records, and a big radio which could bring in dance music from all round Europe. On Saturday evenings, too, pupils and staff, and visitors from Leiston, would dance in the lounge to music from the gramophone. Neill prided himself on his fox-trotting, and Cole Porter's 'Night and Day' – that most haunting tune of the early thirties – evokes at once that crowded, bare-walled room, with Neill leading the way with remarkable grace for such a tall and apparently gangling figure.

There was little overt sexuality amongst the teenage children, and I was surprised to learn from Jonathan Croall's admirable biography* how much of a problem this became for Summerhill. Camaraderie rather than sexuality was the keynote of daily contact amongst the seniors at this stage.

The school clearly enough provided an atmosphere in which the child could become a free person, and it had an impressive record of transforming problem children into children at ease with themselves and society. But did it take the further essential step and fit the child to use this freedom well? In particular did it stimulate and encourage the children to acquire adequate learning and adequate skills to face life after school – to set about the tasks of earning a living and making their way in an outside world where the atmosphere was far from being one of love and freedom? These questions gradually forced themselves upon me as I saw more of Summerhill. And I had to admit that in this second part of his task, Neill was less successful. There was not enough stimulus or enough academic leadership within Summerhill to be sure of engaging the attention and energies of the children so that they ended their schooldays not only well adjusted but with their minds and skills well developed. If children are free to decide whether or not they will attend classes, teachers have to be particularly skilful and astute in attracting and holding their attention. This is particularly true of tough subjects like mathematics. And not all Summerhill teachers were of this outstanding quality. Indeed one of Neill's early difficulties was that the teachers drawn to a free school were likely to be those with unresolved psychological problems, seeking in its freer atmosphere an answer to their own difficulties. By and large Neill managed to avoid these teachers, or to weed them out, but a few remained.

More significant was the question of cost. If you are going to leave children free to do as they please and yet you wish them to discover, and begin to develop their tastes and potentialities, you have to surround them with a wide choice of opportunities – with a wide range of workshops, art rooms, photographic dark rooms, gardens. All of this calls for a substantial

---

* *Neill of Summerhill,* Jonathan Croall (Routledge and Kegan Paul, 1983)

investment in facilities and staff. And Summerhill in the early thirties did not have these. For the smallest children it provided excellent, cheerful quarters in a converted cottage, with small chairs and tables set in rooms with bright walls. There was, too, a small theatre, converted from a former squash court, with stage lighting and curtains and wings. But the other facilities were more makeshift. Some classrooms were mere wooden huts, gaily painted maybe with stripes of blue, gold, green, black and red, but inside bare and none too inviting. The older boys slept in converted railway coaches set in the grounds. These provided a cabin-like bedroom for each boy, which fulfilled the adolescent's desire for a room of one's own, but were hard to keep clean. The beds were often unmade, and the setting was grubby and drab.

Opportunities had not only to be provided. They also had to be taken up by adults, whose example and precept would stimulate the children to turn their own hands and minds to such tasks. Neill himself loved woodwork and metalwork, and his workshop was in fact his true inner sanctum. But not all the staff had a comparable breadth of interest. Neill's dislike of organised competitive sport also denied the children the very real satisfaction which can come from developing and mastering a sporting skill.

Yet such defects should not detract from Neill's massive achievements both with individual children and in changing the over-repressive attitude which dominated most education at that time. By methods which then seemed to many to be outrageous, and which were certainly revolutionary, he brought fulfilment and normality to many disturbed and agonised children, and provided a happy childhood for many others without such problems. Neill proved to society – or reminded it – that faith in a child is a better guide to its upbringing than is fear.

The application of this principle to schools in the state system was always going to be difficult. The high level of facilities and equipment, and the high ratio of teachers to students necessary for Summerhill's methods to work – facts which were already apparent in the 1930s – were not going to be easily found in a state-funded system. Common sense dictated there should be a gradual approach, with an experiment in Neill's methods being first carried out in one or two selected areas. Instead, the Ministry of Education in the late 1960s took the huge gamble of switching the whole state primary system away from traditional teaching methods and over to a child-centred system. It is a gamble which has, tragically, failed. It has hampered millions of children in acquiring the basic skills of reading, writing and numeracy. Without such basic skills, the incentives for children to learn for themselves, rather than to be taught, are greatly diminished. The new methods may have shown gains in easier relationships between teachers and students, and amongst students themselves (though these too are marred by indiscipline and bullying) but in academic terms they have failed.

But such problems belonged to a distant future, into which I had no desire to peer when in the autumn of 1932 I ended my stay at Summerhill and prepared for my first term at Oxford.

PART II

The Oxford Years
1932–34

MEMBERS OF THE HONGI CLUB, 1933–34.

Bertram, J. M.	Waitaki B.H.S. and Auckland U.C.	New Coll.
Campbell, J. A. W.	Mt. Albert G.S. and Auckand U.C.	Merton.
Cox, G. S.	Southland B.H.S. and Otago University.	Oriel.
Falla, P. S.	Christ's College	Balliol.
Lascelles, J.	Christ's College.	Balliol.
Lovelock, J. E.	Timaru B.H.S. and Otago University.	Exeter.
*McCallum, S. P.	Canterbury U.C.	New Coll.
Mulgan, J. A. E.	Auckland G.S. and Auckland U.C.	Merton.
Rapson, W. S.	Mt. Albert G.S. and Auckland U.C.	St. Cath's
Riddiford, D. J.		New Coll.
Riddiford, E. A.		Ch. Ch.
*Sisam, K. A.	Auckland G.S. and Auckland U.C.	Merton.
*Syme, R.	New Plymouth B.H.S., Victoria and Auckland U.C.	Trinity.
*Taylor, F. A.	Auckland G.S. and Auckland U.C.	Ch. Ch.

Graduate.

List of members of the New Zealanders' Club at Oxford, 1933–34. President: J.E. Lovelock; Honorary Secretary: G.S. Cox; Honorary Treasurer: J.M. Bertram.

CHAPTER TWELVE

Oxford

Oxford had been for me such a dazzling goal – one I had hardly dared dream of attaining – that when I went up to the university in October 1932 I was both surprised and dismayed to find myself at odds with the place. I found it unrealistic, dangerously insulated from the realities of either economic or normal sexual experience, cosseted by a high standard of living. It was an escapist atmosphere in which, at a vitally important period of our lives, we were being withdrawn from the hard facts of life instead of being brought face to face with them. I was, it is true, older than the main run of undergraduates, and had already had nearly five years of academic life. I was at the stage when I urgently needed other types of experience. This made me more critical of the unworldliness of Oxford than I might otherwise have been, enlarging its defects as if I were viewing them under a magnifying glass. But they were there all the same, and at first they poured over me like a waterfall, dominating my first impressions, obscuring other good aspects which I came to appreciate only later.

I arrived on a grey, chill autumn evening. A rickety taxi carried me through narrow streets lined with high stone college walls, which were topped with spikes and broken glass, like the walls of New Zealand's Lyttelton Gaol. The gloomy gateway of Oriel was lit by one wan, bare electric globe. Beyond, the buildings of the front quad rose up till they almost shut out the sky. Black, rotting stone flaked off them, like bark from trees in a stretch of burnt bush. No grass softened the quadrangle. It was of brownish beaten earth and pebbles, hard and bare as a barrack-square. Only the great doorway of the hall, above the curved steps, seemed a thing of beauty. From the chapel in the corner a bell tolled in thin, chill tones.

A man in a brown sports jacket and grey flannels, his lean face scholarly in the half light, came out of a small coop-like office that I was to learn to call the lodge. Was he a don? I had no idea. It was on the tip of my tongue to say 'Good evening, sir' when he got in first. 'What name, sir?' He was Shepherd, the assistant porter. It was not the last time in Oxford that I was to take a scout – a college servant – for a don, or a don for a scout.

It was in this setting that I was delivered a body blow. I learnt that I had been denied, for my first year, one essential instrument for getting the best out of Oxford – a room of my own. Instead of having, as virtually all other undergraduates had, a bedroom and a sitting-room study to myself, I found I was to share a sitting-room study with another Rhodes Scholar, a twenty-year-old American from Minnesota called Lynn Beyer. Though he was to prove a good man to share with, someone who combined scholarship with commonsense and who was ultimately to become a leading figure in American naval intelligence, each of us was in the other's way.

I felt doubly in need of rooms of my own. I had lived my life until then amidst the constant pressures of a small community with its vigilant demand for orthodoxy – a community where a multitude of other people were only too ready to live your life for you. I wanted to escape from this, to regulate my life according to my own precepts – even if these proved in the end to be those of the community in which I had grown up. To these personal factors had been added, in my six months in Europe, questions which I wanted the chance to sort out in my own way, on my own ground. There was the drift to war, as the atmosphere in both Russia and Germany seemed to indicate. What could we, who would have to fight in it if it came, do to halt this drift? If, too, I wanted to play some part in public life – and by accepting a Rhodes Scholarship I had accepted an obligation to do so – was there still scope for the type of reformist policies my MacGregor grandfather had pursued, and to which my own instincts inclined me? Or were the Russians and the growing chorus of voices in the West right in arguing that only the root-and-branch change of violent Communist revolution would remedy times so manifestly out of joint? Did Freud, as Neill insisted, hold the key to human happiness, and perhaps even to peace? These were all issues to which I hoped Oxford might have an answer. But to find it, even to search for it effectively, I needed a room of my own. And, by a cruel quirk, fate had denied me that. I knew instantly, as the darkness settled over the Gothic skyline of Oriel's front quadrangle, and I put on my short black commoner's gown to go to dinner in Hall for the first time, that part of the opportunity which Oxford promised, and for which I had worked very hard, had been snatched from me before I began. Even now, as I write about this more than fifty years later, the hurt recurs sharply in my mind.

Oriel's Hall was much smaller, and less grand than that of Christ Church. But it was well panelled in dark oak, with a low gallery looking down on three long tables which ran up towards the High Table dais. Beyer and I found places. The dons entered, the Provost knocked twice, and a scholar recited the long Latin grace. On one wall hung a portrait of Sir Walter Raleigh, in his day a commoner of the college. On another was Cecil Rhodes, also an Oriel man. Portrayed with slightly glaring eyes, he watched the members of the senior common room settle down to a dinner the quality of which had been specially provided for in his will 'so that the dignity and quality of the High Table may be maintained'. We ate soup, roast mutton and sprouts – how often in the next six months was I to eat sprouts! – fruit and savoury, and drank beer from pewter mugs.

After dinner – or after Hall, as I learnt to call it – we had our first glimpse of another marked characteristic of Oxford at that time – its view that women had virtually no place in its life. We newcomers from overseas were invited to take coffee, and advice, from the Dean, the Rev. Dr Brand. He was a clergyman with a future, destined soon to be the Bishop of Brisbane and then of London, a man with a fleshy yet heavily lined face and contented bearing. He urged us to work hard, go to chapel, seek help from religion. His references to sex were, in the manner of the time, carefully indirect: 'You are out in the world now, away from school. Many temptations will be put in your way. And the best advice I can tell you will be that if any bad thoughts enter your mind, get out and have a good row on the river.'

To those of us brought up in the British idiom, the message was plain. But it was less so to a new student from China. His face was suddenly alert, yet baffled. 'What do you mean, sir, by bad thoughts? Anger? Or envy? Or idleness?' For a moment the Dean was disconcerted. 'I think we should talk further of this question, the two of us, later,' he said.

As we filed out into the darkened quadrangle I sensed for the first time how strongly the monastic tradition, from which the first Oxford colleges had grown, still persisted, not only in its attitude towards sex, but in its compensatory interests in good food, isolation from the harsh outside world, and retreat into theory.

The university in which I found myself that autumn of 1932 seemed me to be almost suffocatingly remote from the realities of the world outside. It was at a mid-way stage between the orthodoxy and the dilettantism of the twenties (the era of *Brideshead Revisited*), and the left-wing fervour of the later thirties. As I first got to know it, in those weeks of fog and of intermittent sunshine brightening Oriel's grey walls, Oxford seemed to me to cower away from the harsh facts of the world slump behind a rampart of Kantian philosophy and anchovy toast for tea. At times in my first year I used to feel that when I boarded the train at Paddington for Oxford, I was setting out not for a city set in the countryside of southern England but for another planet, moored somewhere above Didcot.

This unworldliness was emphasised by the university's almost monastic attitude towards women. Rigid rules controlled contacts between men and women students. No woman could visit a man's rooms in college without special permission, and then only if chaperoned by another woman. Similar rules controlled outings on the river or in a car. At lectures women had to wear an austere academic sub-fusc garb – a white blouse, a dark skirt, black stockings, and a dark jacket. When amidst this sombre throng I saw one morning in the High Street an undergraduate in a well-tailored royal blue coat and skirt, she stood out like a colour print in an exhibition of monochrome photographs.

Oxford at this time was, as Goronwy Rees has pointed out, 'an almost exclusively male society … in which for most undergraduates normal biological laws had been for the time being suspended.' To most members of the university, students and dons alike, 'the notion that men should live without women was perfectly natural, to some even it was the only acceptable way of life. It was the idea that women are an essential and indispensable part of man's existence that struck them as abnormal and bizarre.'* What had struck this undergraduate from Cardiff High School came home equally forcibly – and was equally unpalatable – to me. When in my second year, with rooms of my own, I could invite a girl to lunch, it seemed to me that the very walls of Oriel cried out in protest as she made her way across the quadrangle.

My reactions to Oxford were also influenced, I was surprised to discover, by its climate. Its soft, often humid air made me feel lethargic and even oppressed, so that for the first time in my life I had to bestir myself into activity, to resist a desire to sit brooding over a fire. This antipathy to humidity, which I was later to experience even more severely in Washington, was chastening as well as annoying, demonstrating as it did that one's mental state could be influenced by, or indeed conditioned by, such purely physical factors. In time all these impressions were to be softened and modified, as Oxford gradually wove its spell around me, but in that first autumn and winter they were sharp indeed.

Most importantly of all, I was baffled and disappointed by the reluctance of the dons who taught me to relate their teachings to the immediate issues of the day, and in particular by their spurning, as subjects worth studying, the views of Marx and Freud. No doubt had I come up three or four years later I would have been surfeited with such instructions, so rapidly can academic fashions change. But those who taught me in my first year saw no

---

* *A Chapter of Accidents*, Goronwy Rees (Chatto & Windus, 1971), pp. 90, 91

reason why either of these two thinkers should be singled out for special attention – or even merit much attention at all.

Yet these were the two new gods being held up to my generation, and it seemed to me that it behoved us to look closely at them, even if only to establish whether they had feet of clay. I could not accept the view that they should wait their time in the queue for our attention, when we had made our way through the works of Plato and Aristotle, Locke, Descartes and Kant and the other accepted philosophers, or Marshall and the other orthodox economic theorists. Marxism and Freudianism were ideas on the march at that moment, affecting the actions as well as the thoughts of millions of people, and I wanted to get to grips with them right away.

But if Oxford was reluctant to teach me about these two upstarts – as it was until G.D.H. Cole started a private seminar on Marxism late in 1934 – it provided superbly the means for me to teach myself about them. The Bodleian Library had available all I could wish for of their writings. In the high-domed hall of the Radcliffe Camera I settled down day after day to struggle through their works.

And it was a struggle. Karl Marx must be one of the most indigestible writers of all time – and Freud, in his own convoluted way, runs him close. Perhaps this was because I was reading them in translation, but there can be few other thinkers who have exercised such widespread impact and yet who have expressed their ideas in such opaque and exhausting ways.

Of the two, I found Freud the more difficult to comprehend. With Marx there were always the great denunciatory or apocalyptic passages, or the occasional vivid phrase to enliven the whole, even though to reach these one had to cross deserts of arid statistics or lengthy examples. And at least one chapter of volume one of *Das Kapital* I read with avidity – Marx's analysis of Edward Gibbon Wakefield's theory of colonisation, the theory which had brought one of my grandfathers to chance his luck in a country where capital (in the form of land) was abundant but labour was not. But at the end of it all, it seemed to me that you needed only to study closely one document – the *Communist Manifesto* – to hit upon the secret of Marx's appeal in the thirties. That secret lay in his view that, however unpalatable the world might find it, communism was historically inevitable. This was the heart of the Marxist message, expressed in the thunderous prose of his prediction that 'Centralisation of the means of production and socialisation of labour at last reach a point when they become incompatible with their capitalist integument. This integument is burst asunder. The knell of private property sounds. The expropriators are expropriated.'

This faith in the inevitability of communism, this belief that it would, inescapably, be the economic system of the future, looked realistic enough in the depths of the Great Depression. In that autumn of 1932, with unemployment at record levels, with banks collapsing and industries closing, it was possible to believe that capitalism was like a ring-barked tree, doomed to decay and collapse. Signs of hope for its future were rare. Franklin Roosevelt had not yet been elected President of the United States; Keynes had not yet produced his *General Theory*. Further cuts, further deflation, were the only recipes acceptable to those in power in most developed countries. It is not surprising, therefore, that in this atmosphere many Western intellectuals decided that Marx might well be correct, that capitalism was in the process of giving way to communism. This in turn led them to think that if communism was bound to come, it made sense to keep in with the Communist Party – at least as a fellow-traveller – if not as a full Party member. Woodrow Wyatt has said that Kingsley Martin, who as editor of the *New Statesman* exercised great influence over the intelligentsia of the time, was of the view that since communism was bound to win, there was no sense in opposing it. The line between intellectual opportunism and real conviction can be narrow. The danger of fascism, particularly after Hitler came to power in Germany, was no doubt the main factor in drawing so many people towards the Left, and indeed the extreme Left, as the thirties wore on. But the possibility that communism would, owing to inexorable economic forces, emerge as the victor was a powerful further inducement to look leftwards.

Any temptation to accept this view on my part came up against the most important lesson I learnt from my study of Marxist-Leninism. This was the belief that a socialist future would be achieved only by the dictatorship of the proletariat, by the type of ruthless totalitarianism I had glimpsed in Russia. This was to me instinctively unacceptable. All my instincts, reinforced by my upbringing and education in the egalitarian atmosphere of New Zealand (though it too had had its subtle class structure) made the idea of dictatorship, whether from left or right, abhorrent. I therefore drew from my readings of Marx a deduction opposite to the one Kingsley Martin seems to have drawn. If economic forces were bound to carry us towards a system in which productive property had to be publicly owned, then surely the sensible thing was to try to combine that economic system with one of political democracy. Within the contemporary British scene, that was an argument for backing the Labour Party and resisting the Communists. It was to be my personal political stance throughout these years of the troubled thirties.

My first experience of a northern winter provided a dour background to my introduction to Oxford. In New Zealand's South Island the winter was sharp with colour. At daybreak the fields and lawns would be covered with glittering white frost. By mid-morning the sun would be through, and we played football in the afternoon often in bright sunshine under gleaming blue skies. But in Oxford it seemed that each grey overcast day was followed by a starless night, so black that the very sky seemed to have been pulled down into the streets. Only occasionally did the colour come back, with the afternoon sun glowing on the spire of St Mary's at the end of Oriel Street.

Two pieces of news – one personal, one general – arrived with this wintry setting. Early in December my elder brother wrote to tell me that Ongaroto had been sold. The pressure of the slump had been too great, and my uncle had accepted an unusually good offer from an afforestation company that planned to use the area for growing pine trees. It was like the death of a parent or of a close friend. That bronze, grey and green valley, between its high sheltering bluff and its bush-softened hills, had been for me a place of refuge – somewhere to which, if the going got too tough, I could have withdrawn for a week, a month, a year, to replenish my energies before returning to the fray. Now it was gone, and I felt very much on my own.

The second piece of news came at the end of January 1933 when Lynn Beyer and I opened our morning papers at breakfast-time – he took the *Times*, I the *Manchester Guardian* – to read that Hitler had become Chancellor of Germany. (No doubt the news had been on the BBC the night before, but no one at Oxford of my acquaintance had such a thing as a radio.) I knew at once that this was bad, bad news, that the brown-uniformed thuggery I had seen in the streets of Kiel, Berlin and Heidelberg, once released, would do terrible things. It is always easy in hindsight to endow oneself with an appreciation of events which is perhaps imagined. But I am sure I falsify nothing when I recollect pouring out to Beyer the concern Hitler's victory aroused in me – concern less at the increased danger of war than at the possibility that dictatorship, once established in the heart of Europe, would spread until it engulfed us all, until men like Sydney's Colonel Campbell and his kind were able to limit, if not crush, our freedom. I was to make my share of political misjudgements in the years ahead, but on the undoubted evil of Nazism I never had, from that bitterly cold January morning onwards, the least doubt.

Then suddenly, one afternoon in late February when I was walking in the park, there were gold and purple crocuses amidst the grass, and by March the reward of spring. When the vacation came I bought a rucksack (a sombre khaki affair in those days), and made my way, partly walking, partly hitch-hiking, from Dieppe across to Rouen, and then up the valley of the Seine to Paris. Chance brought me to the Hotel du Cygne at Tôtes, which de

Maupassant used as the setting for his short story *Boule de Suif*, and to Vetheuil-sur-Seine, so frequently painted by Monet. My first impression of Paris was vivid too. The bus from Mantes ended its journey at the Porte Maillot, and I stepped from it to see, at the end of the splendid vista of the Avenue de la Grande Armée, the Arc de Triomphe silhouetted against the sky. I stayed in a small hotel in the Latin Quarter, and spent a good deal of my time with a French student who was also in his first year at Oriel. He was a keen boxer, and the price he exacted for showing me the city was that we should first spar for three or four rounds each evening on the parquet flooring of the salon of his family's expensive flat near the Place d'Alma. His father would stand by to offer us a whisky and soda as I applied a hand-embroidered towel or a cold compress to my bruised face – for my friend was a very good boxer. He was somewhat dismayed to find that the only clothes I had were the baggy grey flannels and worn sports jacket in which I had walked from Dieppe. But that did not deter him from taking me with him to attend what was then an event in the calendar of Parisian society, a midday stroll on Thursday in the Avenue des Acacias in the Bois de Boulogne. Women in the high fashion of the day – it was a period of rich fabrics and of a bandbox, lacquered smartness – paused to talk to riders on superbly groomed horses, whilst equally smartly dressed men drove up and down in open-topped tourers. The French bourgeoisie, it seemed, was in no mood to accept Marx's prediction that their day was done.

CHAPTER THIRTEEN

Field Work

I backed my theoretical studies of the Left with some field work. When hunger marchers from South Wales came through Oxford I helped to serve lunch and tea to them. Small and gnarled, they were surprisingly lacking in bitterness. The next morning they continued on their way to London, marching quietly and determinedly down the High Street through the rush hour traffic.

On May Day in 1933 I joined an Oxford contingent for the traditional May Day march in London. The arrival of the coach with its undergraduates in baggy grey flannel trousers and sports jackets at the rallying point on the Embankment caused much excitement among the raven-haired girls with sumptuous plump thighs in khaki corduroy shorts who formed a large part of the East End marchers.

In front of the column, on its march through Aldwych to Marylebone Road and on to Hyde Park, rode eight policemen. Other police marched alongside. Intentionally or not, the benevolent, sheltering way they shepherded the column diminished its militancy. It was hard to look revolutionary with a policeman walking alongside you in a fatherly manner. But the Oxford squad flourished its banners defiantly, proclaiming 'We Declare War on War' and 'Students and Workers Unite'. Communist stewards led chants of 'Scholarships not Battleships' and 'Hitler and Mosley mean Hunger and War'. There were occasional bursts of the *Internationale* and, to the tune of the World War I song 'Keep the Home Fires Burning' this refrain:

Stick to Marx, my hearty
Damn the Labour Party,
Keep the hellfires burning bright
For the bourgeoisie.

In the Temple Gardens two young barristers in bowler hats, striped trousers, spats and black coats, standing amid the daffodils, pointed excitedly to the Oxford contingent's banner; on the Embankment a tiny girl waved a red flag; in Aldwych a tram driver halted to let the column pass, smiled and winked at one of the policemen. It was a gesture which said more about the attitude of the main body of British workers towards the Marxist Left than would have been revealed by a dozen opinion polls – had they existed.

Oxford political clubs, which covered the spectrum from the Communist October Club to the Fascist Club, opened their doors to anyone prepared to pay the term's subscription – usually a shilling – and provided a chance to hear the surprisingly large number of public figures who were prepared to journey to Oxford to address an audience, often numbering only a score or so, of argumentative undergraduates.

In my first term I joined the Communist October Club. This did not make me a member of the Communist Party, but merely of this undergraduate society. I did so for two reasons. Amongst the speakers listed by the October Club were two men I particularly wanted to hear – H.G. Wells and J. Middleton Murry. And it seemed to me sensible that, if I was going to study the theory of Marxism, I should see what the British Marxists were offering to the public. H.G. Wells, one of the gods of my youth, addressed the Communist October Club in a back-street gymnasium, where the climbing ropes were looped against the walls and the mats heaped into one corner. He proved to be a far from god-like creature, small, rotund and with a squeaky voice. But he stood his ground adamantly and courteously when assailed at question time as an issue-dodging petit bourgeois. Another physically unimpressive figure was J. Middleton Murry, Katherine Mansfield's husband, who had just brought out his biography of her. He seemed both pallid and plaintive, an inadequate partner for anyone in whom the fires of creativity had burned so fiercely. But he too stood his ground firmly enough when he argued that change must come through men's hearts, not through revolutionary violence. Of the orthodox Party speakers, Fred Copeman, the former Royal Navy sailor who had been imprisoned for his part in the Invergordon mutiny, made literally the most impact. No theoretician, he became increasingly irritated with a pedantically minded Marxist student in the audience, who kept interrupting him to query some point of Marxist theory. Suddenly the hall was invaded by a group of undergraduates from Brasenose, then a celebrated hearty college, shouting 'Let's get the Reds!' Copeman jumped off the platform, sent one of the invaders sprawling with a left hook, and then turned and for good measure knocked down the Marxist theorist who had been pestering him.

L.S. Amery, then Colonial Secretary, spoke at the Conservative Club. It was hard to see in this small, cherubic man with pince-nez the formidable mountaineer (which he was) or to envisage him as the figure who would

Cox (seated, second from right) as a student at University of Otago, 1930.

Above: During his visit to Russia, (left to right: Intourist official, M. MacDonald, Guide, T. Jarman, Bram Fischer, Geoffrey Cox), Kiev, July 1932.

Left: Cox in Oxford, 1933.

Above: Workers at an Arbeitsdienst labour camp. The slogan over the gate calls on all Germans to work together for the future.

Below: Oriel College, Oxford, founded 1326.

ABOVE: Cox's admission card to the Nuremberg Rally, 1934

BELOW: Hitler talks to the bishops and the generals at the Nuremberg Rally, 1934.

hurl at Neville Chamberlain in May 1940 Oliver Cromwell's words: 'You have sat here too long for any good you have been doing. In the name of God – go!' Personal tragedy too waited in the wings for him. In the war one of his sons, Julian, was to serve with great bravery and skill as a liaison officer with the Albanian partisans, but another was to be hanged in 1945 for turning traitor and serving the Germans.

Kingsley Martin, who as editor of the *New Statesman* was entering upon two decades of great influence, indeed of power, over the intellectual middle class, spoke to the Labour Club. I saw him as 'lean, iron-grey, keen', and noted his description of the Foreign Secretary, Sir John Simon, as 'the outcome of the misalliance of a leech and an eel'. Sidney Webb, a small, self-satisfied man with a goatee, formally introduced as Lord Passfield, held forth on the virtues of Stalin's Russia. At the Liberal Club Sir William Beveridge (as he then was) delivered a talk stiff and arid with statistics. We all agreed that he was one pundit we could disregard. He was clearly far too desiccated a figure to make any impact on events.

CHAPTER FOURTEEN

Viennese Summer

When the long vacation came in June I took myself off to Vienna to study German, to see one more of Europe's still distinctive national states (the days of homogenised, blurred, air-travel cosmopolitanism were still some decades away) and to look at the much acclaimed workers' flats and schools and playgrounds which had been built up in the twenties by the Socialist Municipality of Vienna, and which constituted a welfare state in miniature. Neill had given me, too, an introduction to Dr Wilhelm Stekel, then very much in the public eye as a psychoanalyst much favoured by expatriate Americans. He had psychoanalysed Neill and John Gunther, who in his best-selling book *Inside Europe* was to hold up Stekel as a fount of wisdom. Stekel had been one of Freud's earliest disciples, but was now regarded as a heretic by true Freudians.

The journey by train to Vienna took thirty-six hours, a time we would deem intolerable today. But train travel had many advantages. You had a chance to see and study the countryside of the different countries through which one passed. You had a chance, too, particularly if you travelled third class, to see the people of those countries, as they piled their bundles and their cheap suitcases onto the baggage racks, and filled the air with the reek of their varied tobaccos. You sampled different foods from buffets and food trolleys as the train moved through one country to another. And you had a chance to make friends and share experience with other travellers, in a way which has been glamorised in recollections of the *Orient Express* but which existed as memorably on more modest trains. I am glad that I knew Europe in the days when the train was the usual means of transport, even for statesmen hurrying to yet one more international conference. All you needed to cope with the long hours was enough to read. I took *War and Peace* with me, and read of Prince Andrew at Austerlitz as the train moved across the rolling landscape of Lower Austria in which the battle had been fought.

You could live very cheaply as a student in those days. In Vienna I lodged in a Catholic student hostel. To share a bedroom with an Austrian student cost me a schilling a day – roughly the equivalent of four pence in today's currency; breakfast – coffee and rolls – the equivalent of a penny; and for another schilling I could have a three-course evening meal. But I did not often eat my main meal in the hostel, for it was even cheaper to eat out at one of the municipal restaurants set up by the city council. Distinguished by a big sign of 'WOK', they were to be found in all but the wealthier districts. The initials were useful, as their full name – *Wieneroffentlicherkuchenbetriebsgesellschaft* – was one of those massive portmanteau words in which the German language specialised. The *Donau-Dampfschiff-Fahrt-Gesellschaft* (the Danube Shipping Company) was another of the same breed. A WOK restaurant offered no frills, just tables covered with coarse white cloths, under walls bare of decoration. But for the equivalent of three new pence you got soup, meat, copious offerings of potatoes (I counted them one week: they averaged sixteen per portion), and a slice of cake or tart.

Yet my impoverished room-mate, Karl Bedermann, a law student who was the son of Corinthian peasants, managed on even less. For breakfast he made himself, quite illegally, a cup of tea on a borrowed electric ring plugged into the power socket, and ate some bread or cake sent to him each week by his mother. At the WOK he could get a serving of soup and vegetables for only two pence, though the waitresses often ensured that a slice of meat found its way onto his plate.

Bedermann played the violin well, and sometimes, if I planned to go to the opera, he would sit on the sunny hostel balcony and play me some of the music I was about to hear. When his exams were over, by pooling our resources half a dozen of us from the hostel had enough to celebrate at the Gasthaus zum Roten Ochs, drinking in turn from a huge two-litre stein filled with golden helles beer. Bedermann rounded off the evening by leading us to a nearby block of flats where the most kind-hearted of the WOK waitresses lived. He took up position under her window and serenaded her on his violin. Furious shouts of '*Ruhe!*' and '*Polizei!*' from the other flats did not deter him until, pink-faced with pleasure and annoyance, she came out onto a balcony and pleaded with us to go. I do not think any of us that evening imagined – I certainly did not – that within a few years we would be engaged in trying to kill each other.

The heartland of socialist Vienna lay outside the encircling boulevards of the Ringstrasse, build in the mid-nineteenth century to replace the old city walls. The workers' flats of Sandleiten were its newest and particular pride. The tram from the city centre ran through old slum areas of high, dirty tenements with paint and plaster cracking off them, and the streets dusty in the heat. But Sandleiten was block upon block of new, white buildings, seven to eight storeys high, set around grassy courtyards like Oxford quadrangles, and on many of the dark-green balconies were boxes of scarlet geraniums. In its central square – called after the Italian Socialist Matteoti murdered by the Fascists in 1922 – were shops, a library, a cinema, cafés. A curving building of concrete and glass, set in a garden, was the crèche for the children of workers. Next to it was the Sandleiten kindergarten, with sandpits and wading pools and a bronze statue of a lamb, life size, set in its grassy garden. Brown-skinned children in brightly coloured shorts seemed to be everywhere. In the brilliant July sunshine – the summer of 1933 was one of the best of the century in Europe – Sandleiten seemed like a glimpse of a new world.

There were other similar blocks – the Lindenhof, with the lime tree after which it was named still standing in the midst of a long grassy courtyard; the Karl Marx Hof, its concrete painted in huge areas of blue, red and orange, stretching for a mile along the road leading to the Danube, and within its centre courtyard a statue of the workers of the world, still in chains; Engelshof, its walls red and white; Foriansdorf, with a children's swimming pool occupying one of its courtyards. Elsewhere, even in the heart of the city, you would come across other, smaller, but immediately recognisable blocks of municipal housing, their dark-blue or orange plaster contrasting with the more orthodox apartment buildings amidst which they were set.

Since 1918 Vienna's Socialist Municipality had provided 60,000 workers' dwellings, financed chiefly out of taxation rather than by loans at a time when Berlin was in ever-increasing debt, when even wealthy Chicago was declared insolvent. It had built many new schools, sanatoria, swimming pools and skating rinks, and sent 30,000 children a year for holidays in the mountains. I visited one children's holiday home – a wooden house with wide eaves and flower-edged balconies, which looked across the blue depths of the Vienna Woods.

Not everyone saw this as good. I went one afternoon to the municipal congress swimming pool. At one end of the huge, sixty yard long outdoor pool the red and white Austrian flag waved against a cloudless sky. The wide lawns around the pool were filled with sunbathers. Families picnicked on the grass or drank coffee and beer in the open-air restaurant. From its dance floor loudspeakers blared the hit of the day:

Eins, zwei, drei und vier
Glücklich bin ich bei dir.

The floor was crowded with dancers, mostly in bathing suits, women in backless costumes – the bikini was still two decades away – men in very brief shorts. Many of the young were unemployed, whiling away their days in the sunshine. Two pairs of the dancers were pale boys with heavily lidded eyes and an air of wan listlessness. This roused to fury a young medical student who was with me. '*Ugh, es ist ein Skandal,*' he said. 'This is what the socialists bring. When we chase them and the Jews out of Austria we will have a land, a clean land.' When I argued that at least the socialists had built these baths, and that the homosexual couples on the dance floor were not typical, he shook his head: 'You come from a small country, far away. You do not understand how things are in old, crowded countries like ours.'

The socialist official who showed me round Sandleiten was pessimistic about the future: 'Sooner or later the government will turn against us because we allow the unemployed to remain rent free in their apartments, rather than turn them into the streets. And the Gasthaus and restaurant owners protest against the low prices we charge in the municipal restaurants. When Dollfuss banned the *Schutzbund*, the socialist militia, in March, we lost the means to defend ourselves. If he does not destroy us, in time the Nazis will.'

Wilhelm Stekel proved to be a short, vigorous, assertive man in his early fifties, with heavy eyebrows and a pointed beard. He combined a sardonic manner with a sense of humour – a quality I suspect is not widespread amongst psychoanalysts. He was an ardent tennis player and quickly drew me into playing regularly with himself, his wife, and another doctor. He had a well-developed sense of gamesmanship. Any ball of his opponent which landed in court, but was within six inches of the line, would be greeted with shouts of '*Aus, aus!*', and an indignant waving of his racket in the air. He had developed, too, a technique of returning balls on the second bounce, and would be highly indignant if challenged on this. But he played with such gusto that these modifications of the rules seemed in time merely to add to the challenge of the game. In August, when Stekel and his wife went off to the mountain resort of Bad Gastein for their holidays, they suggested I went with them. Bad Gastein, deep in the mountains of the Salzburg Province, with waters said to be good for both rheumatism and intestinal complaints, had been a favoured resort both of the Emperor Franz Josef, and of the German Kaiser Wilhelm II. Its some 300 hotels stood glaringly white and red in the green elbow of a long valley, alongside a thundering waterfall. Below, the valley – its fields green and gold with the colours of August – stretched away to the red village roofs and white church tower of Hof Gastein; mountain peaks, some snow capped, challenged one to climb;

and a swimming pool cut into a grassy hillside was open to the ringed mountains and alpine sun. I found myself a room in a farmhouse further up the valley, for which I paid a schilling a night – about four new pence – for bed and a coffee and rolls and butter breakfast.

Bad Gastein was a resort of the very rich. French, Italians, Spaniards, Austrians – but very few Germans, for Hitler had imposed a tax of 1,000 marks on anyone visiting Austria. The men in expensive tailored suits, the women looking as if they had stepped from the pages of *Vogue*, took their pre-lunch stroll along the Kaiser Wilhelm Weg or paused to listen to the orchestra in the Kurgarten, or to purchase the newspapers and magazines in a dozen languages on sale in the streets. But Stekel and his wife spent little time in this setting. After taking the waters in the morning, they would set out with me in the afternoon to climb one of the peaks in the valley, following tracks well marked with small coloured signs painted onto rocks or tree trunks.

On these outings, and in later talks over supper in Stekel's Viennese home, I was able to learn something of psychoanalysis, then still a new and tentative practice. I had access to an important source of information, as Stekel had been a pupil of Freud. They had parted company because Stekel believed Freud and his main disciples were wrong in insisting that psychoanalysis required many months, perhaps spreading over two or three years. For Stekel, three months was in most cases enough – and he could point to an impressive list of cures of very difficult neurotic conditions, such as agoraphobia, which he had achieved in that time.

The key to Stekel's shortened form of analysis lay, it seemed, in his swift, intuitive capacity to analyse the dreams of his patients. He required them, he told me, to keep paper and pencil by their bedside and to note, immediately on waking, any dream they had had. This he would interpret for them the next day after little further questioning – a process very different from the lengthy periods of association and recollection other analysts saw as an essential preliminary to any such interpretation. There was much that was empirical, and indeed just shrewd commonsense, in his approach. He saw his task not as unfolding every aspect of the patient's subconscious mind, but discovering and clarifying enough for the patient to be able to live a reasonably normal life. The main thing was for the analysis to reach a point where the patient was freed from the consciousness of guilt which, to Stekel, was a prime cause of neurosis.

In all this Stekel's sense of humour played its part. There was a hint of it in the only occasion on which Stekel discussed one of his cases with me. One of our tennis companions in Vienna had been a patient of his, a Dutch woman in her early thirties whose good looks were smudged by an air of constant sadness. After her treatment had been completed and she had left Vienna, I asked Stekel why she was so sad. She had, it seemed, been married very young to a man who proved to have a voracious sexual appetite, seeking his satisfactions not only every night and often in the morning, but even at lunch time. After some years she had divorced him, and married again. This second marriage had led her to seek analysis. What was the problem? 'Her problem,' Stekel replied with a chuckle, 'is simple enough. Her second husband is just a normal man.'

Stekel had his own views about the world crisis. 'The troubles of humanity begin with the individual, not with the social order. Cure the individual of his psychological disorders and you automatically straighten out the system,' he said to me, leaning back in his chair in his sitting room, his hands folded. 'Psychology gives back the same answer as religion. You must change the hearts of men before you can change society. It is only on method that religion is wrong. You must straighten out the twists in man's subconscious, not just deaden them by prayer.'

On our way back from Gastein, Stekel, who was apt to interpret the highway code as he interpreted the rules of tennis, had a collision with another car on a deserted stretch of mountain road. The other driver, as chance would have it, proved to be a powerful, if theoretically illegal, local Nazi leader. He brought a lawsuit demanding outrageously high damages. As the only independent witness, my evidence became crucial. Since the case was not due to be heard until after my departure from Austria, I was called to a court in Vienna to make a deposition. It gave me a glimpse under the surface of Austrian politics. My deposition was taken by a young investigating lawyer – a clean-cut, fair-haired, cheerful figure. When my evidence placed the blame as much on the other party as on Stekel – which was the truth – he urged me to change it. He made no secret of his reasons: 'What are you, an Aryan and an Englishman, doing in the company of Jews like this? How can you put the interests of this fellow Stekel first? He ought to have been on the road to Jerusalem, not Vienna.' This was at first put in a bantering manner, but when I stood by my story, half a dozen other young lawyers emerged from nearby offices and stood around me in a menacing group. But a British passport in those days was still an armour-plated protection, and I left with my statement intact. Not that it did Stekel much good. He still had to meet a hefty bill for damages.

Under Stekel's buoyant manner were deep anxieties about the future, anxieties he confided to me when in 1937 I returned to Vienna as a correspondent. The Anschluss a year later severed his links with the land he loved, and in 1939 he committed suicide. Mrs Stekel made her way to England, but she too died soon after the war.

In Vienna that summer I saw my first riot. We sup so full of horrors every evening these days – with riots and demonstrations and bloodshed filling the news screens – that it is not easy to recall how rare were such events fifty years ago, or at least how rare was the knowledge of them. One reason was that to be effective then, to gain any real notice in the newspapers or to have any effect on governments, demonstrations or marches had to be on a large scale. There could be no question of gathering a few dozen, or even a few hundred, demonstrators and parading them briefly before the cameras in the hope they would be (as only too often they are) taken as being part of a larger non-existent whole. To make any impact, large crowds had to be mobilised. And it was just such a crowd which the Nazis had mobilised around the Rathaus, the Vienna City Hall, one sunny afternoon in July 1933, to protest against the banning of the Nazi Party in Austria.

Since March that year Austria had been under the virtual dictatorship of the Chancellor, the tiny – he stood only five feet high – but determined Dr Dollfuss. Of the political private armies which had existed in Austria as in the Weimar Republic, only the conservative Heimwehr (Home Guard) under its leader, Prince Starhemberg, was permitted. But the Nazis remained active. On the paths through the Vienna Woods you would find small paper swastikas scattered on the ground or pasted on tree trunks. On mountainsides in the Tyrol great swastika fires would suddenly blaze in the night, a fearsome spectacle. And now, around the university, the tree shaded streets were suddenly full of groups of young men. A police patrol called on them to move on. In a moment there were people running in all directions, with the police after them, batons drawn, hitting out at backs and heads and shoulders.

In the thin traffic along the Ringstrasse, outside the city hall, more people gathered, many of them just passers-by, curious. Suddenly the police charged again, the shrieks of their whistles sounding above the roar of the trams. A woman slipped, and the police were on her, beating her head and shoulders as she tried to rise. A whine of a siren, and an ambulance raced up. At one corner a young Heimwehr man in untidy grey uniform and a forage cap with one green feather at the side was surrounded by a taunting mob of students. White-faced, he unbuttoned his revolver holster. Then a new sound – the clatter of hooves on the cobbles. Across the full width of the Ringstrasse was ranged a dark-brown wave of mounted policemen. Long batons in hand, they crashed towards us at full gallop. The crowd scattered, fighting to get into the side streets. But it was a Viennese crowd, disinclined to take matters too seriously. When the mounted police reformed and thundered back, I jumped behind the nearest tree. A fair girl was already hiding there. She smiled, '*Komisch, ja*?', pointing out a fat, perspiring policeman trying hard to keep up with his fellows. When another policeman tripped, losing his helmet, there was a chorus of derisive laughs and whistles. Vienna had not changed from the time when an Austrian statesman at the turn of the century described the country's situation as 'desperate, but not serious'. Yet the next day the papers reported more than a score of people seriously injured, and over a hundred arrested.

I saw Dollfuss a few weeks later, a tiny figure in grey military uniform, mounted on a brown pony, taking the salute at a Heimwehr parade outside the chancellery building in which, nine months later, he was to be murdered by two Nazi fanatics. Prince Starhemberg, a rather grander figure on a white charger, was by his side. Intended to counter the propaganda spectaculars which had become a feature of German Nazism, the ceremony had an endearing Austrian untidiness about it. The Heimwehr were mere boys in their grey uniforms, with fresh oak leaves on the side of their steel helmets; the red flares which lit up the statue of Maria Theresa gave off black smoke as well as light, lessening the effect; the sellers of red-and-white Dollfuss badges and flags were not young enthusiasts, but old, threadbare professional programme sellers hired for the evening; and when a plane flew over, trailing a large banner, it did not make some patriotic call such as 'Defend Austria', but urged us merely to 'Buy Schroeber's Shoes'.

Far more impressive were the Catholic ceremonies during Holy Week. Night after night Catholics from all over Europe passed in silent, torchlit processions on their way to Mass in the Neue Kirche; a papal legate walked in his robes through troop lined streets towards the cool depths of St Stephen's Cathedral. Peasants from all over Austria marched in the uniforms of the militias they had formed to oppose Napoleon – red or blue or yellow jackets, bright leather knee breeches, white stockings, huge feathered hats – carrying old muskets and sometimes pikes. A white moustached, dignified leader marched ahead of each detachment. In the front rank behind him came the village priest in black cassock, and a girl in bright peasant costume and dirndl carrying a tiny wine cask and glass. Further back were long, straggling columns of brown faced, wrinkled old women in black, upright men, and wide-eyed girls, singing hymns under the leadership of their priests.

Despite political stresses, Vienna's great pride, the opera, continued its season in the magnificent nineteenth-century State Opera House on the Ringstrasse which was to be unnecessarily destroyed by allied bombing in the closing weeks of the war. Entrance to the uppermost gallery was very cheap, and from it I heard most of that summer's repertoire – *Tosca* and *Aïda*, *Carmen* and *La Bohème*, the entire cycle of Wagner's *Ring*, and *Die Meistersinger von Nürnberg*, *Rigoletto* and *Fidelio*. Alas, I am not musical, and the truly deep satisfactions of the music were not for me. Yet I found myself drawn back, week after week. Indeed my attendances were regular enough for the claque to admit me to their ranks. They were a group of about a dozen young men and woman, all opera fanatics, who got free admission to the gallery in return for providing applause to order. Their efforts were orchestrated by a leader, who would bring them in skilfully either to stimulate applause, if the audience were slow in reacting, or to sustain support for a particular singer (often invaluable with a nervous newcomer to a role), or to counter any rare outbursts of disapproval. After the performance they adjourned to a small café behind the Opera, where they were entitled to one free drink for their efforts and where they would be joined by members of the orchestra or singers from the chorus or stage staff, all engaged in a passionate debate about the evening's performance.

Vienna also opened up the chance to learn something about European painting. The collection in its main art gallery had been assembled in the days when Habsburg rule extended far beyond Austria. From Venice, from which Austria's grip had been prised only in 1866, they had brought a magnificent series of Titians and Tintorettos. From the Low Countries, which had been under Maria Theresa's rule, had come works by Rembrandt, Reubens, Breugel, Hobemma, Cuyp and, above all, Vermeer, whose supreme work, *The Painter in his Studio*, was hung here. Perhaps the one good thing which can be said of Hitler was that he loved the paintings of Vermeer – so much so that two of the first works of art he looted in 1940 were Vermeers. Perhaps that reflected a taste acquired in these same stuffy, overheated galleries of the Kunsthistorisches Museum in the pre-1914 days when he was a failed painter living in a Viennese doss house.

It was a city, too, in which you could literally immerse yourself in history. In the grounds of Schonbrunn Castle I swam in a swimming pool built for the imperial guards by the Emperor Franz Josef, and in another in the Belvedere adapted from a pool constructed for a water pageant mounted for the Empress Maria Theresa. At Durnstein, sixty miles up the Danube from Vienna, I boarded a canoe from under the walls of the castle where Richard Coeur de Lion had been imprisoned until he was found by the wandering minstrel Blondel, and drifted and paddled my way in the sunshine down the wide swift brown river to the city's edge.

One warm afternoon in September, as my vacation came towards its end, I made the last of many walks to the Kahlenberg, the highest point in the Vienna Woods. The hillside, bare in the afternoon sun, sloped down to the vineyards of Grinzing, to the first villas of the suburbs, to the brown flow of the Volga. Beyond the river, wide plains stretched towards the distant line of the hills of Hungary. Beethoven had walked on the paths below; the village in the haze was Wagram, Napoleon's battlefield; around us the pine and maple trees of the Wienerwald ran towards the castled headland of Leopoldsberg, when John Sobieski and the Poles routed the Turks. Two girls from the claque, sitting on the grass under the trees, sang an aria in an emotional, unashamed, laughing Viennese manner, pleased rather than embarrassed when other walkers paused to listen. What matter that the sausage in our lunch sandwiches was strong with garlic, that I had still not acquired the local taste for sour milk, that a long journey in a crowded tram lay ahead of us. I felt suddenly very much at home in this distant land.

CHAPTER FIFTEEN

Mosley in Action

I returned to a subtly different Oxford. One change was personal – I now had my own room, with windows looking out on both the front and the inner quadrangles, and could at last live my own life. But other differences went wider. Events in the outside world had impinged on, if not fully penetrated, the cocoon in which the university wrapped itself. Nine months of rule by two of the shapers of the decade, Hitler and Roosevelt, had already made their impact. American Rhodes Scholars, clutching copies of *Time* magazine – then unknown on British bookstalls – were back with excited tales of the New Deal. Hitlerism, though still given the benefit of the doubt by many, was steadily revealing itself not only as a dictatorship, but a brutal one. At home Sir Oswald Mosley's British Union of Fascists, by now a year old, was gaining attention and support. 'Hurrah for the Blackshirts' was the headline of the *Daily Mail* in the junior common room one morning, and if not many of those who read it agreed with it, not many shared my indignation about it either.

That autumn Mosley addressed a meeting in the Oxford Town Hall. The hall was packed, mostly with townspeople. Blackshirt stewards, all wearing a uniform black shirt, but with trousers which varied from grey flannels to differing shades of black, stood round the walls. Many of them wore kid gloves, ready for a fight. They were predominately of two types, grizzled ex-servicemen or young men just out of their teens. There were about thirty girls, all in uniform black blouses and skirts.

Every Blackshirt arm went out in stiff salute as Mosley strode towards the platform. He was dressed entirely in black, with a tight-fitting shirt that buttoned up around his neck, and a wide leather belt around a stomach which was becoming just a shade too obvious. He looked like an actor dressed for the part of Mephistopheles, or for that of an executioner in an historical drama. Arms on hips, with his hands bent slightly backwards, his gaze searching the hall, he stood waiting for the applause to cease.

I knew there would be trouble as soon as I saw John Brown in the audience. He was a student at Ruskin, small, lean, with the high cheek bones and bright colouring of a Welshman. He had got to Ruskin after writing a volume of early autobiography called *I was a Tramp*. The meeting had been underway for barely five minutes when Brown was on his feet, challenging a point made by Mosley. In a flash four Blackshirts were onto him, and he was bundled down the aisle, punched and kicked on the way, and with blood streaming from his nose. This came, he told me afterwards, from the favoured Blackshirt technique of thrusting gloved fingers up an opponent's nostrils.

But John Brown had, at this stage, been spared the full treatment. This was meted out to later hecklers. They were seized by four or five stewards, held face downwards in a horizontal position, and then carried up the aisle. Beside this cortège walked a fifth man who delivered blow after blow upwards into the pinioned man's face. The glint of rings, or perhaps of a knuckle duster, was clearly visible on the punchers' fists. It was brutality all the more sickening for being executed as if by drill.

During these interruptions Mosley would stand silent on the platform, his hand resting on the Union Jack draped over the table. He has been much praised for his oratory, but I found it that evening to be cast too much in a single, hectoring, vehement tone, with too many long words and too few memorable phrases; he tended to make his points more by emphasis than by language. With his dark hair, dark moustache and strongly aquiline features, there was something stiff, Italianate, condescending, in his manner. Mosley's power lay less in his words than in his self-confidence. His bearing conveyed a sense of power, of a man who wanted to do things, not just talk of them. This may have been the secret of his appeal – which is all the more surprising, given that his political career, inside and outside of Parliament, was to be more one of striking attitudes than of achievement.

Mosley's plea that evening was for a self-sufficient British empire, freed from the risk of war because it would be freed from foreign commitments. Only Fascism could bring this about quickly enough, particularly in developing the resources of Africa: 'We cannot wait until every last Hottentot has joined the ILP,' he thundered.

As Mosley moved towards his peroration, I saw John Brown, his face bruised and one eye badly swollen, but with his red tie very noticeable, suddenly slip through the cordon of guards and take his place in an empty seat in the front row, between two Blackshirt dignitaries. It was an act of extraordinary courage. For the rest of the speech he remained silent. But when *God Save the King* was sung, Brown remained seated, shouting out, 'I protest against the use of the National Anthem by a party standing for the ruin of everything really English.' At a sign from Mosley, no one touched him until the singing was finished. Then Blackshirts swept on him from every side, and he too was carried, with deliberate slowness, up the aisle, whilst both men and women rained blows at his face. At the entrance he was hurled down the steps, his face a mass of blood, his collar torn. At the foot of the steps he was arrested by two policemen and was hustled away, still shouting, 'Down with Fascism! Down with Mosley!'

After the meeting the Fascists lined up in King Edward Street, where coaches waited to take them back to London. Mosley stalked around, inspecting and thanking them. There was a look of almost sensual gratification on his face as the blackshirted men and women raised their arms to him in a frenzy of enthusiasm and devotion. A hostile, jeering crowd shouted anti-Fascist slogans from behind a police cordon at the end of the High. But it was not their efforts which broke up Mosley's parade. It was the work of two drunken, cheerful undergraduates, long college scarves swinging from their necks, who lurched around the corner from the direction of Christ Church. Suddenly, confronted by this strange scene in this normally deserted side street, they were at first silent, and then both burst into a tumult of laughter. Holding on to each other, pointing in disbelief at the stiffly parading ranks, their laughter – spontaneous and unchecked – echoed amongst the tall houses. And it proved infectious. It spread first, as chuckles and grins, to the police, and then was taken up by the anti-Fascist crowd, until gales of laughter swept up and down King Edward Street. Mosley turned abruptly, and hurried away to his car. His officers set about embussing their troops. And two undergraduates, cheerfully unaware of the effect they had procured, but still clutching each other in mirth, made their way across the High towards Brasenose.

It would be tempting to see in that incident a proof of how a mature British democracy destroyed Fascism in Britain by ridicule, by an instinctive disdain for uniforms and banners. But that would be to misread history. It was not laughing undergraduates, or jeering leader writers, nor sardonic cartoonists who destroyed Mosley. It was the work of John Brown and his like. For their persistent, constant opposition at BUF meetings, whether at a street corner or in great halls like Olympia, provoked in the Blackshirts a reaction so brutal as to make plain that the rule British Fascism would exercise, if it ever came to power, would be quite as harsh and vicious as that of Hitler or of Mussolini.

By the normal canons of democratic practice, such interference with freedom of speech cannot be justified. But the British Union of Fascists was not a democratic movement. It was not enough for Mosley to claim that he sought power through Parliament, and that his Blackshirts were formed merely to keep order at his frequently disrupted meetings. That is not even a half-truth: at best it is a quarter truth. They did have that function. But they existed also to intimidate their opponents, or the undecided, who needed only to glance across the Channel to see the fate of those who had resisted the black shirt and the jackboot. Even more ominous was the danger these forces posed for the future. If Mosley should ever come to power, the Blackshirts could be a key instrument in imposing his will upon the country. For whatever parliamentary trappings Fascism in Britain might be clothed in, it stood unmistakably for dictatorship. That indeed was the only clear aim and philosophy of Fascism. Nor was it at the time by any means universally regarded as a disreputable aim.

Kemal Ataturk had been lauded for using dictatorship to bring Turkey into the modern world. Even Winston Churchill found good words to say about Mussolini. Adolf Hitler was winning praise for cleaning out what were to many the Augean stables of the Weimar Republic. By adopting the name, the uniform and the salute of the dictatorial regime of Fascist Italy, Mosley revealed his intentions more clearly than any gloss his words might have put on his ambitions. Had events elsewhere in Europe taken a different turn, making it possible for the British Union of Fascists to come to power, only a fool or a simpleton would believe that there would not have been concentration camps on Salisbury Plain and in the Scottish Highlands, and all the apparatus of secret police and censorship by which Hitler and Mussolini, once having got their hands on the levers of power, ensured they kept their grip. That was the fact which had to be faced in those early years of the thirties. It seems to have escaped later writers who have too readily portrayed Mosley as if he were just another politician, though with an exaggerated taste for uniforms, offering policies which could be assessed as if they were merely variants of those proposed by the genuinely parliamentary parties – the Conservatives, Labour and the Liberals.

Since I was now clear in my mind that communism did not offer an acceptable answer to the slump, I did not resume my membership of the October Club. Instead I concentrated on the Labour Club, the stronghold of the social democrats amongst whom I now numbered myself. But Oxford life was far from being all politics. Frieda Lawrence, D.H. Lawrence's widow, spoke to the English Club. Strongly built, with a mass of fair hair, and marked traces of a German accent, she was very much an Earth Mother figure in a long, flowing gown, in striking contrast to the elegant undergraduate in white tie and tails who introduced her to the audience. To his plaudits of her husband she responded with a story Lawrence had often told. A collier had reluctantly attended a lecture on world affairs by a visiting professor. Asked

O.U. LABOUR CLUB.

Meetings are held at 8.15 p.m. at 115 High Street, unless otherwise announced.

Friday, April 28th

TOM WILLIAMS, M.P.

(Parliamentary Private Secretary to Minister of Agriculture, 1924; and to Minister of Labour, 1929-31)

will speak on

"The National Government and Agriculture.

Friday, May 5th

ELLEN WILKINSON

will speak on

"Fascist Germany."

Friday, May 12th

C. T. CRAMP

(General Secretary of the N.U.R.)

will speak on

"The Position of Trades Unionism To-day."

Friday, May 19th

S. O. DAVIES

(Vice-President, South Wales Miners' Federation).

Friday, May 26th

R. H. TAWNEY

will speak on

"A Socialist Policy in Education."

Friday, June 2nd

FRANK HORRABIN

will speak on

"Socialism and the Empire."

Friday, June 9th

LORD PASSFIELD

will speak on

"Russian Communism."

Friday, June 16th

Private Business Meeting and Social.

Programme of speakers at the Oxford University Labour Club, April–June 1933.

what he had thought of the lecturer, the collier commented, 'That bloke knows a bloody sight more than what's true.' Frieda Lawrence made no reference to *Lady Chatterley's Lover*. Nor did the audience expect her to. This was not only because the book was banned in Britain: copies of the edition published in Paris circulated freely in the student and literary world. It was more because to many admirers of Lawrence, *Lady Chatterley's Lover* was an over-explicit statement of a philosophy which was manifest in his other works, the view that we should shake free of our own psychological limitations, and of the constraints of a class-bound sexually inhibited society, and learn to live life to the full. Frieda Lawrence was to this rapt audience not only the legendary companion of a great artist: she was someone who had, with Lawrence, dared to defy convention and put his philosophy to the test. A glow came over her face as she spoke of her years with him: 'He gave a touch of beauty to everything. He was never stale. Life with him was never a routine. It was never dreary. Life with him was always wonderful. Even when he lay dying, he would say "Life is wonderful – a glorious affair. I'm going. But life is glorious."'

Leontine Sagan, celebrated as the producer of *Mädchen in Uniform*, spoke to the German Club. A lithe figure, with greying hair, she was already an exile from Nazism, and had made a film set in Oxford – alas a poor film. She saw no future for film in Hitler's Germany, other than in producing escapist schmaltz – which indeed was to be developed under Goebbels into a remarkable if degenerate art form.

Oxford had by now also given me a number of new friends, several of them Americans. Charles Hitch, an American Rhodes Scholar of Worcester, was one. He was going to prove the outstanding economist of our intake, who after taking a First was to become for a time a don at Queen's. Hitch was a deceptively quiet man, who had not only a sharp, strong mind, but a precise one – a quality reflected in the two sports at which he excelled, rifle shooting and golf. During the early years of the war he was to become the musketry instructor to the Oxford Home Guard. In 1961 he became the Honourable Charles Hitch, an Assistant Secretary of Defence at the Pentagon under Robert McNamara. To Hitch fell the task of informing the new President John F. Kennedy that the 'missile gap' of which Kennedy had made much during his campaign, as proof of the way the Republicans had allowed the Russians to gain superiority in long range missiles, did not exist – or if it did, it was in the Americans' favour.

During the war Hitch served with the American Air Force as an Intelligence Officer, selecting targets for the Flying Fortresses. Several of my Oxford friends were to find their way into military intelligence work.

My room-mate, Lynn Beyer, was to make a career of it, staying in the US Navy after the war and rising to the rank of Admiral. Atherton Bean, of Brasenose, was one of a team of code breakers who, by breaking the Japanese naval code, enabled the United States to win the battle of Midway in 1942, the turning point in the war in the Pacific.

My fellow Rhodes Scholar from New Zealand, James Bertram, was another man whose quiet manner masked remarkable strengths. He was to take a First in English and then – to my considerable surprise – to turn away from academic work to journalism. He became the first British correspondent to penetrate to the remote province of China to which Mao Tse Tung had led the Chinese Communists on their famed Long March, and the first to indicate the long-term potential both of this leader and of the cadres he commanded. Some of Bertram's writings were to command a larger circulation than anything the rest of us wrote, for three of the sayings in the *Thoughts of Chairman Mao*, that small red book printed in hundreds of millions of copies during the Cultural Revolution, bear the words 'as told to a New Zealand journalist'.

Bertram was to have a harsh war. Taken prisoner in Hong Kong, he spent the rest of the war doing forced labour in Japan, working on meagre rations and, from 1943 onwards, under constant bombardment by American planes.

Though Jim Bertram and I became good friends, we did not see a great deal of each other at Oxford. Each of us was keen to take advantage of the chance to meet people from other countries. I needed this, because when I sailed from New Zealand at the age of twenty-one I had not met anyone who was not from either the United Kingdom or Australia, except for one American undergraduate, who had penetrated as far south as Dunedin.

John Mulgan came up to Merton in the winter of 1933–34, though, owing to a bungle in the selection, not as a Rhodes Scholar. Handsome, cheerful, unhurried and seemingly unworried, he was free from bitterness about what, to a lesser man, might have seemed a wanton injustice. He already seemed in some ways older than the rest of us, though he was in fact a year or two younger. We became close friends, and he was to be the best man at my wedding. Yet he had an inner core of reserve which he kept very much to himself. At that stage the rest of us tended, to a greater or lesser degree, to depend upon each other in grappling with our problems. John Mulgan never seemed to need this, but already to have his own quiet source of strength. To that degree he was already the 'man alone' of the novel he was soon to write.

Through John Mulgan I met another Merton student, Bill Williams. A pale, bespectacled former Sheffield Grammar schoolboy, he was on his way to being a history don. He could – and did – out-argue us all, often ending with a quip which would have hurt had it not usually also been very funny. That he had a strong and original mind was not in question. Yet I doubt if any of us had the least conception that before a decade was out, as Brigadier E.T. Williams, DSO, he would be Montgomery's Chief Intelligence Officer in the Western Desert, and from D-Day onwards. Our paths were to cross again in the desert, when I was the Chief Intelligence Officer of 2 NZ Division. After the war Bill Williams became a highly successful Warden of Rhodes House, and was knighted as Sir Edgar Williams.

I came to relish the folklore of Oxford, such as the story of the visiting Frenchman who, on seeing the front of Worcester College with its resemblance to a fine Victorian railway station, exclaimed, '*C'est magnifique, mais ce n'est pas la gare*'. Rhodes Scholars had their own anecdotes, too. There was the law student from the Mid-West who was not enamoured of culture. Asked if he had visited the Louvre during his vacation he replied, 'Yes, I spent an hour there – and I would have done it in half an hour if I had had my rubber heels on.' We added one incident to this folklore when an American Rhodes Scholar, who ranked high among his country's amateur golfers, accepted a bet that he could hit a golf ball from the main quadrangle of Christ Church over busy St Aldates Street and into the quad of neighbouring Pembroke. It required a highly lofted and accurate shot from a number eight or number nine iron, and the least inaccuracy could put at risk ancient building work and ancient glass – let alone modern passers-by. Timing became the heart of the matter, for it involved playing the shot from the grass by the fountain in the centre of Tom Quad before the porters from the nearby lodge could intervene. It was planned like a military operation. On the stroke of three from the bell in Tom Tower a dozen of us, strolling in the sunshine nearby, gathered in a half circle to give cover to the golfer who quickly placed his ball, and shaped up calmly for the shot. The ball rose cleanly against the blue sky, and a distant cheer from within Pembroke told us it had arrived safely. We scattered as porters and scouts rushed on us from all angles and I escaped capture only by taking refuge in the Lewis Carroll library in Peck Quad.

It was in this year, too, that I came fully to appreciate what Oriel had to offer. With my interest in Marx and Freud now sated, I was able to appreciate the quality of the teaching the College offered on the subjects for my degree, and to value the unostentatious comradeship which was Oriel's hallmark. The links I forged with the College then have endured throughout my life.

CHAPTER SIXTEEN

Oxford Revisited

I did not keep a diary at Oxford, but from time to time I noted down moments and events which caught my eye. These notes, and excerpts from letters I wrote to my family, testify across the years to the life we led in those distant days, in that quiet city not yet swamped by traffic and tourism, in the decade leading up to World War II.

✣ ✣ ✣

November 1932; The river, gleaming in the rays of an autumn sun, with the soft colouring of the ragged banners of sunset hung out over Boars' Hill; the pinnacles on Magdalen tower, glimpsed over the black woods, shining white in the sun; the glint of water as the dark-blue blades of the eight are lifted; the poplars beside the Cherwell, with their air of silent aloofness; Magdalen Bridge, with red buses and cars roaring over it, a reminder that there exists another world busy with other things than beauty and the river. Coming forward slowly, squaring the blade. Over square two, drive those legs down.

The tow path white with snow in the winter, and the dark water; the eight crossing in the punt, their yellow-shafted dark bladed oars held erect like spears; the coach on the tow-path with megaphone and bicycle, cursing the crowded straight; struggling beginners being coached in tubs by some old hand, wrapped in overcoats and scarves; the trial eight, imperiously claiming its right of way, its cox bellowing, 'Look ahead!'; another coach trotting on a big bay gelding; girl undergraduates walking in pairs, watching the rowers; the boatmen in blue caps; the swans sailing in and out of the craft.

The Labour Club – as do many Oxford clubs – meets in an unpretentious hall on the High. You enter through a long narrow passage – 'very good for defence, we chose it because two or three men could hold it against a crowd,' one man told me the first night I attended. There was a note of superiority, of pride in his voice, as if he were proud of belonging to a club which talked such dangerous stuff that at any time one might have to turn and defend one's principles by blows as well as words.

Last evening at the Labour Club I talked with a young miner, wearing the red shirt which seems to be the Ruskin uniform. He described pit conditions, and told me that his brother and his father are working for 39s 6d a week at the moment. He did not seem to resent pit work. 'There is something enjoyable about the feeling of battling with nature,' he said, 'though it's a feeling which soon wears off.' He is studying at Ruskin on a scholarship which leaves him £35 a year to live on when his fees and expenses are paid. 'There must be a tremendous difference between Oxford and a mining town, isn't there?' I asked.

'I've learnt to live since I came to Oxford,' was his reply.

He said his local miners' debating society had echoed the Oxford Union anti-war resolution. Not many of the miners were Communists; most were Labour Party Socialists. They felt keenly on political matters.

This man, at least, was no fighter determined to rise and lead his class to victory in a class struggle whether in Parliament or behind the barricades. He seemed content to carry on so long as the system worked and provided a living for the men and women in it. A man has to be very hungry, either for food or for life, to be a revolutionary. And the average working man has, socially, a surprisingly full life so far as human contacts are concerned. The friendliness, the sociability of a miner's life are quite different from the complex-making isolation of a petty bourgeois city clerk.

As I came back to college I noticed, outside the House, a great sports-model Bugatti, with gleaming radiator pipes outside the long bonnet. A man wearing a fur coat drove off with an Alsatian curled up on the seat beside him. As he started I heard him shout, above the roar of the engine, 'Cheerio, old man. The Dorchester will find me for the next fortnight,' I remembered that my Ruskin friend had told me that he bicycled home for the vacations – a hundred miles a day.

First term of 1932. An undergraduate audience, in grey flannels and buff jackets, smoking pipes and cigarettes, listen to a young, dark-haired alert German, a Social Democrat, explain the present position of Socialism in Germany. His speech, read in slightly faulty English, is nevertheless succinct and informative. Social Democracy in Germany has reached the crossroads. It has shown, by failing to oppose the dictatorial measures of von Papen in July last in Prussia, that evolutionary socialistic methods are of no avail in a crisis. It is moving towards the Communists, and preparing to take up a position in which unconstitutional methods will be employed.

The speaker described vividly the scene in the Trades Union hall at Kiel on the night of 26th July, when the SDP members waited all night for word of the Executive's policy towards the declaration of dictatorship in Prussia. Would they, by a general strike, fight for socialism? Or would they stand by and let the forces of reaction consolidate their position? It was a momentous decision. Would they act courageously, declaring they would not retreat? Was SD strong enough to oppose reactionary capitalism and Junkerdom? Yet, after waiting all night, the SDs were forced to go home at dawn disappointed. No call for action came through.

May Day 1933. At 6 a.m. I watched the Morris dancers in the misty, grey early morning. A crowd, mostly women and children and one or two tourists in the Broad outside the gates of Trinity. The dancers, and the jester, undergraduates, wore white flannels with coloured sashes and, on their legs, little jingling bells. There was an air of robustness and fellowship which spoke of the days of Merrie England and cakes and ale. They were definitely folk dances, portraying the spirit of a time when each town, and almost each village, was a separate unity socially and economically. Even this rather bald presentation of the dances conveyed a feeling of roistering and 'sunburnt mirth', of village greens overhung by chestnuts, and country-folk 'a-maying'.

I am afraid the days of maying are almost over. My scout told me that he could remember when people went about the streets in costume during the day, and danced maypole dances where now the red buses roar, at Carfax, and an effigy of Jack the Green was carried in procession. 'There was real fun in those days,' he said. 'But the cinemas have killed it. Can't get anyone to dance round a maypole when they can sit in the cinema for sixpence.'

The Colleges still slept in the faint grey mist as I walked back to an early breakfast before boarding the coach for the May Day demonstration in London against Fascism and war.

Autumn 1933. There was a note of tragedy in Zimmern's lecture today. His subject was the same as that of last term – the League of Nations – but his treatment was different. Gone was the rather strained optimism, the idealist faith in peaceful, constitutional internationalism, in facts and treaties and conferences. He admitted that the League of Nations has not fulfilled all that he and others had hoped. In a forcedly jocular manner he exposed its weaknesses – its failure to take over the functions of the Postal Union and the International Health Office; the failure of bands of experts to entangle the Giant of War in a tangle of red tape. From an opponent of the League this might not have seemed strange, but from Zimmern, Professor of International Relations, ranking with Lord Cecil and Gilbert Murray as a staunch supporter of all that is comprehended in the words pacifism and internationalism and hope, it sounded like the death knell of all half-way measures.

As I came out in the Lobby of the Schools building I passed a group of five men wearing Fascist badges in their buttonholes – Mosley's men.

Walking down to row in the early afternoon. Through the gloomy, shaded ravine formed by the walls of Oriel and Corpus; past Merton tower, a little too squat and rich, like some prosperous merchant; past the dark stone and grey slates of Merton library, with a single birch tree leaning against it and casting its leaves on the lawn.

Out into the spaciousness of Christchurch Meadow; the glimpse along the sunny old city wall, towards Magdalen tower. The avenue of elms; schoolboys playing soccer, being coached by a young man seeming more anxious to show his own worth than to teach others.

The wide avenue running down to the river sees all sorts pass up and down it during the afternoon. Rowing men with hairy legs and white shorts and brightly coloured woollen scarves twisted round their necks; two nursemaids talking eagerly, whilst their charges play tig around the rugged boles of the elms; pairs of undergraduates, deep in conversation, striding along – parsons of the future discussing all that they will do; a young man showing his people around; a fair-haired man in a polo-neck sweater, arm in arm with a radiant-faced girl in a fur coat – he walking a little proudly, no doubt aware that he is the object of the jealousy of the sex-starved throng off to take 'a little strenuous exercise. So good for one – approved by the Church'. Groups bound for rugger or hockey, wearing blue shorts and blazers, carrying football boots; a girl in a brown beret, tugged along by an eager, rough-haired terrier; a thin-legged runner in white shoes, white shorts and a sweater, red in the face, and with one arm swinging loosely as if in protest on behalf of a body being subjected to such undignified treatment.

The barges, like gaily ornamented Noah's Arks, lie moored in a long line along the northern bank under the elm trees. Each barge has a flagpole, but since there are no races in progress today, none of the banners is raised.

In the Oriel barge: stove, bicycles, drying clothes, a broken gramophone, book of photos, weighing machine, photos of Eights, sawn-off oars, the whistle used when the 1st Eight bumped 6 and the Second Eight bumped 5 (in 1877!).

Chart of races, broken-backed books, on rowing, boating, in the Badminton Library – Grammar of Rowing, Henley Days, History of the University Boat Race, *Marshall's* Zoology, Last Will and Testament of Cecil John Rhodes, Letters of Gabriel d'Annunzio.

In BNC Hall I said to Bean, 'Who is the lady?' pointing to a portrait on the wall.

'Sarah, Duchess of Marlborough.'

'That's the damsel whose Blenheim Park we visited, isn't it?'

A man sitting opposite joined in. 'The Duchess of Marlborough? That's the person whose concert I gatecrashed in town last vac. We thought we were crashing a dance, and walked in the door of the house as if we owned the show. There were just masses of footmen in livery standing round, but once in we couldn't retreat. So we went upstairs, and then didn't know where to go next. All the doors were shut, but from one room we could hear music. Then we looked down, and found that all these flunkey chaps had gathered in a big band at the foot of the stairs, and looking as if they were ready to charge. But one of them was a genius. He noticed we were smoking, and called out in a stentorian voice, "No smoking up there, please". We just grabbed the hint, and walked downstairs and out of the door. Damn funny.'

'Damn funny,' we echoed.

Rhodes House. Amery, small, cherubic, doll-like man, talks of Kingsley Fairbridge with guarded enthusiasm. It's hard to believe that Amery climbed the Minarets in a 19-hour tramp across the Southern Alps with Arthur Harper.*

Stonehaven† introduced him and thanked him in two speeches which amounted to much more than did Amery's.

Stonehaven, screwing up his cheek to keep his monocle in place, said, 'Well, I mean, we all know we don't want another war, but if there is another war, well, we'll all turn and fight in the right spirit.' He liked the scheme, which 'gave those boys and gels born under an unlucky star' a chance to become cogs in the Imperialist machine, propagating Empire patriotism. I

---

* Founder of Child Emigration Society. A Briton of Rhodesian origins, he advocated establishing farm schools – schools which were also farms – at which children from British slums could get a new start. He set up the first near Perth in the early 1930s. It met with mixed success.

† Lord Stonehaven. Governor General of Australia 1925–30

like the scheme, too. It's easy to say that it doesn't touch the root of the system – of course it doesn't – but it accomplishes what is possible within the system, and gives an example for future systems.

*I am not surprised that after Stonehaven the Aussies appointed Sir Isaac Isaacs.**

Midday. Man with cocktail shaker at the window of rooms in Corpus, opposite my window: 'I'm too weak to shake the damn thing until after I have drunk one.'

Overheard in the Oriel Shower Room. 'Do you know what sort of party I did last night? The Society for the Prevention of Cruelty to Animals. Uphill work – dance first with the kitchen maid, then with the housemaid, then worked gradually up the scale. Uphill work, what?'

Hargreaves was my tutor in Economics. In a letter to my father in February 1934 I wrote:

> In my tutorial yesterday, Hargreaves, like everyone else here, was discussing what attitude we can take up when this war breaks out – because it's certainly no longer a question of 'if', but of 'when'. Hargreaves is a gentle little man with a good knowledge of economics but without many other qualities in the way of self-reliance. He and I were picturing London wiped out by gas bombs, and with only Hargreaves left alive. He thought he would live so long as the tinned foods in Selfridges last. After that he supposed he'd have to starve, because he didn't know how to grow a crop of any sort. And if he couldn't find a tin opener he supposed he'd starve from the start.

✣ ✣ ✣

Laski†, at the Labour Club, speaking seriously, more absorbed by his topic than by his delivery. His manner confidential. Both he and Salter‡ spoke confidently. The need for determined, militant socialism. The Labour Congress with 365 points for its manifesto, and Laski and Arthur Henderson§ in the backroom of the Harrogate pub, working on simplifying them.

---

* Governer General of Australia 1931–6.

† Harold Laski. Professor of Politics, London School of Economics. Leading left-wing theorist in 1930s. Active member of the Labour Party, and Chairman of the Labour Party at the time of its great election victory in 1945.

‡ Sir Arthur Salter. British civil servant who did important work in WWI as Director of Merchant Shipping. After the war he became a top official in the League of Nations. MP 1937–53. Raised to peerage 1953.

§ Labour politician and Minister. Home Secretary in first Labour Government 1924. Foreign Secretary 1929–31. Strong advocate of the League of Nations.

The High, on Saturday afternoon. Undergraduates, well developed, well fed, in flannels and brown jackets, some on bicycles, with squash racquets, hockey sticks, rugger boots. Two white-stocked, black-capped men are motoring to the Hunt in a long, sleek Lagonda; red buses, and then the Town – women shopping, pushing their prams along the crowded pavement; girls, pretty, but unsure of themselves, in cheap brown or green coats, giggling in shop doorways, waiting silent by the bus stop, thronging into Woolworths. Youths – bank clerks, office employees, mechanics – on their half-holiday, many dressed like undergraduates in flannels and sports coats. But there is a difference in their bearing, their expression. Less confidence, less assurance. In their faces is an undeveloped, slightly hungry look, not for food but for something else – mental training, responsibility, culture. What a hell of jealousy many of these must suffer, living in the same town where a picked band of people of their own age live full, care-free, developing lives. To imagine that every youth in the Oxford streets is a mass of thwarted intellectual desires would be nonsense; but to imagine that they are all 'content in their station', and generally inferior to the undergraduates in mental calibre is equally false. Undoubtedly, the pick of Oxford are, physically and mentally, far above the average man. But there is a big section of Oxford – the dim, unadventurous, about-to-be-schoolmasters – who row in their college's second togger, acquire a taste for beer and a third in schools, who differ from millions of other men in offices, factories and shops not in mental ability but only in position and opportunity.

During one Oxford vacation I spent some time at Summerhill. The Parrot and Punchbowl was a village pub near the school:

Saturday night. The little Tap Room at the Parrot and Punchbowl is thronged. On the wooden benches sit the labourers and farmers.

'Did you see the new fence ole Charlie is amaking down there?'

'Yes, he's quick at it.'

'Ay, finish it in a week, I'll warrant.'

'Week? More like three or four days. He's a right fair fencer, is Charlie. Same again, Ted, please – two halves of cider and a pint o' bitter.'

In the tiny room next door an accordion strikes up, disturbing a game of darts. The players make their last throw, and retire to the Tap Room.

'Come on, Alf, give us a dance.'

Alf and Charlie rise and, arm locked in arm, swing in the rough melody of a clog dance. Then Alf does a sword dance, alone, over two crossed belts.

'Ah, this place be right old. Stood here since Queen Elizabeth's time.

Road to the sea used to go past here.'

'Here be Alf again, doing another clog dance.'

The simple, shrewd, inarticulate wisdom of these people, closer to the soil than the average New Zealand farmer, asking little from life. But they are chiefly all old or middle-aged men. Where are the young men? 'Oh, they be away on their bicycles to the pictures at Aldeburgh, or playing cricket for the village at Yoxford.'

Asking so little of life. They are men who have grown on the land like the trees, unlike so many new world farmers, who have been bank clerks, soldiers, racehorse trainers, labourers. They live in a complete acceptance of life, working long hours, asking little – food, lodging, enough for their pint at night. The dying race of the peasantry.

A warm May night, the moon swaddled in soft grey clouds, the elms dark masses against the sky. Drifting downstream in a canoe, a boy and a girl. From a punt moored under the willows comes the thin, heart-fingering music of a mandolin, playing Adieu *and then* Baccarole. *Other punts move silently downstream, each with an erect figure at the stern, silhouetted, with his lance-like pole, against the sky. A crowded punt follows, with a gramophone playing, and a scent of pipe tobacco that carries across the water. Over everything is an air of stillness and peace and calm that no one wishes to break.*

In the distance a train roars, and a motor cycle throbs its incessant way into the night – reminders of another world than this of the gentle, quiet moving Cherwell.

Another punt, with a noisy party joking and laughing together.

Then a punt, silent, drifting. 'From the silence, I should think that one's mixed,' says Anita. A woman's voice, a slight laugh, shows she is right.

In the branches of a willow tree an owl sits, a still figure, coagulated darkness. He sees many things, that old bird.

The value of an Oxford education lies to a great degree in its freedom. Despite the masses of petty regulations concerning the undergraduate's social and emotional life he is, in intellectual affairs, free to think what he likes. But he must think. He must not merely act on prejudice. The Oxford don will, on the whole, give credit for any idea, provided it can be defended on rational grounds. You can be a Communist or an Oxford Groupist or a nihilist, provided you can justify your position on rational grounds.

The Dominion student finds he is left free to work as much or as little as he pleases, to attend lectures only if he so wishes, and is not bludgeoned into study by regulations requiring attendance at frequently uninteresting and unoriginal lectures, by frequent tests and examinations. At Oxford he is free to work or not as he likes, the assumption being that any man who, in a term or two, cannot show that he is keen enough to study of his own free will is not worth teaching, and is better out of the University.

In the autumn of 1934, as leftish politics became increasingly fashionable at Oxford, I tried my hand at play-writing, in an attempt to capture some of the ironies of those days.

THE SCENE: A college sitting room. Enter MACDONALD. He looks round the rooms, sees that no one is there, wanders over to the bookcase, glances at an opened book on the top, puts it down with impatience, finally picks up the newspaper and settles in an arm-chair to read. Enter PARSONS, with a tray of glasses and a sherry bottle, which he puts on the sideboard.

MAC: Good evening. Is Mr Atherton likely to be long?

PAR: I don't imagine so, Sir. He isn't usually out at this time. I expect he's just gone into the town for a few minutes, Sir. I should wait if I was you, Sir.

MAC: I will. (*He glances at the paper*). Do you read the evening papers?

PAR: Well, not exactly, Sir. Sometimes I glances at the football or the racing news. But I do read the *News Record* every morning.

MAC: *News Record*. Pretty conservative, eh? Never has much to say about the working class, does it? Well, what do you think of this new reorganisation of the dole? Pretty harsh?

PAR: Well, it does seem a bit hard, Sir. But then times is hard, Sir, for everyone, so I suppose the working man can't grumble.

MAC: Why shouldn't he grumble? It's a pity he doesn't grumble a lot more. Why, look at this news only this morning. I expect even the *News Record* published it – dole reorganised so as to cut a lot of poor devils down a bit more, and at the same time money voted for an increase in the air force. How's that now? Is it unfair or is it not? It seems to me to be damned unfair.

PAR: Well, now you put it like that, Sir, it do seem a little hard. But with all this talk about war I suppose we got to be prepared.

MAC: Be prepared – for another damn Imperialistic slaughter. Tell me, what will you do if another war breaks out?

PAR: Well, I suppose I shall do my bit, Sir. I shall fight if they need me. I always been taught that that's my duty, Sir, and I'm going to do it.

MAC: But doesn't it ever seem to you – no I don't suppose it does – but doesn't it ever seem to you to be just so much wasted lives for no reason at all? No, I don't suppose it does. You are loyal, aren't you? You know, King and Country and all that.

PAR: I hope I am, Sir. I know what I've been taught, Sir, and I'm going to carry it out. If you'll excuse me Sir, I'm no bolshie. Don't hold with them at all, Sir. Just a lot of foreigners interfering where they don't belong. And now Sir, if you'll excuse me Sir, I must be getting along, Sir. *Exit.*

MAC: Always the same. I expect there are more convinced conservatives among the College's staff here than amongst the undergraduates. Duty, do my duty. My God, when will these fellows realise they are being led by the nose.

Enter STEPHEN.

STE: Hullo Mac. Sorry to be late. Just had to rush up to town to get some things. Well, how is it?

MAC: Not bad. I've filled in the time trying to convert your scout to anti-war beliefs.

STE: You damn fool. You only unsettle the old chap and make him think I'm a dangerous character.

✣ ✣ ✣

January 1935. This morning, around the corner of BNC came three men in single file, each bearing on his right shoulder a silver mace. They wore black gowns, and soft black hats like those worn by female undergraduates. Three or four steps behind them followed a small, white-moustached, insignificant little man in cap and gown, and white tie. The Vice-Chancellor was processing to St Mary's.

There was little impressive about the procession, save the unsmiling lack of self-consciousness of all concerned. The mace bearers did not march. They sloped along. One of them had grey flannel trousers, which showed under his black gown, and light grey socks. The Vice-Chancellor blew his nose as he walked, and seemed quite oblivious of either his harbingers or of the passers-by. But for the complete lack of self-consciousness on the faces of all the party, they would have looked foolish; as it was, they looked merely amusing.

I thought of Berry, who went down on his knees when the Vice-Chancellor passed him in the Broad.

An Indian student nearby joined me in a grin, his teeth very white against his dark skin. 'The Vice-Chancellor. Eh?' he said.

CHAPTER SEVENTEEN

Encounter with Storm Troops

In the spring of 1934 I found myself drawn into an argument about Nazism at a meeting of the Bentham Society, a discussion group at Queen's College. Baron von Oppen, a German Rhodes Scholar, spoke quietly but angrily against criticisms I had made of Hitler. A tall, fair-haired upright man, von Oppen looked exactly what he was – the descendant of an aristocratic East Prussian family, who owned great estates along the Polish frontier, a frontier they had helped to hold for centuries against the Slavs. He insisted that my knowledge of Nazism was incomplete, and challenged me to come to Germany and see the new order as the Germans themselves knew it. He was prepared to arrange for me to serve for a time in the German Youth Labour Service, the Arbeitsdienst, which ran Labour Camps in which young Germans worked on land drainage and road building.

I took up his challenge readily. Not only would it give me a chance to see Nazism from the inside, but it would provide some physical labour during my vacation, something which I had had in New Zealand and which I now missed. Von Oppen wrote off to Berlin. The arrangements were made, we shook hands on the plan, and did not meet again, for this was his final year at Oxford. The Register of Rhodes Scholars records him as having been 'Killed in Action 25 Oct, 1944'.

Chance opened another window on the Third Reich. I met a schoolteacher from Nuremberg who was staying with a Sussex family to improve his English. A quiet, responsible, manifestly decent middle-aged man, he was an ardent supporter of Hitler who had, he declared, brought back order and discipline into a country in political and social chaos. He was horrified at my insistence that Hitler's ambitions for Germany must bring war to Europe, and invited me to come to Nuremberg to see and hear Hitler at that summer's Nazi Party Rally. His brother owned a bookshop on the main square at Nuremberg, directly opposite the stand where Hitler would take the salute during the march past of the SA and the SS. I could watch the parade from seats they would place in the shop window. They would, too, secure a ticket for me to attend the mass rally at which Hitler was to speak. This offer I also accepted eagerly.

Germany was very much in the news by the time, towards the end of July, when I was due to leave for Berlin. On 30 June Hitler had turned against his former Storm Troop colleagues, had had Roehm and hundreds of other SA leaders shot, and had at the same time had General von Schleicher, the one Nationalist leader who might have caused him trouble, put to death, together with leading members of Schleicher's staff – an event which was later to have repercussions for me, in my days as a foreign correspondent. On 25 July James Bertram and I came out of Covent Garden (after watching a matinee of the newly formed ballet company) to see the newspaper placards proclaiming 'Dollfuss Murdered'. The Austrian Chancellor had been shot by two Austrian Nazis in his office in the Ballhausplatz, the building in front of which I had watched him take the salute some ten months earlier. I had little personal sympathy for Dollfuss, for he had used the field guns of the Austrian Army to shell the workers' flats at Sandleiten and the Karl Marx Hof in February 1934, to crush the Austrian Socialist Militia, which had taken to arms to resist the removal of the elected socialist municipal authorities in Vienna and Graz. This action by Dollfuss's conservative regime had considerable repercussions. Perhaps because it was directed against a party which bore a marked resemblance to the British Labour Party, it was a major element in reinforcing Hugh Gaitskell's socialist views (he was in Vienna at the time). It has also been cited – though the evidence for this is somewhat dodgy – as the event which turned Kim Philby towards Communism. Certainly the pictures in the newspapers and magazines of the shattered walls and archways of the blocks of flats, and of socialist militiamen, in working clothes and cloth caps, being marched off to prison camps, seemed to me doubly horrifying because they had been accurately forecast by the men and women who had shown me round Sandleiten in the summer. Even so, Dollfuss's regime was preferable to the Nazis, and his murder was a reminder that it was only a question of time before Austria, too, fell to Hitler.

One more major event was still to come. On the morning of 1 August, a few hours after I had reached Berlin, I was walking along the pavement in the Unter den Linden when a crowd began to gather around a loudspeaker set on a lamp post. I could catch some of the words, spoken in sharp tones '… has passed into the beyond … the nation will mourn'. Dr Goebbels was announcing the death of President Hindenburg.

Half an hour later a procession of men in brown shirts – some with long trousers, some with knee breeches, all carrying great swastika banners –

ABOVE: Cox (second from left) as a junior reporter for the News Chronicle *at a press conference given by Fred Perry, 21 June 1935.*

BELOW: Report by Cox from Madrid, November 1936.

CAPITAL CONFIDENT OF VICTORY

From GEOFFREY COX
"News Chronicle" War Correspondent

MADRID, Friday.

THE fourth week of Franco's attack on Madrid closes today with the city in apparently a stronger position than ever. Streets which a month ago had only a few paving stones or a pile of sandbags as defence have now scientifically-constructed barricades, deeply-dug trenches, well-placed gun positions.

And, more important still, the men and women manning them now believe that victory is certain to be theirs.

This afternoon the rebels launched their heaviest air attack so far on the district behind the Government line near the Model

GEOFFREY COX

Above: *With Cecily on holiday in Switzerland after return from Spain, 1937.*

Below: *Cox during his time as Paris Correspondent for the* News Chronicle, *1938.*

ABOVE: Pacific War Council meeting at the White House. Representatives left to right: Cox (NZ), T.V. Soong (China), Lord Halifax (UK), Dr Evatt (Australia), Winston Churchill, (UK), President Roosevelt (USA), Mackenzie King (Canada), Canadian Ambassador, Dutch Ambassador, Philippines President. May 1943.

BELOW: Cox with General Freyberg, to whom he was Chief Intelligence Officer, Italy 1944. (Photograph courtesy the Sir John White Collection.)

Pioneering editor of television news, London 1960. (Photograph courtesy The Times.*)*

marched down the central alley of Unter den Linden, under the lime trees. I followed them to the former Guard House, where a fire flickered unceasingly above the Unknown Soldier's grave. Nazi officials, they were paying the Party's first tribute to the dead President, swiftly seeking to capitalise on the sentiment which the death of Germany's patriarch aroused. They were not a pleasant-looking body. Many had the hardened expression of men from whom harsh experience had burnt away all human sympathy.

The Unter den Linden that day was a very different place from the boulevard I had first seen two years earlier. The street walkers in their pastel-coloured dresses had gone from the corner of the Friedrichstrasse, the crowds in the cafés had thinned. Now a great aerial torpedo had been erected at the crossroads, poised as if it were rushing in full flight to earth. Beside it a map showed Germany, denuded of all war planes, surrounded by countries whose territories were thronged with squadrons of bombers. 'Join the Air Defence League! Every German Must be Air Minded' was written above it.

The shoppers on the pavement were not fashionable people, but simply dressed women or heavily built men in suits bought off the peg. On a seat under the lime trees a group of unemployed in threadbare plus fours sat talking. An official passed them, portly in a new yellowish brown uniform with red shoulder tabs, and with a bulging briefcase under his arm. Reichswehr privates in grey uniforms, with sunburnt boyish peasant faces, strolled along, herding together. They saluted two SS officers in black uniforms who strode briskly past. Then came a Storm Trooper in brown shirt, brown breeches and a yellow-topped cap. A woman in a homemade frock, with a child clutching her hand, walked beside him. Under his left arm the Storm Trooper carried a parcel loosely wrapped in newspaper. But the other arm was free to be raised stiffly, in salute, to the official SS men, even to the Reichswehr party. Each time his face glowed with pride. The child whimpered and tugged at his mother's hand, hurrying her along the pavement.

I had some ten days to spend before going to the Labour Camp, so I took a course for foreigners on 'The Theory and Organisation of Modern Germany' being run at the Berlin School of Political Science, a massive, heavily ornamented building opposite the ex-Kaiser's palace. We had lectures ranging from 'The Theory of Dictatorship' to 'Agricultural Marketing', and from the events of 30 June to the position of women in the Nazi State. We visited schools, housing estates, slum areas and factories. Some of the lecturers were ex-Army or Naval officers. Some displayed no Party insignia. Only the theorist on racism wore a full Storm Trooper's uniform. Yet by now the Nazi Party had won respectability with many of the nationalist forces who had previously sneered at this upstart organisation headed by an ex-corporal. One student, a German who was taking the course as part of his preparation for the diplomatic service, invited me to his home for supper. His father had been a governor of East Prussia in pre-war days, and had known Hindenburg personally. To my surprise, the student appeared at the door to greet me in SA uniform. His brother, a barrister, arrived in black SS uniform; another guest had in his buttonhole the badge of the Air Sport Federation, the unofficial but very active air training force.

Something of the isolation into which the mass of Germans had been plunged since the war – and which was indeed widespread in Europe in those pre-television days – came home to us when we toured a slum area in East Berlin. Despite their theories on racism, the school had accepted as one of the class a black American student. The moment she appeared in this street of high, shabby apartment buildings, her appearance fascinated the children playing here. Within no time about fifty of them had gathered round her, staring at her as if she were literally a visitor from Mars. It was clear they had never before seen anyone like her. It soon became almost a stampede. Small boys whistled to their friends, bringing them racing around street corners or out of archways. Little girls taking the baby for a walk rushed up, pram and all. Ground-floor windows were opened, and children lifted out by their parents to join the procession. The young American student took it wonderfully. 'It's a good thing Hitler isn't here, or he would sue me for alienation of the country's affection,' was her only comment.

Hitler had acted against Roehm partly because the SA had been getting too powerful even for the Führer's liking, and partly to appease the Army, the Reichswehr, who wanted no rival militarised forces in the land. Hitler moved swiftly to claim his reward from the generals. When Hindenburg died, he merged the post of President with that of Reich Chancellor, which he already held, and – most importantly of all – had all ranks of the armed forces swear personal loyalty to him, Adolf Hitler, as Führer and Reich Chancellor. This sealed his dictatorship, ensuring that he could be removed from power only by a revolt or by death. A plebiscite a fortnight later gave public endorsement to this move.

On the day that Field Marshal von Hindenburg was buried at Tannenberg in East Prussia where, in 1914, his troops had defeated the advancing Russians, I stood in the crowd in front of the Rathaus, the Berlin City Hall, listening to Hitler's funeral oration. Through the loudspeakers his voice was jarring, tense, filled with emotion. He was followed by the sound of '*Deutschland Uber Alles*', played by the massed military bands at

Tannenberg. Immediately every arm in the crowd swung up in salute, till the square showed a forest of white hands and white faces, impressive and yet menacing in their silent, drilled unanimity. I felt that there were hundreds in that crowd who would tear to pieces any opponent who disturbed the semi-religious solemnity of an occasion like this.

The bands checked, the hands wavered, but a moment later they were outstretched again as the sound of the Nazi anthem '*Horst Wessel*' thundered out from the loudspeakers: *'Die Fahne hoch, die Reihen fest geschlossen ...'*

That this support for Hitler rested on fear as well as on faith I had no doubt, for the British and American newspaper correspondents in Berlin had bravely chronicled the repression launched over the past eighteen months against every trace of organised political opposition. Later that day I was to acquire my own evidence of this fact. Neill had given me an introduction to a former Summerhill pupil, Charlotte Reimer, a woman in her early twenties who had a German father and an English mother. Her parents had left Berlin, but she had stayed because Karl, the young German to whom she was engaged and who had been a leader of the Communist Youth Movement, was now imprisoned by the Nazis.

Charlotte proved to be a small, dark, vital figure, speaking perfect English. She surprised me by asking if I would take her to lunch the next day in the restaurant on the top floor of the leading German department store, in the heart of Berlin's West End. It was a fashionable and costly place, the Fortnum and Mason's of Berlin, and my funds did not run to such luxuries. 'I will pay,' she explained. 'If we get there early, and get a table by the window, it is possible to see into a corner of the courtyard of the Moabit prison. The prisoners are allowed into the yard for exercise between midday and one o'clock. If I can see that Karl is amongst them, then I know he is still there, and has not been taken off to Dachau or some other concentration camp. The police have beaten him terribly, but so long as they hold him, he has a chance. Once he is handed over to the Nazis, they will destroy him.'

We were in good time, and secured a window table, from which it was possible to see, some blocks away, a small patch of courtyard surrounded by high grey walls, and to detect tiny figures moving across it. Charlotte sat, outwardly nonchalant and talkative so as not to arouse the suspicions of the waiters or the people at other tables. Only one hand, clenched around her napkin until her fingers seemed almost bloodless, revealed the strain she was under. Around us women, in the flowing gowns of the time, furs draped across the back of their chairs, their lacquered hair showing under expensive hats, laughed and talked to their escorts – many of whom were in well-cut Storm Trooper uniforms. As cover for her scrutiny of the prison yard, Charlotte pretended to be pointing out the sights of Berlin, spread out in the sunshine below us. We were halfway through ordering our meal when I noticed her grip on the napkin suddenly relax. Her eyes softened with relief, and once the waiter had gone she nodded, and began to ask eagerly for news of Summerhill. Only when later we got to the relative privacy of the street outside did she say that she had seen Karl walking with two other prisoners, and with an apparently undamaged stride.

We met again that evening and went to a cinema, and afterwards had a drink in a café on the Kurfurstendam. Soon after we had taken our place a young man with close-cropped hair entered and seated himself a couple of tables away. 'He's a detective who shadows me from time to time,' Charlotte said. 'The waiter will have telephoned him to say I am here. But if we speak English he won't give us any trouble. They don't want to offend the English at present.'

Charlotte faced the constant risk of imprisonment because of her links with a known Communist. Yet she was uncomplaining and full of courage. But when I left her at the doorway of the ponderous, old-fashioned apartment building in which she had a room, and I watched her small, neat figure start briskly up the stairway, she looked very vulnerable and very much alone.

Charlotte's spirit of defiance may have had something to do with my own actions a few minutes later. The street from her flat led towards a broad main thoroughfare which ran from the Gedachtnes Kirche towards the station. At that hour – it was nearly midnight – it was ill lit and there was no traffic. Marching down the roadway, close to the pavement, was a detachment of some thirty or forty Storm Troopers, one of many such units which had been passing along the Berlin streets throughout the evening, on their way to entrain for Nuremberg and the Party Rally. As they approached the corner the three or four passers-by on the pavement turned and held their arms out in salute. But I was determined to do nothing of the kind. In what I realise must have seemed a deliberately provocative gesture, I thrust my hands in my pockets and stood, feet apart, at the kerbside.

Murmurs rose from the marching ranks, and the squad leader called them to a halt. Three or four men rushed towards me. I pulled out my passport, and turned towards the leader, saying, 'I am an Englishman.' As he bent down to look at the passport, I saw him give a swift signal. Out of the corner of my eye two men detached themselves from the rear rank, and moved out of my range of view. A moment later I was struck heavily on the back of the head. I came to a minute or two later on the pavement, to hear the tramp of the squad marching on their way. One of the onlookers picked me up and took me into a nearby chemist's shop, which was still open. As the pharmacist staunched the blood from a cut on my scalp, the man who had helped me spoke in English, 'It's really only excessive zeal that makes these fellows do this sort of thing. Wait until Mosley is in power in England and you too will appreciate what discipline and soldierliness really are.' Then he left the shop abruptly, before I could decide whether he was speaking sincerely or sarcastically.

I woke the next day with an aching head, and a long but fortunately superficial scalp wound. I debated whether I should seek out the *Times* correspondent and tell him my tale, but to do so could have added to the risks Charlotte already ran. So I kept quiet and rested up until, two days later, it was time for me to take the train to Hanover and the Youth Labour Camp in a nearby village.

CHAPTER EIGHTEEN

A Nazi Labour Camp

A week later I was wearing a brown uniform myself, though of the darker khaki of the Arbeitsdienst, the Labour Service, and was marching along cobbled roads to staccato orders shouted in German.

The camp in which I was to serve for three weeks was on the edge of a village in Hanover. It consisted of low wooden buildings, painted red and black, forming three sides of a square round a parade ground of beaten earth. Beyond stretched heather-covered moors. Over the gateway was painted in big letters the slogan 'Make Germany Bread Free' (free, that is, of imports of grain from abroad). It was flanked by tall white poles, from one of which hung the red, white and black flag of Germany, from another a swastika flag on a red ground, and from a third the flag of the Arbeitsdienst, with its emblem of a spade set between two ears of wheat. In front of a sentry box by the gate stood a sentry in khaki uniform, with a spade sloped like a rifle on his shoulder.

They wasted no time in drawing me into the life of the camp. I was issued with the same uniform, bedding, sports clothes, even underwear, as went to every one of the 170 other trainees – Arbeitsmänner – and was assigned to a troop. The sixteen of us slept in a small bare barrack room. At five o'clock the next morning I was bundled out of my bed to the chill notes of the German Army reveille, followed by whistles and shouts of '*Alles Auf!*' Ten minutes of loosening up exercises on the parade ground were followed by washing, shaving and bedmaking and, at 5.45, breakfast of coffee, bread, margarine and jam. After breakfast we fell in, in fours (a drill formation which the British Army was only then abandoning for the triple rank formation of World War II), roared a '*Heil Hitler!*' at the Camp Commandant, and saluted the flags as they were run up. Ten minutes later we were on our way to the Baustelle, the worksite, wearing our working fatigues – a worn, drab grey uniform and a crushed cap that made us look like a column of German prisoners on the Western Front in 1918.

The work was shovelling earth from a wide, canal-like drain being cut across swampy moorland, or cutting undergrowth to be bound into faggots for the ditch sides. I had great difficulty in convincing the section leaders that I really wanted to work, that I wanted the exercise, the chance to harden my muscles and test myself physically which farming work in New Zealand had provided. That I had come to see their camp they could understand. But they felt that the best hospitality they could offer me was the chance to sit in the sun and take things easily, whilst Obertruppfuhrers and Underfeldmarschals explained to me the significance of the swastika facing east, or questioned me as to why Germany should be denied equality of armaments, or why Britain allied herself with France: 'We are all Saxons, the English and the Germans, and we ought to hold together.' But in time I got onto the work itself.

It was not very hard. When Ude, the sharp-tongued little section leader, was away on another sector, the sector would take a spell in the sun, or hunt adders in the heather. We worked from about seven till nine o'clock, when we had a half-hour break for a second breakfast, of bread and sausage sandwiches we had brought with us in our pockets. Work continued until one o'clock, after which we would march back to the camp. Lunch was usually a stew, with innumerable potatoes. Then came a period of rest, followed by two hours of drill or sport.

It was not so much military training, as pre-military training. We did the basic barrack-square drills with spades being sloped or presented as if they were rifles. But there was no weapons training, unless you classified under that heading a game in which you sprinted a hundred yards, crawled another ten, and then threw long-handled, dummy German hand grenades towards a bull's-eye traced in the dust. I proved proficient at this and represented my section in a camp contest.

Each evening we had a *Befehls Ausgabe*, a parade at which the orders for the next day were read out. At the first one I attended we were told that the password for the day was 'Tannenberg'. What was Tannenberg? The man asked sprang to attention with a heel click that sounded like the crack of a whip, and gabbled off at top speed: 'Tannenberg-was-a-battle-won-by-Hindenburg-against-the-Russians.' This was typical of all our formal dealings with the officers. We were expected to reply to orders in this unnaturally fast voice, and to give the Hitler salute whenever we approached them.

Service in a Labour Camp was at that time theoretically on a voluntary basis, becoming compulsory only on 1 November 1934 for all young German men between the ages of 17 and 25. It served to take young unemployed off the labour market, to put some health and strength into the puny and under-nourished from the cities, and to provide a taste of military drill and discipline until conscription was reintroduced early in 1935. And it did something to improve land drainage and to repair and build roads in rural areas.

For three weeks, in that gloriously sunny August of 1934, I enjoyed the camp life, but without it changing my view that it was part of something both wrong and dangerous. I got very fit, in a countryside like East Anglia, where we marched across fields in the early morning with the woods on the horizon still hazed with mist, or where at midday great cloud masses moved across the wide blue North German sky. Working, scrubbing out the barrack room, playing football, stealing out at night to secure a supply of pears from a nearby peasant orchard (there was a bumper fruit crop in Hanover that year) I quickly merged into the easy camaraderie of the young, particularly of those sharing the same daily life and work. Nazi indoctrination – by lectures, by posters and by books – was constant rather than insistent, concerned more with glorifying militarism and soldierly virtues than with theories of National Socialism. Had I not had the evidence provided by the foreign press of the brutal oppression of all opposition – and indeed the direct evidence of the still sensitive scar on my own scalp – it would have been easy to be won over by this, to forget that the whole Nazi structure rested not only on persuasion but on fear. We in the Labour Camp were deployed as part of that process on the day of the plebiscite held to confirm Hitler as Führer and Reich Chancellor. We paraded in our best khaki uniforms and Sam Browne belts and marched into the nearby village. There we were drawn up for about an hour outside the main polling booth, a manifestation of the regime's activity and presence, a means of encouraging – or intimidating – the voters.

My fellow Arbeitsmänner guarded their tongues carefully, and none would be drawn into anything but the mildest criticism of the regime. Equally, few were ardent Nazis. The camp authorities tried to get them to sing propaganda songs as they marched. One of these proclaimed that '*Wir sind deinen Arbeitsoldaten*', whilst another, in the Nazi *geist* of 'Blood and Soil', declared:

> We are the Lower Saxons,
> Storm-tried, rooted in the soil,
> Hail to the Viking Duke's race

This part of Lower Saxony was indeed proud of its ancestry. Crossed wooden horses' heads, like figureheads on a bowsprit, indicated that both the farmer and his wife were of pure Lower Saxon stock.

But the labour servicemen preferred more homely songs, and we would swing along the village street, our heavy leather calf-high boots ringing on the cobbles, to the strain of a seaman's ballad:

Weil in Hamburg wohnt ein blondes Kind
Und das bist du, Marie

or a hiking song:

Steig Ich den Berg hinauf
Das macht mir Freude

I thought I should counter with some Antipodean culture, so I taught them a Maori haka. They took readily to its drilled, rhythmic gestures and its full-throated chants. On the night before I left camp to go on to Nuremberg our section, burnt by the sun as dark as any Maori, gave the haka in the parade ground, in the light of the head-lamp of the section leader's motor cycle. The Camp Commandant was, I decided, worried about the ideological rights or wrongs of allowing the dance of a very non-Aryan race, but the Deputy Commander, who had for eight years prior to 1914 been a sheep farmer in South Australia, backed it firmly. I have since wondered whether fate decreed that any of those who chanted or watched the haka that night were later, as soldiers in Crete or the Western Desert, to hear its like roared out in reality as the Maori Battalion of the 2 NZ Division came towards them.

CHAPTER NINETEEN

Hitler at Nuremberg

The schoolteacher from Nuremberg had been right. The window of his brother's bookshop on the city's main square offered an excellent view of the stand where Hitler was to take the salute at this 1934 Nazi Party Rally. The square, lined with stands, was already packed with onlookers and official guests by the time I battled my way through the crowds and the police and SA guards to the backdoor of the shop. Long red banners with the black swastika in a white circle on them hung from the brown stone medieval buildings which formed the square. Garlands were slung across shopfronts. Only the serrated front of Nuremberg's great church, the Frauenkirche, its pinnacles rising like stone pine trees on either side of its triangular façade, went unadorned by bunting or flags.

At ten o'clock, amid a frenzy of '*Heil, Heil*', a long black Mercedes drew up, and Hitler took his place on the stand. He wore the brown uniform of the SA, but with a well-cut jacket, collar and tie, Sam Browne belt, knee breeches and knee-high leather boots. The Iron Cross hung on his left breast pocket, and on his left sleeve was a swastika armband. But for this, and the high boots, his uniform could at first glance have been taken for that of a British Army officer wearing rather an odd shade of khaki. He was hatless, and his hair looked dark, brushed down closely and sleekly, except for the long lock which tended to slip down over his forehead.

The bookseller had binoculars, and I could study Hitler and the other Nazi leaders closely as, for four hours, column after column of Storm Troopers marched past the stand. Hitler's face was a strange blend of ordinariness and strength. The nose was somewhat prominent, the moustache a shade larger – and to that degree less comic – and certainly the chin more determined than I had expected. It was perhaps the low forehead, sloping back abruptly, and the fleshy cheeks which made it seem so ordinary, the kind of face one would not have glanced at twice in a crowd, had it not been that of the dictator of Germany.

Hitler's stamina was remarkable. For four hours he stood, with only intermittent breaks, as twelve abreast the brown ranks of the SA and the black ranks of the SS passed in front of him. As the standard carried by each detachment came abreast of him, Hitler would swing his right arm across his chest, then sweep it out in the Nazi salute. At the same time his eyes would fix on the faces of the men in the ranks with an intent, concentrated stare. He would then move his arm slowly to the right, following the flag, through an arc of about fifteen degrees, and then cut it back abruptly to his side, hooking his right thumb into his belt until the next column approached. This skilfully designed movement, military and precise, enabled him to alternate two or three minutes of saluting with a similar period of rest – without the rest appearing as slack or untidy. Even though the parade was organised so that from time to time there was enough of a gap between units for Hitler to move about on the stand and talk to the other leaders, the strength necessary for four hours of such activity was considerable. Yet such is the stimulus of power that he seemed relaxed, laughing with Goering and Hess, and showing no signs of irritation even when Leni Riefenstahl, who was filming the parade for her propaganda epic, the *Triumph of the Will*, plucked at his sleeve to attract his attention. In a cream-coloured silk suit, with a close-fitting hat shaped rather like a Reichswehr helmet, she came and went from the saluting platform, giving orders to the cameramen packed around its base, and to others set at the windows of buildings around the square.

Goering and Goebbels wore uniforms of the same cut as Hitler's, though Goering's Sam Browne sagged low over his bulging stomach, and his flesh seemed to slop over at every point within his brown shirt. Goering was in high good humour, chuckling and slapping his thigh as he talked to the burly bald-headed Julius Streicher, who was on the platform not so much in his role as the principal Jew-baiter of the Party, but because he was the local leader – the Gauleiter – of Nuremberg and as editor of *Der Sturmer*, the Party's virulently anti-Semitic journal. Goebbels, a small figure under a wide, flat cap with a swastika badge, his club foot disguised by long trousers – he was the only Party leader not wearing jack-boots – looked at first sight like a boy among adults. Only when one looked closely did one see that his sharp, wary expression was far from that of a youth. Rudolf Hess wore no tunic, but a brown shirt with a black tie, as if to mark the fact that, though Deputy Leader, he was in a different grade from the others. And in sharp contrast to these brown uniforms was the garb of Himmler, clad in the severe black of the SS.

Power is intoxicating, whatever its cost, and perhaps that is why on the platform in Nuremberg this morning an air almost of jollity prevailed. Even Himmler, his spectacles glittering in the sun, allowed himself an occasional smile.

Physically they were an ignoble lot, far from being the embodiment of the 'master race' which they proclaimed Germans to be. Only Hess, erect and stern, like an overgrown Boy Scout in his brown shirt and black tie, had any physical presence, and that was marred by the deep set, harsh fanaticism of his eyes under their heavy eyebrows. Even Baldur Schirach, leader of the Hitler Youth, was already running to fat within his calculated boyish uniform. Yet my bookseller host and his Nazi family and friends saw no such defects. To them these were demi-gods, the men who had protected Germany from Bolshevism and corruption by international Jewry. Any defects were to be glossed away. Goering was to them a merry figure, a man who enjoyed life, admired now for his lustiness, 'Der Dicke' – the Plump Fellow. Goebbels, I was assured, was a clever man, 'the kind the Führer needs to combat the many enemies threatening the Reich'. And when Hitler smiled patiently as Leni Riefenstahl posed him for yet one more shot, my hosts were almost in ecstasy at these signs of the humanity in this Supreme Being, so understanding even with so many weighty concerns on his mind.

That evening Hitler delivered his main speech of the Rally, in the vast new concrete exhibition hall on the outskirts of the city. We were there early to secure a good place in the body of the hall. Once again I had a better vantage point than that available to the foreign press, for I was part of the audience in the midst of the Party faithful, caught up in its reactions and its moods, not observing it from a place set apart. Around me were the men and women from whom National Socialism derived its basic support – peasants in dark suits, clearly their Sunday best; shopkeepers, small businessmen; clerks. Amongst them were many women. Behind the platform a huge metal swastika was ringed with red paper flowers above the words *Alles für Deutschland* (All for Germany) painted in blood-red letters six feet high. The pillars along the walls bore the swastika surmounted by the German eagle. High up in the wings electricians were busy with batteries of arc lights. From the rostrum in front of the platform a voice called, '*Achtung, achtung*, silence. We are testing the loud speakers.'

Slowly the minutes passed. A man in front of me ate tomatoes from a paper bag. A Storm Trooper walked up and down the aisle spraying the sultry air with eau de cologne. Then, a sudden blare of trumpets and everyone was on their feet: 'Yes, there he is, there! *Heil, heil!*' Through the thicket of outstretched hands the dark head of Hitler could be seen as he made his way with his officers down the central aisle and took his place on the platform.

The trumpets sounded again. In the entrance stood a black-uniformed standard bearer holding the 'Blood Flag', the banner carried in the first abortive Nazi *putsch* in 1923. It was borne swiftly up the hall, in the glare of the arc lights. Behind came the SA section standards, three abreast, sweeping up the central gangway in a stream of gleaming metal, their Storm Trooper bearers hidden by the tasselled swastika banners.

One of Dr Goebbel's most astute techniques then came into play. Instead of the meeting launching immediately into vehement political oratory, an orchestra played the prelude to Act II of *Löhengrin*. It was mood music on a grand scale, preparing the audience's mind for higher things and deeper thoughts, and at the same time throwing a cloak of respectability and legitimacy in advance over whatever outrageous assertions or claims Hitler might make. Opponents of Nazism even argued that classical music of this kind purged the audience of its better feelings, leaving its baser instincts open to exploitation by Hitler's oratory. Certainly an almost religious hush had spread over the whole vast audience by the time the prelude finished.

The mood then abruptly changed. Rudolf Hess, looking more than ever like a grown up Boy Scout, strode to the rostrum, curtly declared the meeting open and then cried, 'The Leader speaks!' In a tumult of cheering and heiling, Hitler's brown-uniformed figure took its place at the rostrum.

He spoke for an hour and a half. It was a speech not for foreign consumption but aimed at the German people, emphasising that he now embodied Germany and that the Nazis had supreme power. His long, convoluted sentences, his high-sounding, abstract words and sudden bursts of slang were difficult for me to follow, so that I was not caught up in the emotions he roused. But the crowd clearly were. A mother in front of me turned to her teenage son, her eyes bright with tears. No one seemed to notice the stage management behind it all. As Hitler worked towards a climax the arc lights came on, one after another, until he rounded off his sentence, fist in air, in a blaze of purplish light. When he brought his fist down on the rostrum and turned to his text again, every light would go out except one beside him, illuminating his face. At his feet crouched cameramen, and a film camera on a moving trolley rolled up and down the aisle.

Whenever he made a deliberate pause, brushing back his thin, shining hair from his eyes, the crowd were on their feet shouting, '*Heil, heil!*' One woman broke into hysterics, and went on with a shrill '*Heil, heil*' after the others had ceased, until she was pulled down into her seat. The tense, straining, menacing voice continued: 'The world outlook of the German people, the whole character of the German race demands … '

The Führer finished amidst a tumult of cheering, clapping, heiling. The SS guards smiled with pride. Hess mounted the rostrum. His voice sounded deep and calm after Hitler's: 'The Party is Hitler. But Hitler is Germany. All for Germany means all for Hitler'. The band broke into '*Deutschland Uber*

Alles' and then '*Die Fahne Hoch*'. Hitler stalked out through the cheering throngs, the standards followed in their gleaming stream, and the crowd surged to the doorway.

Outside it was raining. The trams were crowded, and in the trampled mud by a corrugated iron refreshment booth a child was looking for a dropped handkerchief. Wearily, I made my way to the railway station, and took the train for Berlin.

PART III

Apprentice Journalist
1935–36

CHAPTER TWENTY

Towards Journalism

My Labour Camp experiences were to provide me with an entry into British journalism, for I returned to Berlin from Hanover to find myself in the possession of a scoop. I had an introduction to the Berlin correspondent of the *New York Times*, and when I told him that I had come from working in an Arbeitslager his face lit up with interest. A row had just blown up about these camps because the High Commissioner in the Saar, then ruled by the League of Nations, had accused the Nazis of drawing young men from the Saar into Arbeitslager to give them military training. Were the camps militaristic? Were they indeed a hidden form of military service, designed by the Nazis to get around the compulsory military training banned by the Versailles Treaty? These were questions to which the foreign press in Berlin were seeking an answer. If I could provide it, the *New York Times* would consider an article from me.

I wrote two thousand words for them, thankful that I had kept my hand in by intermittently contributing articles to New Zealand papers ever since I came to Europe. But I was not optimistic about getting into a paper of the standing of the *New York Times*. A week later I was called to the telephone from the breakfast table in the Bloomsbury boarding house in which I had a bedsitting room – one of the admirable places offering clean and, by today's standards, remarkably cheap accommodation which then abounded in London. The call was from the London bureau of the *New York Times*. The paper proposed to use my piece as the cover story for the magazine section of their Sunday edition. Would I accept seventy-five dollars – fifteen pounds – for it? That was the equivalent of at least £300 in today's money, so I tried to sound as nonchalant as I could when I answered 'Yes'.

This encouraged me to try a shorter article on the Labour Camps for the *Spectator*, who paid me the then going rate for a 'middle' of three guineas. It was printed in the same edition as an article by their art correspondent, one Anthony Blunt, who in terms of the purest dialectical materialism dismissed the work of Salvador Dali as belonging to 'psycho-sexual exposition, not to art'. Other sales of my article followed, to a French journal, and to newspapers in New Zealand and Australia.

All this sharpened in my mind a resolve which I had been formulating for some time, to try my hand at journalism before turning – as I still planned to do – to the law. My contemporaries in the law faculty at Otago were all having a hard time in the continuing slump. If I could make a living, if only for a few years, reporting on these mighty events which were clearly underway in Europe, that seemed a reasonable thing to try. Perhaps subconsciously I had long had it in mind to become a journalist, a course indicated, if not acknowledged by me, when I had six years earlier decided to study history as well as law. Whatever were the forces guiding me, I decided that I would look for a job in Fleet Street once I had taken my degree.

My decision did not commend itself to the secretary of the Rhodes Trust. He was Lord Lothian, soon to be reviled or revered, according to your viewpoint, as one of the main advocates of appeasing Adolf Hitler. When I told him of my plan, in his office in the Haymarket, he was coldly scornful. Journalism, he made clear, was not a career for a university man. Teaching, yes; the law, yes; better still, government service or politics – but certainly not journalism. If one wanted to achieve something in life, one must first gain power. And journalists had no power.

Surely, I countered, they helped to shape that most formidable power, public opinion. 'Public opinion,' he snorted. 'The press don't form public opinion. We in Government do so. We decide what is to be done, and then send for Fleet Street and tell them to sell it to the public. You will exchange the reality of power for the shadow if you go into journalism.' His voice rose with a scorn close to contempt – so much so that the secretary in his outer office, a former Army officer, said to me as I came out, 'I expect you could do with a drink after that', and took me off to lunch at Stone's Chop House. I was shaken, but Lothian had power only to advise, not to rule, on what path I followed after Oriel, and I held to my plan.

Oxford in that winter of 1934–35 was becoming rapidly more and more left-wing. Labour Club meetings were packed. A proclaimed socialist from Canada became President of the Union. G.D.H. Cole at University College set up a study group on Marxism. No Marxist himself, he examined Marx's ideas sympathetically, almost as if he wished he could accept such certainties because of the basis for action they offered. Under his quiet, rather pallid manner, Cole hid a great deal of passion. This showed unexpectedly when, during a speech to the Labour Club, he admitted that much freedom of speech would go during the period when a socialist government was crushing the capitalists. 'Why would you support that infringement of our freedom, Mr Cole?' queried one undergraduate from the audience. Cole suddenly flushed a deep red and replied angrily, 'Because I think capitalism is a dirty, rotten state and ought to be destroyed.'

We were now well into the era of the fellow travellers, that special phenomenon of the thirties. Many motives combined to produce it. Genuine idealism, the instinct of the intellectual to hitch his wagon to a star, was an important element. But so too was the instinct, usually unacknowledged or indeed unrealised, of intellectuals to put their talents at the service of power, and particularly at the service of what looks like tomorrow's power. This instinct is a major cause, I believe, of the recurrence, generation after generation, of the phenomenon of *la trahison des clercs*. Personal factors – dominating parents, harsh schools, sexual inhibitions – no doubt had their place too, as many memoirs of the time reveal. To these influences was now added the very real desire to buttress the Soviet Union against the Fascism which threatened not only world peace, but the survival of democracy in the west. All of this amounted to a potent force, which released a torrent of favourable reporting about the Soviet Union into the press, not only of the Left, but of the centre, in Britain, France and the United States. Visitor after visitor came back from Russia with glowing accounts of the country's progress under the Five Year Plan, and with a determination to overlook or disregard the dictatorial basis of the system.

Kingsley Martin and the cartoonist David Low had made much the same journey at much the same time, as we had, to Moscow, Leningrad and the Volga. But in their book, *Russian Notebook*, they had either not seen or had ignored the mass surges of the displaced peasantry, the drunks in the streets, the underlying air of menace. From Moscow Walter Duranty, the *New York Times* correspondent, W.H. Chamberlain of the *Christian Science Monitor* and Louis Fischer of *The Nation* not only recorded constant economic success for the Five Year Plans, but stressed that democracy was increasing under Stalin's guidance. Reports of famine in the Ukraine were dismissed as fabrications. 'I backed Stalin the way you back a horse' was to be his later justification. George Bernard Shaw, having assured American listeners in a trans-Atlantic radio talk that 'Russia is so successful she has the laugh on us', continued to declare 'Stalin has delivered the goods.' Julian Huxley and Harold Laski, J.B.S. Haldane, John Strachey and Joseph Needham came back from the Soviet Union praising what they saw. The Webbs were about to remove the question mark from the title of their book *Soviet Communism: A New Civilisation?*

In the face of such assertions, I began to doubt not only the interpretation

I had put on what we had seen in Russia, but whether in fact I had witnessed anything like the spectacle of the kulaks in Kubyishev marching into imprisonment.

One man's writings cleared these doubts. On a winter afternoon early in 1935 I came across in Blackwells bookshop in Oxford a novel by an author at that time unknown to me – Malcolm Muggeridge. His *Winter in Moscow* not only confirmed the mass deportation and mass starvation in the Ukraine, making clear that we had glimpsed a huge and hideous reality, but it also portrayed and parodied the readiness of the fellow travellers to see only the good about Russia. In the civilised tradition of Blackwells no one disturbed me as I stood devouring much of the book then and there. Only later did I read, in back copies of the *Morning Post*, Muggeridge's detailed reports of collectivisation in the Ukraine, reports which the *Manchester Guardian* had refused to publish. Yet it was not the reports of these events but the reflections on them in the pages of the novel that had the greater impact on me – the first evidence I had had that fiction can get nearer the truth than all but the rarest of journalism. No statistics of kulaks exterminated or hectares collectivised could have for me the force of Muggeridge's picture of the Commissar 'in a high gilded room in the Kremlin', planning his next step in 'rooting out mercilessly all hostile elements in the villages'. As the Commissar 'lay in his bath he brooded on the reports; soft limbs, white and hairy, relaxed in hot water; red pate glowing in a mist of steam; little eyes half closed.' Enemies, he determined, must be crushed 'enemies at work everywhere; secret underground enemies, corroding the Dictatorship of the Proletariat; enemies in the Party, perhaps even in the Polit Bureau; enemies all around him night and day, intriguing, sabotaging.'*

Equally important was Muggeridge's brief introduction, in which he described the forces brought to bear in Russia to ensure that only a favourable picture of the Soviet Union reached the outside world: 'In consequence of all this' he concluded, 'the credulous organs of the Left in England are systematically misinformed about Russia, whilst the credulous organs of the Right, lacking genuine information, make their case against the Dictatorship of the Proletariat absurd by over-statement and invention'.†

I do not know how many people were influenced by *Winter in Moscow*. They may have been few. Indeed it was many years before I met anyone else who had read the book. But for me it was a work of prime importance. It prevented me from being caught up in the new wave of blind fellow-

---

* *Winter in Moscow,* Malcolm Muggeridge (Eyre and Spottiswood, 1934), p. 63

† *Ibid.*, p. 146

travelling faith in Stalin's Russia which was to sweep along so many of the British intelligentsia in the thirties, a faith which became all the more tempting as right up to the Nazi-Soviet pact of August 1939 the Soviet Union appeared as the one sure bastion against Hitler. Muggeridge restored too my faith in my own judgement of events, that essential element in the make-up of a journalist.

Today, fifty years on, Soviet Communism has shown itself economically so inefficient, and politically so brutal, that it is difficult to realise that for those of us who were young in the thirties, and who wanted to do something about the manifest injustices of the slump, and to halt Fascism and the drift to war, Communism was an option which had to be examined. The Russian Revolution was not yet two decades old. The idealism which had animated many of its supporters had not been stifled or distorted by Stalin. The major Soviet show trials did not get really underway until after the assassination of Kirov in Leningrad in December 1934. And we had this constant assurance by so many western intellectual leaders that Russia did indeed hold the answer to the future. At the same time social democracy seemed to offer no effective alternative on the Left. It had crumbled before fascism in Germany and Austria. In Britain its leader had split the Labour Party, and gone in with the Tories. Labour at Westminster was a mere rump, with an ageing, garrulous pacifist as its leader. In these circumstances the wonder is not that so many intellectuals gave their backing to Communist ideas, if not to the Communist Party itself, but that even more did not do so.

My article in *The Spectator* on my Labour Camp experience brought me an invitation from the Conservative MP Sir Arnold Wilson to tea at the Athenaeum Club in London. It was the first time I had been in a London club, and the Athenaeum in York Place was one of the grandest, with high-ceilinged rooms, deep leather armchairs, and servants in the club livery. Sir Arnold urged me to use my knowledge of the Arbeitsdienst to advocate peace and understanding with Hitler. A brave soldier in World War I, who had won the DSO in action in the Persian Gulf, he saw in Hitler not only the saviour of Germany, but a man who could ensure a peace in Europe. When I argued that against what was good in the Arbeitsdienst had to be set the bad of the dictatorship of which it was a part, his disappointment at my stance verged on anger. Did I not realise that I might be helping to prevent another world war if I helped to build trust in Britain for Hitler? I was flattered that this brave and impressive public figure, speaking in the heartland of British power, felt that I could influence public opinion. But I thought of Charlotte keeping her lone vigil in Berlin; of the concentration camps into which opponents of Nazism were being herded at Dachau and Buchenwald, a fact already well documented in the British press; of the sense of wary fear in Berlin, and I told Sir Arnold that I did not trust Hitler to keep the peace. He shook my hand sadly on the steps of the Athenaeum, disappointment in his tone as he urged me to think again.

In the five years which followed that talk, Sir Arnold Wilson emerged as a leading advocate of appeasement, whilst at the same time calling for conscription and British rearmament. When in 1939 his policy of trusting Hitler fell into ruins, he did the honourable thing. Although he was already in his fifties, he enlisted in the RAF, trained as an air gunner, and was killed in action over France in 1940. He had been proved wrong, but he was a man.

I made too an unexpected friendship as a result of my Labour Camp experience. I was questioned closely on my views about the camp, and about the Nazis, by a Scottish undergraduate at Balliol, Lord Douglas Hamilton. He was the younger brother of Lord Strathclyde, who had won fame a year earlier for having piloted the first aircraft to fly over Mount Everest. (The cameraman on the flight, Ronnie Read, was to be my chief cameraman, and my good friend, at ITN, twenty-five years later.) Lord Douglas and his brother had visited Germany, and had seen much there to admire. My view that there was much to deplore troubled him and he questioned me closely on what I had seen and experienced. He was very much a Tory, and took me to lunch at the Carlton Club, the inner sanctum of High Toryism in Oxford. On another occasion, when he was called upon at short notice to gather some students for a talk the Prince of Wales was to give in a committee room at the House of Lords, Douglas Hamilton enlisted me for that task. We drove to London at high speed in his Morris Minor, in time to hear the Prince, flanked by the Conservative leader, Stanley Baldwin, urge the virtues of child emigration to the Dominions. In a letter to my father I noted 'the Prince was bored, but charmingly so, and read a speech as if he meant everything in it. Baldwin was sentimental and a little clumsy. Neither of these speeches got to the four or five wealthy people invited to the meeting so much as the news that Woodful was on the platform, and the Prince had given the Society a £1,000.'

Despite the difference in our political attitudes, Hamilton and I established a sincere friendship, and I was due to visit his family home in Scotland when, in 1935, the opening I gained into Fleet Street plunged me into a different and all-absorbing world. In 1940 his brother succeeded to the dukedom – and was to find his place in the history books as the man whom Rudolf Hess had hoped to meet when the Führer's deputy made his extraordinary flight to Britain in 1941. By another of life's ironies, Hess's flight was to be the lead story in the first edition of the *Crete News*, the Army newspaper I brought out on Crete. Preparing the headlines for it during an air raid in Canea, I recalled those eager debates on the nature of Hitlerism in the Balliol quadrangle seven years earlier.

CHAPTER TWENTY-ONE

Into Fleet Street

It was one thing to decide that I would like to get into Fleet Street: it proved quite another to do so. Armed with my cuttings from the *Spectator* and the *New York Times*, where my piece had been made the cover story and impressively illustrated, I set about during the winter vacation of 1934–35 knocking on the doors of all the national newspapers. Surely such a direct approach, together with printed evidence of my work, must be a commendation in itself. I was quickly disillusioned. Most of the news editors on whose desks landed the slips I filled in, under the eye of world-weary commissionaires in the ponderous hallways favoured then by the major dailies, refused to see me. Occasionally an assistant news editor, or a senior reporter, would come down to deliver the refusal in a more kindly way. It steadily became clear to me that a university degree and an interest in world affairs were not recommendations for the post I was seeking, as a reporter. Reporting the news was seen in Fleet Street in those days as a craft to be learnt the hard way by apprenticeship on a local newspaper, a job for youngsters recruited direct from school. If a graduate had ambitions for journalism, he should seek a post as a leader writer or a feature writer, not among the Other Ranks facing the hurly burly of news-gathering. 'Get yourself three years' experience on a provincial daily, and then try again,' was the burden of the advice I received. But I had come from the remotest province of the Commonwealth, and had no intention of making any such detour.

Nor had I any desire to sit in a back room writing editorials telling people what they ought to think or do. I wanted to see and learn much more about the world at first hand before I started proffering my own advice or, worse still, putting my pen at the service of proffering someone's else's advice. My instincts were those of the historian, not of the preacher. I wanted to be up at the sharp end, where history was in the making. That meant being a reporter, even if to become one I had to defy or circumvent Fleet Street's unwritten demarcation lines.

Only on one paper did I penetrate the inner recesses of the management. Ian Coster, the only New Zealand-born reporter then in Fleet Street, worked on the *Evening Standard*, and persuaded Frederick Doidge, a senior management executive on the *Daily Express*, to see me. Doidge was a New Zealander who, after service with the New Zealand Expeditionary Force in France, had joined Beaverbrook in his early days on the *Sunday Express*, and had risen with his master – 'the loyalest friend I ever had' Beaverbrook said of him to me some years later. Doidge was also a kindly man whose true character was belied by his appearance, for with his long, lined, saturnine features he looked cast for the role of crooked gambler in a Mississippi showboat film. He could not offer me a job, but he did offer me one valuable piece of advice. If I wanted to crash into the preserve of the reporters I would need influence from the top.

I could deploy little such influence. Rhodes House, given Lothian's attitude, was no help. Oriel, an inward-looking college, had no links with anything as worldly as newspapers. G.D.H. Cole was my best hope. He agreed to write to his friend Aylmer Vallance, who had recently become editor of the *News Chronicle*. This sounded an ideal suggestion, for the *News Chronicle* seemed to me the one popular paper at the time which was trying to give its readers a relatively unpartisan view of events. And I wanted to work on a popular, mass circulation paper because I wanted to record, and try to explain, events for the type of people I had lived and worked amongst in New Zealand. One man in particular embodied the audience I had in mind. Jim Gallagher was a skilled sawmill operative who had lost his job in the slump and made a precarious living for himself and his wife and five children by splitting logs for fence posts in the winter, and general farm work in the summer. Self-educated, he followed and argued about events with an Irish combativeness. When we had been forking hay together during my last summer in New Zealand I had told him of the attractions journalism had for me, but had also expressed my doubts as to whether it really was a worthwhile job. Would one not be too much of a spectator of life, too little of a doer? He dismissed these doubts: 'If you can get out into the world and tell us the truth which those bastards of the *New Zealand Herald* try to hide from us at all times, you'll be doing a real job all right.' His approach may have been unfair, for in fact the *Herald*'s world coverage was more copious than that of most daily papers today. But his attitude stayed in my mind. There were, I was sure, a multitude of Jim Gallaghers and their like, responsible if baffled men – and women – who wanted their news in words and terms they could readily understand. I believed I could bridge the gap between what the pundits were saying, and what these people could take in amidst the pressures of their lives and their work, and I saw the place in which to do that as being the popular press.

Vallance's reply dashed my hopes. He had no openings on the *News Chronicle*, and could see none likely in the near future. I went off to do a winter vacation job on a farm near Peterborough in a chastened mood.

Sacrewell Farm, outside the village of Wansford on the Great North Road, was managed by John Abbott. I had met him through the Institute of Agricultural Economics in Oxford, who respected him as a farmer who, at a time of severe depression in British agriculture, was paying his way. Abbott liked New Zealand, and gave both John Mulgan and myself vacation jobs. He could not pay us anything but he provided our board and lodgings, and we got the exercise we sought. That winter it proved to be hard exercise – forking sugar beet in the bitter early morning cold, from clamps on the roadside onto lorries for transport to the processing plant in Peterborough. Two aspects of Britain in the thirties provided a background to our work. All day down the Great North Road passed a steady stream of tramps and unemployed, making their way from the deeply depressed north to the more affluent south. Some were like tramps out of picture books, trousers caught under the knee by string, and with their belongings tied up in a red spotted handkerchief and slung on a stick across one shoulder. Others pushed their belongings in battered prams. A good proportion of them were women, with wispy hair escaping from under battered cloche hats or men's cloth caps. 'You have to watch yourself with them,' my forking mate advised me. 'One of them once offered it to me for sixpence, and got real nasty when I refused. They'll be over the hedge, with their skirts up around their ears, if you give them half a chance.' The size of this sombre procession was extraordinary. Very seldom was there not at least one figure in sight, from early morning until evening, on the long straight road.

The Quorn, who held their New Year meet just north of Sacrewell, presented the other extreme. Scarlet coats rose above the brown line of the hedgerow as if a squadron of cavalry were forming up, interspersed with the black habits of lady riders and the bronze tweeds of the farmer members. Many of the women rode side saddle, neat booted feet showing from under capacious black folds of their riding habits as they sat confidently aloof on their big gleaming hunters. There were few if any motor horse boxes in those days. Instead grooms in brown leather leggings led superbly groomed horses down the side lanes, to hand them over to men in tight-fitting white whipcord breeches and long black boots who clambered out of waiting Rolls Royces and Bentleys. Assured voices rang out in the pale winter sunshine, greeting one another with the prep school nicknames beloved of the rich:

'Hullo, Buffy.' 'Good morning, Chatty. Have you seen Tibs today?' As the mass of horses stirred and shifted and eddied, and the moment grew near for the huntsmen to lead off the hounds, you could sense a carefully concealed concentration and the excitement of risks, if not dangers, about to be shared. There was, too, a noticeable undercurrent of sensuality, conveyed in a swift smile from very red lips behind a black veil or the shared glance of a couple ranging their horses side by side.

It was a scene reeking of wealth, all within yards of the highway along which that day's members of the drab southbound contingent made their way. But the two farm workers who watched with me shook their heads when I said, 'What a waste of money in a slump.' 'No, no,' they countered. 'It makes employment, does the Hunt. You take it away, and you take a lot of jobs away, too.'

Back in Oxford I had two last cards to play in my bid to enter Fleet Street. The assistant London correspondent of the *New York Times*, Ferdinand Kuhn Jnr, had liked my work and took me to meet the foreign editor of the *London Times*, Mr Deakin. He worked in a small dark room up a narrow stairway in Printing House Square, and proved bluntly discouraging. He had no openings, and he saw no chance of anyone with my limited experience getting into Fleet Street. But Kuhn, a small, quiet, ever-courteous man, a member of the Jewish family who had owned the *New York Times*, continued to give me both encouragement and friendship of a kind invaluable to me. He gave me occasional freelance jobs, mainly in tracking down scientists in Oxford who might contribute to the scientific section of his paper's Sunday supplements. He once sent me on a trip, organised by the Ministry of Labour, to show overseas correspondents a rehabilitation camp in Norfolk for the long-term unemployed. In it men could, over a period of six weeks, get back into some sort of physical condition on ample if plain food and in carefully graduated physical labour. The scheme had some resemblances to the German Arbeitslager but with one major difference. In Germany we had worked on building installations which would last: in Norfolk the men were literally digging trenches one week and filling them in again the next, to avoid claims from the union that these camps were a form of unpaid labour.

My one further possibility of influence was that of the Conservative MP for Lowestoft, Colonel Loftus. His son, whom I had come to know at Oxford, where he had some reputation as a minor poet, asked him to give me his backing. The Colonel suggested I might dine with him at the Commons, and he would see if he could introduce me to some of the Lobby's correspondents. We dined in some style, consumed a bottle of claret, and went down to Annie's Bar for brandies afterwards. Annie's Bar was in a tiny room off the Inner Lobby, at most some thirty yards from the doors of the Commons chamber and, alas, was never restored when the House was rebuilt after being bombed in the war.

In the bar, as luck would have it, was David Keir, the political correspondent of the *News Chronicle*. And, as even more luck would have it, he wanted a favour of Colonel Loftus, in the form of information about a forthcoming Bill on the White Fishing Industry. The Colonel readily supplied this, and in return, as a further round of brandies circulated (this time on the *News Chronicle*) suggested that Keir might get me an interview with his editor.

The outcome was that forty-eight hours later I found myself facing Aylmer Vallance across his desk in the editor's office of the *News Chronicle* in Bouverie Street. He began by saying, 'Well, at least you've got one journalistic quality – persistence,' but went on to deploy the same case as Doidge had put – that Fleet Street newsrooms did not want graduates from the universities, but from the barrack-squares of provincial journalism. I countered that it was time for a change, that I believed from my New Zealand experience many ordinary people would value their daily news presented in some greater depth, provided this was done in terms they could comprehend.

Though I did not know it, I was stating Vallance's own aim. He was a newcomer to Fleet Street. His previous experience had been in the more rarefied world of *The Economist*, which he had helped, under Sir Walter Layton's guidance, to turn from a dry-as-dust economic journal into an influential and readable intellectual weekly. Layton, who had become Chairman of the Daily News Ltd which owned the *News Chronicle* and the *Star*, had persuaded Vallance to move to the *Chronicle* in order to give the paper a sharper intellectual edge.

Vallance heard me out, and then said in his restrained, abrupt way, 'The most I can do is to offer you some holiday relief work next summer. It may be for only two or three weeks, but at least it will enable you to say you've worked for one Fleet Street paper when you next knock on the doors of the others.'

It was one of those offers which, however sincere, can fade into nothingness. But fortune once again favoured me. In March 1935, when I was in London during the vacation, I got a telephone call in the tiny Chelsea flat I was sharing with John Mulgan. It was the secretary of the *News Chronicle*'s news editor. My name had been given to him as a likely freelance. They had a flu epidemic in the office and urgently needed staff. Could I do a reporting shift tomorrow? Indeed I could, and at eleven o'clock the next morning found myself crossing the threshold of a newspaper in the street which was to be my working base – except for the war years – across the next twenty-one years, and with which my links were sustained until, in the 1980s, its great newspapers were dispersed to Docklands, or the South Bank, or Kensington. That brought to an end the institution which was Fleet Street, none the less powerful for having had no formal existence than that of being grouped in one corner of a great city – a city, in those years of the thirties, utterly confident about its future.

CHAPTER TWENTY-TWO

Learning on the Job

Fleet Street in the mid 1930s had much the same glamour as television has today, and it attracted much the same attention and criticism. For the popular papers in particular the decade was to mark the peak of their influence and success. Sharpened public interest in events and intense and costly circulation wars carried their sales to unprecedented levels. By 1933 both the *Daily Express* and the *Daily Herald* could claim circulations of over 2,000,000 copies, and by 1935 the *Daily Express*, under the editorship of Arthur Christiansen, was climbing steadily towards the 3,000,000 mark. Newspapers remained, too, the main source of news, unchallenged as yet by radio. Though the BBC's news bulletins were increasingly trusted, the corporation was not yet in a position to challenge the national press. The newspaper barons had seen to that, securing from the government limitations that the BBC should put out no bulletins before six in the evening – limitations which were to last until war broke out in 1939. The BBC were also forced to draw their news from the agencies rather than to cover it themselves.

The stars of the media – though that hideous, if inescapable, word had yet to be invented – were the newspaper columnists and special correspondents. Vernon Bartlett and A.J. Cummings, Sefton Delmer and G. Ward Price, G.E.R. Gedye and W.N. Ewer were names almost as familiar to the public as those of today's newscasters and reporters. Their photographs appeared on newspaper posters and often accompanied their by-lines on the page, making them recognisable – and recognised – in railway compartments and restaurants.

The national daily papers in 1935 fell into three clear groups. There were the quality papers – *The Times*, the *Daily Telegraph* and the *Morning Post*: the populars – the *Daily Express*, *Daily Herald*, *Daily Mail* and the *News Chronicle*; and the two picture papers, the *Daily Mirror* and the *Daily Sketch* – though the *Mirror* was in the process of transforming itself into a tabloid version of a popular newspaper, providing a strong if encapsulated news service, supported by trenchantly opinionated columnists. The *News*

Chronicle had the smallest circulation of the populars at around 1,300,000; it was at one and the same time both the oldest and the newest of them. Its name and structure dated only from 1930, when two Liberal papers, the pro-Asquith *Daily News* and the pro-Lloyd George *Daily Chronicle* had merged.

The *Daily News* dated back to 1846, when its founder editor had been (briefly) Charles Dickens. A bronze bust of him stood in the entrance hall of the *News Chronicle* in Bouverie Street to remind us of our ancestry. The paper had had a libertarian policy from the outset, backing the North in the American Civil War (by no means a popular stance at the time) and supporting Garibaldi. It opposed the Boer War and lost circulation as a result, just as half a century later the *News Chronicle* was to suffer from opposing Suez. George Cadbury of the Bourneville chocolate-making family, and a Quaker, was also opposed to the Boer War; he stepped in to save the *Daily News*.

In the twenties the *Daily News*, like other papers in the then over-populated national daily field, was in financial difficulties. George Cadbury's nephew Laurence turned to the man who had been his economics tutor at Cambridge, Walter Layton. Layton was not only a theoretical economist. He had shown himself, in the Ministry of Munitions during World War I, to be a remarkably practical statistician, with rare ability to assemble data and clarify issues for his political masters. Both Lloyd George and Winston Churchill greatly valued his work – so much so that Churchill was to bring Layton back in 1940 for the key negotiations with the Americans about arms production after Dunkirk. Layton's success in World War I led him, in the years which followed, to a triple career in business, journalism and politics, winning acclaim as the editor of *The Economist* which he built up into a major journal. His dry, hesitant manner hid a massive self-confidence in both people and events, which made him throughout the thirties and forties the main power in the *News Chronicle*, of which he had been the architect. Brought onto the *Daily News* Board in 1927, he organised a merger first with the *Westminster Gazette*, and then with the *Daily Chronicle*, becoming chairman of the paper which emerged from these dealings and gaining a knighthood at the same time.

The first editor of the *News Chronicle* had been news editor of the *Daily Mail* in its most celebrated Northcliffe days, Tom Clarke. But Clarke was too much of a populist, too much of a smash-and-grab news man for Layton. He wanted to recapture the great days of the *Daily News*, when Chesterton, Kipling, John Masefield and Joseph Conrad had been amongst its contributors, and Winston Churchill – a cigarette smoker, it seems, at that time – would drop in from the House of Commons to write an occasional leader. So Layton replaced Clarke with Aylmer Vallance who had been his assistant editor at the *Economist*.

The past of the *Daily News* was, however, of less interest to me in 1935 than that of the *Daily Chronicle*, for it was a writer for that paper, Philip Gibbs, who had first stimulated my interest in Fleet Street. Gibbs had not only written of his own experience in his *Adventures in Journalism*, but in the immediate post-war years had poured out articles, travel books and novels which had brought Britain, Europe and the Middle East vividly alive to me, as they arrived on the tables and shelves of the Invercargill Public Library. His work more than any other, planted in my mind the idea of journalism as a form of instant history, and held out the fascination of making a living by portraying events as they unfolded. Sir Philip Gibbs had opened his novel, *The Street of Adventure*, with his hero at the corner of Bouverie Street and Fleet Street, on his way to report for his first day's work on a national daily. I found myself, one sunny morning in March 1935, at that same corner, waiting until it was eleven o'clock, the hour at which I was to begin my first stint on the *News Chronicle*. I waited with some apprehension.

I was well aware that though I had written dozens of articles which had appeared in newspapers, I had never covered – except for an undergraduate paper – a hard news story. Somewhere between Aylmer Vallance's office and the *News Chronicle* newsroom the limits of my experience – about which I had been quite open to Vallance – had become obscured. The news editor's secretary clearly took it that I was a trained reporter. I was not going to let this one chance slip by drawing his attention to the fact that I was not. Given luck, I could train myself on the job, before anyone probed too deeply. My luck held. The first job I was given was to write about the preparations being made along the route to St Paul's for the Silver Jubilee procession of King George and Queen Mary due to be held in May. I had noticed stands being erected in Green Park and Trafalgar Square, so I talked to the foremen and workers, and eked out the information they gave me with descriptions of the half-built stands. But I needed some statistics to give body to the story. So I rang the Ministry of Works. Public relations officers existed in those days in only two Ministries – the Post Office and the Air Ministry. I was passed from one civil servant to another until at last I was told that information was not given to strangers over the telephone. If I called at the Ministry someone, after verifying my credentials, might be able to help me. It was by then too late for that, so I made my way anxiously back to Bouverie Street with what, even to my inexpert eye, was a thin story.

As I entered the newsroom the news editor's secretary, a friendly, boyish man called Wilson – we all used surnames in those days, even when we came to know people quite well – gave me a few sheets of material torn from a teleprinter: 'There is a line or two from the PA on your story.' I was by no means quite clear what the PA – Press Association – was, but I saw that its report carried a statement from the Ministry of Works about the miles of tubular scaffolding, tons of planking and number of men being employed on the stands. One branch of the Ministry, it seems, had been busy giving out the very information another was denying me. I blessed the PA, took its information into my story and typed out the five hundred words I had been asked for. At seven the next morning I was outside the newsagents in the King's Road when the day's papers went on sale. To my relief and delight my story was in the *News Chronicle*, cut back but with its main structure intact. I was over my first hurdle.

My next story brought me to Golders Green crematorium, where flowers had been arriving all day for the funeral of a famous High Court judge. I was looking at the cards on the wreaths and sheaves of flowers when a middle-aged man dressed like a bookie spoke to me. He wore spats, had a pearl pin in a wide cravat, and his suit was a colour midway between ultramarine and purple. His thickened nose and lined, red-veined cheeks spoke of a hard life, leavened by hard drinking.

'I'm Marvin Johnson from the *Express*,' he said, in reassuringly friendly tones.

Proudly I replied, 'I'm from the *News Chronicle.*'

'Did you notice the small bunch at the side?' he asked.

I had not, but scrutinised the card. 'You were always a fair man,' it read. It was signed, 'From an old lag.' Its presence, amidst this heap of tributes from the Bar and Parliament, gave the story an added human dimension, and I felt a glow of thanks and comradeship for one who was clearly an old hand in Fleet Street and who was giving a newcomer help in this way. It was only after I had telephoned in my story, and was in the tube on my way home, that another interpretation of the event occurred to me. Had my new-found *Express* colleague perhaps another motive than friendliness? Had he perhaps written the card, and placed the bunch of flowers there himself, and shrewdly ensured that I reported their presence to add authenticity to his tale? It seemed to me highly likely. But my story was in now, and I certainly was not going to change or withhold it at this stage. I noted, however, the next day that we were the only two reporters who seemed to have come across this moving human tribute.

Later that summer I found myself once again on a story with Marvin

Johnson. This time we met in a park at St Albans, where a summer pageant was due to be staged. It was a day of blazing sun, and he had exchanged his magenta-coloured suit for a light tweed check which confirmed his bookie image even more sharply. He greeted me as an old friend, put an arm around my shoulder, and drew me aside from the other reporters and cameramen. 'I'm on to a damn good angle to this otherwise dead story,' he said. 'Make your way quietly to the caravan by the trees. That's the producer's headquarters. Don't let the others see you go.' On the far side of the caravan I found him talking to a worried woman in a tweed coat and skirt. 'All you've got to do, my dear,' Johnson was saying, 'is kneel on the grass by the caravan steps, and hold your hands in prayer whilst we get a photograph.' Then he turned to me: 'We've got to get some relief into this story somehow, so I've persuaded the producer to kneel here and pray that it stays fine for the pageant.'

This the pageant producer rather embarrassedly did, under a blue sky devoid of clouds. But this time I was determined not to be an accomplice, and confined my story rigorously to a description of the pageant. The next day the news editor gave me a chiding: 'Interesting angle the *Express* had on the St Alban's story,' he said, pointing to a photograph of the kneeling producer, spread across much of an inside page. 'Marvellous eye for the unusual they've got.'

Johnson and his kind of amiable jokers were a dying breed in Fleet Street, and he was soon to be replaced on the *Express* by the new generation of younger, leaner, keener reporters brought on by Arthur Christiansen. The Johnsons may have tampered with the truth in spicing their stories but they did so without malice, and certainly without any political or propagandist aim.

I got through the three weeks of holiday relief work, which Vallance had warned me might be the most I could hope for, without any disasters, but also without any triumphs. When the duty rosters for the next week went up, I was gratified to find my name on them. This continued for a fifth, a sixth, and a seventh week, and gradually the unbelievable prospect emerged that I might be on my way to a regular job. The truth, I discovered later, was that I was the unintended beneficiary of a power struggle between Vallance and the old guard of sub-editors and senior reporters. Champion, the news editor, was caught between these two forces, and was understandably anxious to keep a foot in both camps. Since I was a Vallance nominee, he hesitated to lay me off. Vallance, on the other hand, gave no sign of recollecting who I was. Whenever I passed him in the corridor – he never appeared in the newsroom – he looked at me blankly. It is highly likely that he took me for one of the general reporters whom the paper had inherited from the *Daily News* and the *Daily Chronicle*. Certainly during the nine months I was to serve under his editorship he never exchanged a single word with me.

My cover, in this anomalous role, was intensified by the fact that my name appeared on no salary list. I was a freelance, paid on space rates, which were determined not by what stories I covered but what stories of mine appeared in the paper. Every morning a cheery figure from the accounts department, Mr Turner, would appear in the newsroom with a copy of the paper on which, in bold black pencil, the origin of each story was marked, Ex-tel, PA, Reuter, Staff or, in the case of freelances – and there were many in the provinces – with the contributor's name. Some days there would be no sign of 'Cox' on any page. On others I might have two or three entries. For a story of some length I could expect a guinea; for a shorter piece, ten shillings; for a paragraph, a mere five shillings. And since my role was essentially to do the bits and pieces, I averaged no more than three guineas a week. I had a toehold in Fleet Street but certainly not one paved with gold, or even silver.

My tenure was, however, helped when I discovered a niche few staff members wanted to fill. This was the night reporting shift on which two reporters were rostered from eight in the evening until four the next morning. Not only were the hours unsociable: the night news editor, Robert Mackenzie, had a reputation if not quite as a tyrant, certainly as a martinet. I discovered this on the first story I did for him. I had been warned that Mackenzie had one unbreakable rule. Reporters out in the field must ring in every hour to the news desk to report progress, even if the story was far from finished. I duly rang in at six o'clock, to be met by angry questioning from Mackenzie about first who I was, and, secondly, the state of the story, which was far from complete. By seven o'clock the one person who could provide any information (it concerned a businessman who had disappeared overboard from a Channel steamer) had still not returned home. I duly began to report this to Mackenzie. He interrupted me. 'Have you got the story?' he queried. 'No,' I replied. 'Then don't come on the phone until you have got the bloody story,' he retorted.

Fortunately in the intervening hour the woman for whom the businessman had left a note returned to her Knightsbridge flat, to find a *Daily Express* reporter and myself waiting. I can still recall the look of shock and pain which passed over the woman's face when we told her the purpose of our visit. She said, 'I can say nothing now, but if you wait half an hour I will see you.' Ten minutes later she emerged from the flats, walked up the road to the Brompton Oratory, and knelt and prayed in a front pew. The *Express* man and I watched from the shadows. 'Never let them out of your sight. It's the only way,' he had insisted to me. We followed her back to her room, and in due course knocked at her door, when she told us that the businessman (whose mistress it was clear she had been) had been told the day before that he had incurable cancer. Suicide stories are today – rightly – not investigated by the press or, if investigated, information is not published prior to the inquest. In those days they formed an element in the reporting even of the quality press. This story secured a place in the paper, and a grunt from Mackenzie which could have meant either approval or scorn.

Mackenzie was a survivor from Tom Clarke's short editorship of the *News Chronicle*, having been brought over by him from the *Daily Mail*. The bravadaccio of the Northcliffe era attached to him, expressed in orders which were shouted as often as spoken, in desks thumped with the fist, in glaring eyes. It took me some time to realise that behind this noisy manner Mackenzie had two great news editing virtues. He was decisive, and he could arouse enthusiasm. But I soon learned his bluster hid a shrewd mind. Something in my work must have revealed to him my lack of reporting experience. Midway through my first week on the shift he sent for me and said abruptly, 'How much reporting experience have you had before coming here?'

Instinct told me this was no man to prevaricate with. 'None at all,' I answered. After a moment's silence he exploded with wrath: 'Good God, what sort of paper has this become? Half the best reporters in Britain want to join us. And what do they give me? An untrained New Zealander who doesn't even know his way round London.'

He fell silent again – a silence I later realised must have been due to the fact that, with this new-fangled Vallance regime, even he had to tread carefully. Then he burst out: 'All right, if they won't give me trained reporters, I will bloody well train them myself. And I will start with you.'

That was the beginning of what could have been for me a nightmare period, had I not been convinced that if I could meet Mackenzie's standards I would not only be well trained, but could have in him an ally. He scrutinised every line of my copy, and if the least detail was lacking or any point, however minor, at all obscure, he set me to putting it to rights.

Fear of Mackenzie's tongue, but also respect for his standards, brought me many exhausting late night safaris. Provided only with the name of a street, but not the number of the house, I knocked my way at midnight from door to door down a seemingly endless row of houses in Wood Green, seeking a woman who that day had been reunited with a brother she had not seen for fifty years. Windows were thrown up, furious voices shouted for quiet, one man in his dressing gown threatened me with a garden rake for disturbing everyone's sleep. But Mackenzie's voice rang louder in my ears than any Wood Green accent, and I continued on my path until – glory be – I found brother and sister drinking cocoa in a front room, and only too happy to talk. And if North London provided problems, South London was a fearful place, where roads of identical houses seemed to stretch on for ever; where a wrong turning in dockland could bring you a walk of two or three miles round a high, unbroken wall, as you sought the site of a fire long since dealt with.

The most unpleasant task Mackenzie ever set me came later, after I had been on the paper for about a year. The *Sunday Referee*, one of the least scrupulous of the popular Sundays, had reported that in a village in Sussex a woman had kept the dead body of her son, embalmed in an attic, for the past twelve months. The day news editor had decided not to cover the story. When Mackenzie came on duty, I could see him, through the glass partition which separated his desks from those of the reporters, pacing up and down in unusual doubt. Then he emerged, and abruptly told me to cover the story. A train deposited me in this remote corner of Sussex about eight in the evening. It was a black winter night, and nothing I had experienced was blacker than high-hedged English by-roads on a starless night. The house was up a long drive. Fortunately the village pub was nearby, and in a corner of its bar I sought the advice of the landlord. 'Don't go near the place,' he said. 'There's an Alsatian in the grounds. I've already had two of you chaps in here, scared out of their wits.'

Was the story true? 'Yes, it is,' he said. 'The old lady could not bring herself to believe the boy was killed, when he was in a road crash a year ago. He was only in his middle twenties. She's had the body embalmed, and believes he will still come to life.'

The bar by this time was almost empty, and I consumed another pint whilst I gathered my nerve. The landlord suddenly came to my aid. My accent had revealed I was a New Zealander. 'Look,' he said suddenly. 'I served alongside the New Zealanders at Messines. I reckon I owe you a thing or two. I'll ring the chap at the house – he's the older brother – and see if he will talk to you.'

The subsequent conversation took me completely by surprise. Instead of rejecting my inquiries angrily, the brother confirmed what the landlord had said, and then pleaded with me not to publish them. 'If my mother sees them in the morning papers, it will be terrible for her. She will never see the *Sunday Referee*, but a daily paper would be different.' And he added, 'I know you journalists have to find news to fill your papers. But if you agree not to print this I will do anything I can tomorrow to find something else instead. Anything at all.'

Despite this plea, poignant as well as chastening, I could give him no such guarantee. But I passed every word he said on to Mackenzie after I had telephoned in the story. For good measure I had added at the foot of my copy a memo reading: 'I think it would be very wrong to publish this story.'

It did not get into the paper, but when I reported the next day Mackenzie sent for me. 'In the future, mind your own business. Your business is to get the news; mine to decide whether it goes through for publishing.' But there was as much warmth as wrath in his words, for at least he had had the story available, if only for the spike, and that was the job he – and I – were paid to do.

But in that spring of 1935, when I was still struggling to keep going as a freelance, I had another unexpected problem to contend with. What started as a nagging pain in my right side became an ever more insistent stabbing pain. The doctor diagnosed a rumbling appendix and urged me to have it out. Alan Small, a New Zealander who had been my contemporary at the university in Dunedin, was house surgeon at Queen Mary's Hospital at Stratford at Bow. His consultant agreed to treat me as a panel patient, and operate on me for no fee. Riven with anxiety that my foothold with the *News Chronicle* might be lost, I decided I must get the operation over and done with.

Chance was, however, to decree that my spell in hospital would not weaken but greatly strengthen my link with the paper, for a week after my operation a news story fell into my lap – or, more precisely, into the orchestra pit of the nearby Stratford Empire. A trapeze artist in a music hall show missed his grip and hurtled into the midst of the orchestra, breaking the cellist's arm and his own leg. He was brought into the bed next to mine in the ward, and as he waited to be X-rayed he told me exactly what had happened. I persuaded the night nurse to let me borrow her telephone, and phoned the story through to the *News Chronicle*. The next day, marked 'exclusive', it was on the front page. Though I never knew it until I left the paper two years later, this clinched my position with Mackenzie. When I came back to the paper three weeks later I was told I could regard myself as having a job at least until the end of the summer. Mackenzie has asked for you for the night shift, I was told.

I utilised the last weekend of my convalescence to get married. In the village church at Fernhurst, in Sussex, on 25 May 1935, I married Cecily Turner. She has already appeared in this tale, for she was the undergraduate whose well-tailored dark-blue coat and skirt had caught my eye, and raised my spirits in the High in Oxford one grey autumn morning in my first term at Oriel. I have had many strokes of good fortune in my life, but none matches that which linked me, for fifty more rich years, with someone who became not only my wife but also my closest friend.

CHAPTER TWENTY-THREE

Two New Zealanders

During the summer months which followed I was so absorbed in the struggle to survive, and in learning the craft of daily journalism, that I had little time to scrutinise the wider flow of events. The stories we covered late at night were seldom of political or social significance. Fires, accidents, robberies were our staple diet. Occasionally there would be a scuffle at a Fascist meeting, but none that I covered in London's East End that summer matched the calculated violence of the one I had attended in Oxford. On the Continent it was, too, a relatively quiet period. Mussolini was lying low before his assault on Abyssinia, and Hitler was not yet ready to assert the armed strength he was secretly amassing.

With the autumn, however, came increasingly menacing reports of Italian forces gathering along the frontier of their colony in Eritrea. Then, one sunny afternoon in October, from the top deck of the bus on which I was riding to work, I saw the newspaper sellers in Victoria Street hurriedly putting up placards saying 'Adowa Bombed'. I felt a sudden chill to the spirit – the knowledge that, inescapably, the long slide to war for us all had begun.

That evening I sat with Vernon Bartlett in front of the big wireless set in the *News Chronicle* top floor boardroom (the only set in the office) straining our ears to catch Mussolini's voice carry through the static, as from the balcony of the Palazzo Venetia in Rome he announced the invasion of Abyssinia. The frenzied baying of '*Duce, Duce!*' from the crowds only too easily increased the feeling that the dogs of war were indeed being let slip – that metaphor which Shakespeare had put into Mark Antony's mouth in a scene set close to the spot where Mussolini was now speaking. When Britain imposed sanctions on Italy, the possibility that we might get caught up in the conflict became a reality. If it became a shooting war, we who were in our mid-twenties would be the obvious candidates to fight it. Between stories in the newsroom we would discuss what life in the trenches would be like. To cheer us up, Wigley, one of the senior reporters, coined a recruiting slogan – 'Join Up and Take a Pop at a Wop'.

My thinking about sanctions and our policy towards the dictators was sharpened by contact with a New Zealand Government official who was to become a close friend. This was R.M. Campbell, who held the post of official secretary at the New Zealand High Commission, then housed in the Strand. He was the only political and economic adviser to the High Commissioner, and constituted in effect the entire New Zealand overseas diplomatic service. The few other New Zealand officials stationed abroad were all primarily concerned with trade.

Dick Campbell – even in those more formal times everyone used his first name – was in 1935 thirty-eight years old. With his high-domed, balding head and spectacles he gave at first an impression of pedantic seriousness. But when he spoke this was quickly offset by his swift, darting intelligence, his humour (a quality he could deploy to puncture pretensions of manner or thought) and his originality of mind. Campbell had started as a clerk in his teens in the New Zealand Civil Service. By attending night-classes he had taken a degree in economics at the University of New Zealand, and followed this with a post-graduate degree from the London School of Economics. The label 'intellectual' – which Campbell not only was, but looked – was not a commendation to the New Zealand politicians of the 1920s. Yet he won the trust of the most powerful figure of the day, J.G. Coates, the New Zealand Prime Minister from 1925–29. Coates, a tall, upright man with a dark moustache that made him look like a blend of Oswald Mosley and Anthony Eden, headed the conservative Reform Party which was in power when the slump first hit New Zealand. He was a big enough man to listen to the unorthodox ideas put forward by Campbell, then a young economic adviser on his staff. One of Campbell's proposals for coping with the collapse in world meat prices, which had glutted New Zealand's cold stores with unsold lamb and mutton, was daringly simple. He suggested that the government should provide a free weekly ration of meat to the public, buying the meat from the farmers and paying the butchers a fee to cut and prepare it. The money which in this way would flow into the economy would save the farmers from bankruptcy, lessen the cost of relief payments to the unemployed, and generally stimulate recovery. It was pragmatic Keynesianism some years before Keynes had produced his *General Theory*. It is to Coates' credit that he seriously entertained the idea, but the orthodox economists in the New Zealand Treasury ensured it was shot to pieces.

I came to know Campbell well in my last year at Oxford when I was working on a thesis on the New Zealand exchange rate in the early years of the slump. My mail one morning at Oriel brought me a letter from him. Campbell had attended a meeting at Downing Street to discuss quotas on

New Zealand meat. He had found himself waiting in a room where the desk was stocked with official Downing Street notepaper. He borrowed a sheet of it to write to me. His letter ran: 'Dear Geoff, As you will see from the above address, I have at last arrived. Of course I am only here temporarily. But then who isn't?'

Campbell had another great gift, that of encouraging and stimulating others. He exercised this by treating me as someone whose views merited respect, who should be encouraged to put forward an opinion, and then to defend it in the face of his own sharp, deft, probing mind – a process in which banter and candour took the sting out of any sharp criticism. He was a remarkable exponent of the Socratic method of clarifying by questioning, and would not hesitate to draw me into discussion with other officials, and on occasion the High Commissioner himself. In his large, rather dark room at the back of the ground floor of the High Commission in the Strand, or over the lunch table at nearby Rules Restaurant he made himself accessible and companionable not only to me, but to a host of British as well as New Zealand politicians, civil servants, university lecturers and businessmen attracted by his cheerful and empirical unorthodoxy.

Campbell was a close friend and admirer of our fellow countryman David Low, then at the peak of his influence as a cartoonist. 'The great god Low' was how Campbell, only half in jest, would refer to this compact, quiet-voiced figure with a black goatee beard, looking in the flesh exactly as he appeared, very occasionally, in his own cartoons. By 1935 Low's cartoons in the *Evening Standard* were a political force of remarkable power. Within minutes of the *Standard* appearing on the streets his latest offering would be the subject of applause or denunciation in clubs, Government offices, the corridors of Westminster, and the newsroom of every other Fleet Street paper. Low's draughtsmanship was superb, with its confident, strong lines, but above all there was a warmth and generosity in his work – something lacking in so much modern cartooning, which often seems impregnated with hatred not only of its victims, but of human nature itself. Low's Hitler was a Chaplinesque figure, menacing yet comic; his Mussolini a low-grade opera singer; Goering a fat boy fond of dressing up, yet playing with toys which could destroy us all. The danger these men presented was never underrated, but their pretensions were constantly punctured. Low was instinctively in touch with the opinion of ordinary people at the time, with the British inclination to mock rather than revile their enemies.

David Low's faith in collective security as a way of halting the dictators has been criticised as naive, as has been his tendency to portray Stalin as a sardonic rather than a wicked uncle. His choleric, reactionary Colonel Blimp has too been regarded as building a dangerous distrust in the armed forces, who were in due course to have to rescue the country from the mess the politicians and statesmen got us into. But in backing the League, and in not attacking Stalin until the Nazi-Soviet pact of 1939, Low shared views widely held at the time. And who can deny that until events – and Montgomery – took the British officer corps by the scruff of the neck and shook it hard, there were not only old Blimps but young Blimps in its midst? When Hitler's blacklist of people to be dealt with once Britain was conquered was published after the war, Low's name was prominent on it. His comment was succinct: 'I'm not surprised. He was on mine.'

Over the years Campbell, Low and I became the core of a small group who used to meet for lunch on New Year's Eve and write down our predictions for the year ahead, though reading these a year later was often a chastening experience. Even at the peak of his influence, Low never took himself too seriously. 'All I am really selling is vitality,' he told me many years later. 'People buy my work for the feelings I express, not the ideas. At the end of the day I am just making a living selling the energy I gained bicycling to school along frosty roads across the Canterbury Plains.'

Low and I were in Campbell's office on the afternoon on which, at Geneva, the British Government announced its support for sanctions against Italy. Philip Noel Baker, who was also there, was aglow with excitement at seeing his hopes for the League of Nations fulfilled in this way. I felt somewhat less enthusiasm, in my role as a possible inhabitant of the trenches, yet I was rather shocked, when Campbell asked, 'But will we stick by it?' That seemed to be carrying discussion by questioning a shade too far. Surely the British Government could not, indeed would not, withdraw from such a commitment? Yet within two months I was interviewing Sir Samuel Hoare, just after he had been made the government's sacrificial victim, when he had been discovered negotiating (with Baldwin's full approval) a secret deal with Pierre Laval of France to give Mussolini most of what he wanted. Ensconced in a richly furnished, high-ceilinged, rather gloomy flat in a block of red brick mansions off Sloane Square, Sir Samuel had one foot in plaster after an accident on the skating holiday which had been interrupted when the Hoare-Laval plan was exposed. He was a model of urbane courtesy – and of the art of saying nothing to a questioner, least of all to one from a newspaper which had castigated his role. In the nearby Abyssinian Embassy, just off the Fulham Road, a friendly muddle prevailed, which increased when the deposed Emperor Haile Selassie made it his refuge. He brought his family with him – and the young princes, quick, darting boys with gleaming white smiles were apt to interrupt press conferences as they pursued one another in a game of chase. I was standing one evening in the entrance hall, as the Ambassador was about to usher Sir Anthony Eden into the lift. Suddenly a small boy appeared from nowhere, slipped quickly into the lift, slammed the gates, pressed the button, and departed upwards, roaring with laughter in the face of an astonished Foreign Secretary and an embarrassed Ambassador.

They deserved their fun, those boys, for they and their own children were in due course to end their days in the gaol of the Marxists who were, in the 1970s, to impose upon their country a far more onerous regime than ever Mussolini contrived.

CHAPTER TWENTY-FOUR

An Editor is Sacked

In the autumn of 1935 Aylmer Vallance's editorship of the *News Chronicle* came dramatically to an end. In his two years in the chair he had done much to establish a more intellectual tone for the paper, to reinterpret in the terms of the thirties the character the *Daily News* had had under A.G. Gardiner. He had brought in Gerald Barry, who had been a highly successful editor of the *Week End Review*, as features editor, and given him as an assistant Tangye Lean, who had won attention by writing an undergraduate novel about Oxford, and who was to go on to become the controller of the European Service of the BBC. When in 1933 Vernon Bartlett, then the best known commentator on current affairs for the BBC, got into difficulties with the Corporation about the amount of opinion in his talks, Vallance made him diplomatic correspondent of the *News Chronicle*, and plastered London buses with posters declaring 'Vernon Bartlett – Still Broadcasting – in the *News Chronicle*'. Even more important in the long run was the appointing in 1933 of Oscar Hobson as city editor, when the *Financial News*, which Hobson had edited, was absorbed by the *Financial Times*. Hobson, ably flanked in due course by Paul Bareau and, after the war, by Patrick (now Sir Patrick) Sargeant gave the *News Chronicle* city pages of the highest standard, in what became virtually a distinct – and distinctive – paper within the main paper, and held many readers who might have found the main body of the paper veering too often to the Left.

Another key – and durable appointment – was of the brilliant and idiosyncratic Ian Mackay as industrial correspondent. Lionel Hale became assistant literary editor, under Robert Lynd.

The weekend supplement to the paper, printed on distinctive green newsprint, anticipated the Sunday paper supplements which did not appear until the fifties, and today's copious Saturday editions.

These developments were real strengths, but they were offset by the tactless and high-handed attitude, not so much of the editor, as of some of the newcomers he had brought to the paper. They gave an impression of scorning the older hands, of seeing the reporters and sub-editors as mere hack journeymen. In the summer of 1935, for instance, a tall, very assured, well-dressed young man called John Arrow suddenly appeared in the reporters' room. He was designated as a special writer, engaged by Vallance to give flair and distinction to major news stories. His talents were not, it seemed, to be wasted on run-of-the-mill reporting. In fact Arrow had had even less news experience than I had brought to the paper, and it was soon clear that nothing he wrote was as good as the copy of some of the older, more reticent reporters who had come up the hard way. Arrow was a protégé of another Vallance appointee, the fiction editor, Helen Chisholm, the granddaughter of Sir Edmund Gosse. She was a spectacular, six-foot blonde, strikingly good looking, superbly dressed, and with an imperious manner. She would stride confidently into the reporters' room, past the desks where other reporters were hammering out their stories, to discuss some ideas with Arrow, or to arrange for them to lunch at the most expensive restaurant in Fleet Street. It was not calculated to endear the editor to the rank and file newsmen upon whom the essential news service, and the production of the paper, depended.

Vallance made, too, the mistake of bringing his private life into the paper. One woman executive was widely assumed to be his mistress, and he broadened the interpretation of the concept of editorial freedom to comprise the freedom of the editor to make love in the office. Layton once came upon him in the act. 'They did not even stop when I came in' is reported to have been Layton's rueful comment.* Collin Books, who was a leader writer on the paper at this time, noted in his diary that Vallance 'fornicated all over the place. Even Arthur Cummings' sacred desk was violated.'†

Other senior executives thought the idea worth copying. I was typing a story late one night in the newsroom when the door of the office of one of Vallance's senior colleagues was flung open. A candidate in the *News Chronicle*'s contest for The Best British Typist emerged. Stifling a shriek and gathering her unbuttoned dress around her, she ran along the open corridor through the newsroom to the ladies' lavatory. The sub-editors were disgusted, but, conditioned by films like *The Front Page*, I was not greatly surprised. I had expected to find Fleet Street full of such happenings, though the flagship of the Quaker Cocoa Press did seem an odd place in which to encounter them.

Editors in those enlightened times not only often had their dinner at the

---

* *No Ordinary Press Baron,* David Lubbock (Weidenfeld and Nicholson, 1985), p. 138
† *The Rise and Fall of the Political Press* Vol. 2, Koss, p. 524

Savoy Grill or the Café Royal, but wore evening dress to do so. In dinner jacket, black tie, and gleaming stiff shirt front, Vallance would return to look at the proofs of the first edition at the end of the subs' room, followed by glowering glances from the shirt-sleeved sub-editors up to their elbows in copy, men whose weekly wage only just stretched to the cost of their austere lives in semis in Petts Wood or Bromley. Only too often it was also apparent that their editor had not only dined but wined exceedingly well. Legend had it that he slipped whilst bending over the stone – the bench on which the type was assembled – and came up with the front page printed on his shirt front. Certainly the night editor, John Davis, a burly Welshman who had lost his left arm and wore a steel hook in its place, and who played the cornet in a Salvation Army band at weekends, looked more and more antagonistic each time the editor made one of these visits.

The climax came on the night of the 1935 General Election, on 14 November. A raucous party, men and women all in evening dress, had gathered in the editor's room, and Vallance's voice could be heard leading the cheering every time the radio announced that one more Liberal (the Party the paper had backed) had lost. Suddenly Davis struck. He marched up the stairs to Sir Walter Layton's room, and told the chairman that the editor was drunk, and that the staff would not bring out the paper so long as he remained on the premises. Ten minutes later Vallance had left Bouverie Street for good. A week later his resignation was announced, and Gerald Barry took his place as editor.

With Vallance departed many of those whom he had appointed. I waited with some concern to see if I would be amongst them but together with Ian Mackay I survived the purge. I was fortunate that at the time these decisions were being taken I had secured a scoop of the kind to which Fleet Street, if not necessarily the outside world, pays close attention. It concerned a possible 'mercy murder', the name which had been given to the action of a girl whose fiancé had been diagnosed as having a swift and incurable cancer. She had smuggled poison into the hospital, had given him one dose and taken another herself, falling dead across his own deathbed. Ten days later another very ill patient died suddenly, in suspect circumstances. The evening papers all confidently asserted that another mercy killing had taken place. So did the early editions of the morning papers, our own included. But Mackenzie had one of his sudden hunches, and despatched me to the Southwark Mortuary to see if the results of the post-mortem were yet available. In a dark street, hemmed in by high warehouses, I rang the doorbell of the mortuary. It was well after midnight, and I expected a hostile reception. But relief spread across the face of the mortuary keeper when he learnt my mission. 'I thought you were an accident case that would keep me up all night,' he said. 'Come upstairs and have a cup of tea.' The post-mortem had indeed been completed. He showed me the doctor's report. No trace of poison. Death from natural causes. I studied it as we drank tea in his small office, just opposite the slab where the body lay covered by a green sheet, and then hurried out to the nearest telephone box. The next morning alone of all the national papers the *News Chronicle* carried the news that this was no mercy killing. The others continued to claim that it probably was. Mackenzie was delighted. Not only did he ensure that I was not fired, but he also got me taken onto the staff, at the trainee rate of seven guineas a week. I had made my way through the eye of the needle.

CHAPTER TWENTY-FIVE

The *News Chronicle*

Under Gerald Barry the *News Chronicle* flowered into a paper with a substantial and devoted readership. Even today I meet people whose faces light up with pleasure as they recall the *News Chronicle* of the late thirties and early forties. It became very much the paper of people who carried responsibility without necessarily getting much credit or reward for it – schoolteachers and factory foremen, clergymen and trade union officials, the non-commissioned officers of civilian life. Like their uniformed counterparts in the armed services, they were a vital element in keeping the country going at a time when amateurism was widespread in the upper echelons of power. In modern jargon they were middle-management, at a time when many top management posts went to those from the right family, the right school, the right background.

These people found in the *News Chronicle* from 1936 onwards a paper which not only gave them news they wanted in certain specialist areas, like education and the arts, but which above all seemed to share their attitudes and their aspirations. This was reflected not so much in the leader columns, which often wavered and wobbled between an Asquithian individualistic liberalism and modern socialist collectivism, plus at times a dash of fellow-travelling wishful thinking, as in the paper's selection of its news and feature articles, and the tone of its special writers. Above all the paper was permeated by a sense of hope and faith in human nature, a belief that life for ordinary people should and could be improved without revolution or violence, that unemployment and slums and malnutrition were man-made evils which man could end, and that peace could not only be maintained, but go hand-in-hand with justice. This could have seemed wishy-washy and unreal – 'piling up a daily heap of sand under which Liberal ostriches could thrust their heads' was one critic's view of its role – had the paper not stood firmly from the outset against Mussolini and Hitler and other regimes which were beginning to be classified under the broad label of Fascist. On this central issue of the day the *News Chronicle* was forthright and tough. At home it not only denounced Mosley in its leader columns, but followed his activities – and his brutalities – closely in its news columns. Its detailed reporting of the scenes at the Blackshirt meeting at Olympia in 1934 – where organised interruptions were met by organised brutality – helped to swing Conservative opinion against Mosley. Gerald Barry had been a member of a self-appointed group of observers who testified to the violence they had witnessed at that meeting. And when the Spanish Civil War broke out in 1936, the *News Chronicle* ranged itself unhesitatingly on the side of the Republic.

It had also an authority, bordering on the prudish, in its treatment of stories of sex and crime. At that time the evidence in divorce cases, the publication of which has since been banned, was a rich source of salacity drawn on abundantly by the popular Sundays, and certainly not spurned by the other popular dailies. The *News Chronicle* rationed the amount of such material it would carry, and – together with coverage of the more gory or garish court cases – would tuck such stories away, under deliberately restrained headlines, on an inside page. Crime stories were covered with care and in detail, but given as little prominence as was compatible with the news values. One house rule forbade photographs of boxing matches being used on the front page. These attitudes owed something to the Cadburys, who were staunch Quakers (the rule on boxing certainly did), but more to a sense of what was decent – a sense which was part of the philosophy of the Left at the time, reflecting the fact, as Morgan Phillips has pointed out, that the ideas of the British Labour Party owed more to Methodism than to Marx. It was a far cry from today's often-held view that sexual freedom, and indeed sexual aberration, seasoned with a dash of pot smoking, are essential aspects of left-wing progress.

One further strength of the *News Chronicle* owed nothing, however, to any political or social stance. This was the excellence of its sports coverage. Both the *Daily Chronicle* and the *Daily News* had had good sporting staffs. Combined they produced wide, reliable coverage and excellent sports writing, with the great Charles Buchan providing an insight into football unequalled in its day. In all its later vicissitudes, the *News Chronicle* sustained this high quality of news and comment upon sport, a fact which added to the impression that it was a healthy, trustworthy paper.

Journalistically the *News Chronicle* had for me a virtue which went beyond any political stance. It gave its reporters and its writers a degree of freedom remarkable in those days when, at least in the popular press, the proprietor was all-powerful. In the *Daily Herald* Labour policy, and in particular trades union policy, regulated the news as well as the opinion columns. The *Daily Mail* reflected Lord Rothermere's narrow, dark conservatism, which enjoined its staff, amongst other things, to print nothing hostile to Hitler, Mussolini or Emperor Hirohito of Japan. The *Daily Express* was unmistakably Beaverbrook's paper, however far he might claim to have withdrawn from its operation. On the *News Chronicle*, however, once you were appointed you were treated as a professional with professional standards, and left to get on with the job in your own way. Reporters' stories might be cut or trimmed, but were very seldom rewritten, and were certainly not revised in a way which altered their tone or sense. No one in Bouverie Street ever preached to me the dictum of C.P. Scott, the great editor of the *Manchester Guardian*, that 'facts are sacred, comment is free'. It went unpreached simply because in the Bouverie Street newsroom it was taken for granted. No schools of journalism or courses of media studies had yet arisen to debate at length such issues as whether impartiality was a true goal or merely the illusion of those who, blinkered by their class origins, were just propagandists for the status quo. The assumptions of the craft journalists, amongst whom I now found myself, were the same as those of good scholars in universities – that there was such a thing as truth, and our task was to seek it out, to the best of our powers, in the time available to us. Not that the reporters and sub-editors of the *News Chronicle* in the thirties were given to theorising about their work. They were for the most part men and women who had learnt their craft by apprenticeship rather than study. They brought to the gathering and presentation of news a self-reliance and self-discipline that had its roots deep back in the yeoman tradition of a job well done – and independently done. This editorial stance seemed to be reflected in the typeface and the layout of the paper, which was strong without being strident.

Gerald Barry was thirty-seven years old when he took over the editorship. He had been schooled at Marlborough in the period when it combined classical scholarship with harsh discipline. Barry, whose sense of humour was one of his virtues, used to tell the anecdote of the two Old Marlburians who found themselves in World War II as prisoners of the Japanese, working on the deadly Burma Road. Each morning they would encourage each other to face another day of horror by saying 'whatever happens it can't be as bad as Marlborough'.

From school Barry had gone into the Royal Flying Corps, serving as a fighter pilot, and rising to the rank of captain. After the war he went into periodical journalism, and soon became editor of the *Saturday Review*, a literary and political weekly with left-liberal tendencies. In 1930 the paper abruptly changed its character when it was bought by the fiercely patriotic and eccentric millionairess, Lady Houson. Barry and his key staff resigned en bloc, and within a matter of days had merged with the *New Statesman*.

Barry became features editor of the *News Chronicle* in 1934. With a rounded, open countenance and an easy, approachable manner, he could at first sight convey an impression of softness. 'A melting snowman' was one of Beachcomber's crueller pen pictures of him. But in fact Barry was decisive not only in his editorial judgements but also in his choice of people, and was calm in a crisis. He quickly emerged as a skilled editor, with a gift for quiet, effective leadership. With his background in the intellectual weeklies, he could well have been regarded by the craft journalists as yet another highbrow put over them. But Barry differed from Vallance – perhaps indeed he had learnt from Vallance's mistakes – in that he respected, and showed he respected, the professionalism of those whose task was to get and present the hard news. Though at the two daily planning conferences he guided, quietly and unobtrusively, the selection of news to be covered, and though he took an active and increasingly direct role in overseeing the coverage of foreign news, he did not seek to interfere in the technicalities of subbing and the layout of the news pages. That task he left to the night editor – at first to John Davis, and then to the formidable talent of the Welshman, Noel Joseph.

I was to observe later that a change of editorship can release within a newspaper a sudden gust of vitality and effort. This may derive from the fact that the adherents of the old regime are keen to prove to the new boss that they should keep their jobs, whilst those held back in the past feel themselves freed to give of their best. This helped to get Barry's editorship off to a good start in the opening weeks of 1936. But a further element of true journalistic leadership came from Barry himself. This stemmed from his strong sense of creativity, and his capacity for detecting and encouraging creativity in other people. One outstanding example of this was to be his nursing of the talent of Vicky, who developed from being a good foreign artist into one of the century's greatest English cartoonists. 'Has he got the spark?' was the question Barry would pose about a potential recruit for the paper, as he sought out that special ingredient which provides star quality, whether in a newsroom or on the screen. His ability to detect that spark, and nurture it, was to make Barry into an outstanding editor – certainly, with the exception of Arthur Christiansen, the best editor of his time of a mass circulation paper. And Barry was actively concerned with the paper's political and social policy to a degree which Christiansen, who left such issues to Beaverbrook, was not.

CHAPTER TWENTY-SIX

Death of a King

In January 1936 I found myself caught up for the first time in the coverage of a sudden, big news story which deployed all the resources of the paper. On Saturday 17 January it was announced that King George V was ill at Sandringham. On Tuesday evening at 9.30 the BBC broadcast the words of the King's doctor, Lord Dawson of Penn, which were to become famous: 'The King's life is moving peacefully to its close.'

Despatched to Buckingham Palace, I hurried up Bouverie Street where the lines of red newspaper vans were waiting to carry the early editions to the railway stations. It was a mild night, and outside the palace railings half a dozen members of the public, and as many reporters, had gathered. Just before midnight a small, middle-aged man in a bowler hat, a minor palace official no doubt, walked across the courtyard carrying a small noticeboard. 'E's gorn,' he said, as he hooked onto the railings the official announcement of the King's death. We noted down the words and sprinted for the phones. With my story dictated, I returned to the palace. The pavement was deserted. With the radio to inform them, people were clearly in no mood to gather here at this hour. During the next half hour, only one car drew up. From it emerged a neatly dressed young man, his face vividly made up with scarlet lips and darkened eyebrows. He read the notice, clambered back into the car, and was driven swiftly away. It was – particularly given the mores of the time – a strange footnote to a moment of history.

No such bizarre figures were in the long lines of people who waited to pass by the dead King's bier in Westminster Hall later in the week. On Sunday evening, the last of the four days of the King's lying in state, the queue at midnight stretched back to Vauxhall Bridge. It was made up very much of the ordinary people of Britain, many of them in the cloth caps and white or grey mufflers which were the uniform of the working class, employed or unemployed. One young man with a black band round his sleeve, and a pretty girl in a black beret faced a three-hour wait in the queue, and then a two-hour walk home to Hackney – for by then all public transport would have stopped. 'I'm a housemaid, you see,' she said. 'I have to get back in time to help with the breakfast.' Another was a farmer from Kent, his face, roughened and reddened by the wind, in sharp contrast to the pallor of the Londoners around him. What drew these people? Affection for the Royal Family? That certainly had been shown in unexpected warmth at the Silver Jubilee celebrations eight months earlier. A desire to share in an historic event? Or was perhaps some deep instinct drawing the British people together, as they felt the world around them growing more dangerous every day? Whatever the reason, the size and patience of that queue emphasised to me one thing – the British people, despite the slump, were far from being the antagonised masses of class war theory.

Westminster Hall itself looked immense, its wide stone floor stretching away into the darkness under the great oak hammerbeams. The only bright lighting was on the catafalque, where the coffin, covered with a Union Jack, stood on a raised platform. At each corner stood a soldier of the Household Cavalry, his hands clasped over the guard of his down-pointed sword, white horse-hair plumes falling across his gleaming helmet. Two nights earlier the new King and his three brothers, all in service uniform, had mounted this guard, in this same posture. The queue moved steadily down the wide steps, past the brass plaque marking the spot where Charles I had stood trial.

Twenty-nine years later I was to witness almost exactly the same scene in the same place, as Sir Winston Churchill's body lay in state, with the same long queues stretching along the pavement in the winter darkness outside. But then my task was different. It was to organise transmission by satellite to the outside world of television pictures of the scene.

Amongst the Soviet representatives at King George's funeral was the Vice-Commissar for Defence, Marshal M.N. Tukhachevsky. He had been the outstanding general of the Red Army during the wars of intervention. Whilst still in his twenties he had defeated in turn both the main leaders of the Whites – Admiral Kolchak and General Denikin – and had led the Red Army in 1920 into the outskirts of Warsaw. That city might have fallen had not Stalin, as Commissar of Budyenny's Cavalry Army to the south, overridden orders for Budyenny to join in the attack on the Polish capital. It was to prove one of the decisive battles of the century, for the Soviet defeat in front of Warsaw ended for the time being any attempt to spread communism by military conquest beyond the boundaries of Russia.

I interviewed Marshal Tukhachevksy, through an interpreter, in a panelled, high-ceilinged room in the Soviet Embassy in Kensington. Upright, quiet in manner, with few signs on his face of the strains he had been through, he spoke readily of his escape, as a Tsarist lieutenant, from a German prison camp in 1917. On his fifth attempt he got over the frontier to Switzerland and then to England, spending several hours in London's Waterloo Station during an air raid. From Edinburgh he returned by boat to Russia, to rise swiftly to a senior command in the Red Army.

His eyes kindled when I asked about the attack on Warsaw: 'We had to win on the first onrush, or not at all. We were outrunning our supplies.' He was more wary when I asked if it was true that a new patriotism had arisen in Russia, and that people were thinking more in terms of their country than of communism. 'The way we beat back the enemy in the civil wars shows that what is called patriotism is not new in Russia,' was his reply.

There was nothing arrogant in Tukhachevsky's bearing. I had had little to do with soldiers then, but I was to meet his counterpart a score or more times over the years ahead, particularly among the brigadiers and colonels of 2 NZ Division. It is the bearing of men who have been tested in the fire, and not found wanting.

Eighteen months after that quiet Sunday evening in Kensington Palace Gardens, Marshal Tukhachevsky was dead, shot in the back of the neck in an OGPU prison, the leading victim in Stalin's purge of the Red Army – the purge he carried out as soon as he had completed the extermination of most of his former political colleagues amongst the Bolshevik Old Guard.

To keep my knowledge of German in some sort of trim, I got into the habit of listening to the news on the *Berlin Deutschland Sender*. From its bulletins, just audible through crackling static, I learnt that on the morning of Saturday 7 March German troops had been sent into the Rhineland, the zone forbidden to the armed forces of the Reich under the terms of the Versailles Treaty. As with his announcement of the reintroduction of compulsory military service a year later, Hitler had acted at the weekend, knowing that the statesmen of the Western democracies, and particularly those of Britain, would have dispersed to the countryside. The habit, particularly favoured by Baldwin, of politicians and diplomats and editors gathering for the weekend at the great country house of one of the ambitious political hostesses, such as Nancy Astor's Cliveden, or Mrs Ronnie Greville's Polesdon Lacy, or Mrs Ronald Tree's Ditchley Park became increasingly inappropriate for these more urgent times. Not only did it remove ministers from their offices, but it must also have been tiring rather than restful, giving added force to Baldwin's view that 'half the mistakes since 1918 have been the work of tired men'. There can have been little chance for a busy man to recharge his batteries at a house party where the hostess was anxious to have the country's affairs discussed and determined around her dinner table or on her lawns. At least Chamberlain had the good sense to get away fairly often to a trout stream or a salmon river – even if, as I saw it at the time, he misused the energy this gave him.

This Saturday morning Dr Goebbels was using the most modern instrument of mass communication, the wireless, with consummate skill to tell Germany and the world of this further flouting of the Versailles Treaty. The on-the-spot reporting which came over the air from Berlin to the yellow Bakelite radio set in our Fulham flat was brilliantly done. Microphones picked up the rumble of gun carriages over the cobbled streets of Cologne; the menacing tramp of the marching infantry; the barked orders; the powerful brass and the insistent drums of the military bands with their incongruous admixture of the tinkling cymbals of the Glockenspiel; the constant baying of '*Heil, heil*' from the crowds. Interwoven with this was a commentary from reporters placed along the route, not only describing the scene but doing so in terms both exultant and threatening. This was a new and more direct form of reporting than we writing journalists could offer, but for the moment it posed no threat to us as no such coverage was offered by the BBC. They were still tied down by agreements with the newspaper proprietors which prevented them doing their own direct reporting. Only later that year did they appoint their first reporter, Richard Dimbleby, and even so they had to disguise his role under the title 'eyewitness'.

None of the great events of the next two years in Europe was covered directly by the BBC. They were to have no correspondents in Spain during the civil war, or in Austria during the Anschluss, or in Prague during the Munich crisis. Not until Dimbleby, at the end of 1938, persuaded his masters to allow him to go to the Franco-Spanish border to describe the retreat of the defeated Republicans into France, did the BBC deploy the powerful instrument of the microphone to cover these historic events. The news which reached the British public from Portland Place was clear and authoritative, but was all indirect, drawn from written agency copy. None came in spoken words from eyewitnesses on the spot, let alone from microphones which relayed the live sound. In fairness to the BBC it must be added that the American networks, though uninhibited by any deals with the press, were also slow in getting off the mark with direct radio reporting. The only live American coverage of the Spanish Civil War resulted from the private initiative of the leading American commentator of the day, H.V. Kaltenborn. At his own expense he sent a vivid eyewitness account from the top of a haystack in France of the frontier with Spain. The links were, ironically enough, arranged by BBC engineers. But it was a once-only effort. Not until March 1938, at the time of the Anschluss, did a young CBS producer, who was in Europe arranging talks for an arts programme, seize the opportunity to arrange coverage from Vienna, Berlin, Paris and London. This initiative by Edward R. Murrow was an instant success, bringing into being on the American networks regular, on-the-spot reporting from the news centres of Europe, and setting Murrow on the path to a well-made and well-deserved fame. But if this inability of the broadcasters in Britain to provide direct coverage was a deprivation for the listeners, it was a boon for Fleet Street, for it left the field open to those of us who were descriptive writers to use our pens and typewriters to provide the main record of the events which now raced in, one after the other, like breakers on a wide Pacific shore.

Gradually the scope for me widened. I began more and more to be rostered on the daytime shift. I was glad to end the upside-down life forced on night workers, and to grapple with stories which called for more background and perspective. But night work had called for two other journalistic qualities, speed and accuracy. Fleet Street papers in those days liked to have on the front page or in the stop press column a story that showed they were close on the heels of the latest news. Very often these were fires, which had to be covered in a matter of minutes against the deadline of the last (4 a.m.) edition. You had to dash from the office, get a cab from outside the milk bar in Fleet Street (the only one of its kind in London), race to the scene, force your way through police cordons and crowds, establish where the fire was exactly (an error in the address could bring a claim for damages) gather in any eyewitness interviews, and sprint to the nearest phone and dictate a story from your notes. It was not profound work, but it tested your wits. Occasionally it produced scenes of drama. I arrived at one fire in Soho to see a woman, trapped at a third-floor window, jump into an outstretched raincoat held by three men below. It broke her fall enough to save her life, though she was badly injured. Another woman tried to jump, but fell back, overcome by the smoke and flames billowing around her.

With the job done, I would catch the four o'clock bus back to Fulham, alongside my fellow night-workers. From Fleet Street we were mostly newspapermen and printers, and a few office cleaners. At Charing Cross railwaymen and postmen joined us. And as the bus moved through the Strand and Piccadilly it would gather in a score or more of whores, ending their stint on the West End pavements. Garishly dressed, lavishly made up, with large hats and gleaming high-heel shoes, they would clamber aboard, chattering like magpies, filling the lower deck and smoking despite the rules, bound for flats in Fulham and Hammersmith. In Trafalgar Square and along Haymarket, the Westminster City cleaning squads would be out – huge men in gleaming mackintoshes and sou'westers, hosing down the streets until they were as clean as a parade ground.

Work in Fleet Street brought, I found, an unexpected boon – the comradeship which journalism engenders, and which is one of its intangible rewards. Daily newsgathering resembles warfare in that journalists are striving, side-by-side with others, to deal with the unexpected and the difficult in conditions calling for swift decisions and common action, and it thus engenders something of the comradeship of war. It has other unifying characteristics. You are grappling not only with the problems of getting the news, and handing it on to the public, but you are doing so in highly competitive conditions, where your successes and your failures will be patent for millions to see and read the next day. You are often doing this at very unsocial hours, when other people are asleep or at leisure, and in conditions frequently of discomfort (though sometimes of luxury) and sometimes of danger. In the thirties journalists were, too, bound together by the sense of being an outlawed tribe. Only in its uppermost regions, where editors and columnists and special correspondents mixed with politicians and statesmen, did the idea fade that there was something not quite respectable about the reporter's craft. To the upper and middle class at least, you were someone who ought to be directed to the servants' entrance – as indeed I once was, in the stockbroker belt in Surrey.

Each Fleet Street paper had a nearby pub which served as an unofficial office club. For the *News Chronicle* and the *Star* the Feathers filled this role. It stood in Tudor Street, just outside the wide green-painted gateway into the Inner Temple, with the red brick Georgian buildings of King's Bench Walk – Charles Lamb's 'place of my kindly engender'. This brought a leavening of barristers into our midst. The Feathers was like hundreds of English pubs at this time – heavy oaken bar counters, walls covered in khaki plaster, black shiny seats stuffed with horse-hair flanking the few tables, high stools at the bar. The printers gathered in the public bar, the journalists in the saloon bar – not out of social prejudices (a sub who had been working on the stone with the printers would often take his pint in the public bar), but out of convenience, for the talk would be of shop and that drew like to like. Journalists tended to drink a lot in those days, though in my time on the *Chronicle* in the thirties I never had the money to do more than pay for a single pint, and perhaps contribute towards the two-shilling charge for hiring the snooker table during a supper break. It is surprising indeed how much good work got done by people who thought three or four pints a normal ration at lunch time, before settling down to some serious drinking in the evening once their copy had been handed in. But those drab Fleet

Street bars were more than just places of camaraderie and gossip. They played their part in the maintenance of standards, for here stories – in one's own and in rival papers – were discussed and dissected, and anyone tempted to distort known facts, or trim a story to meet someone's interest or whim, or breach a deal between colleagues would swiftly learn what others thought of him. This need to meet the unspoken yet clearly perceived levels of good journalism was a more powerful force for decent professional standards than any press council has since proved to be. To gain and hold the respect of one's fellow journalists was no mean goal.

The company into which I was admitted in Bouverie Street was a goodly one, full of people remarkably different in character and appearance – a much more varied band than are found today in newsrooms, staffed as they are almost entirely by more uniform products of universities and schools of journalism.

Only four of us in that pre-war *Chronicle* newsroom were university graduates. Paul Winterton had been at the London School of Economics, Wilfrid Sendall at Magdalen, at Oxford, and Richard Greenhough at Balliol. Sendall had won his post for an essay he had written on Lloyd George, a one-off recruiting method (or stunt) adopted by Tom Clarke.

Richard Greenhough looked very much the man about town, with sideboards down his cheeks at a time when anything but a short back and sides looked exotic, and a habit of spending his holidays in wealthy company at Salzburg or Venice. But he was a resourceful reporter, who secured a masterly scoop by getting himself equipped with a white coat and attached to the staff of the film projectionists at the Porchester Hall. There he was able to witness a strictly private Nazi-style meeting of the German community in London in 1935, with the Ambassador von Ribbentrop being greeted with shouts of '*Heil Hitler*' and the Nazi salute, and much lauding of Hitler.

CHAPTER TWENTY-SEVEN

Civil War in Spain

Hitler's military re-occupation of the Rhineland brought much scurrying of ministers between Paris and London, but no action beyond a ritual appeal to the League of Nations. On the whole, the British public concurred. 'After all, he's doing no more than move into his own backyard', was the general view. It was now clear too that we were not going to take any effective action to halt the Italian advance into Abyssinia. My belief that we might soon find ourselves in khaki proved unfounded. By April the Duke of Aosta's armies had reached Addis Ababa, and Haile Selassie sought refuge in Britain. Sanctions were not formally raised until June, but as they had never covered oil supplies they had been ineffective from the start.

In July began one of the great upheavals of the decade, the Spanish Civil War. In July a group of senior Spanish Army officers rose against the Popular Front Government which had won power in a general election in February, and which had found it increasingly difficult to maintain order in a spate of political murders from both Right and Left. I learnt of the generals' *putsch* in the small Austrian lakeside town of Zell am See, in the mountains south of Salzburg, where Cecily and I were on our first holiday since our marriage. (The only honeymoon we could afford had been a walk in Hampton Court park.) As I spelt out the news from the black print of the ornate Gothic script which German and Austrian newspapers then used, I expected that within a day or two the generals would have triumphed, and one more democracy would have gone to the wall, just as socialist Vienna had been crushed only two years earlier under the field guns of the Austrian Army. It was a chilling prospect, for it left only a thin line of democracies in Central Europe – Czechoslovakia and Switzerland, France and the Low Countries – which must increase the pressure for totalitarianism in Britain.

Perhaps my background in a new country – New Zealand in 1936 had been formally a state for less than a hundred years – had led me to underestimate the strengths and the depth of the roots of parliamentary democracy in Britain. But the friends of Fascism and dictatorship within

Britain were then numerous and well placed. Mosley's Blackshirts stalked the streets of British cities every evening. Not until after the major East End riot – the Battle of Cable Street – in October 1936 was the wearing of political uniforms to be banned under the Public Order Act. Lord Rothermere, under pressure from Jewish advertisers, had muted his 'Hurrah for the Blackshirts' campaign, but all three of his newspapers lauded Hitler and Mussolini day after day, and were quick to give the same blind support to Franco. Even if there was little likelihood that the British people would ever vote a Blackshirt Party into power, there was still the danger of a more subtle right-wing totalitarianism creeping up on Britain as a result of pressure from abroad, as dictatorship strengthened its hand in the neighbouring European countries. Geoffrey Dawson, the editor of *The Times*, was, for instance, already calling upon his correspondents in Germany to avoid giving offence to Hitler in their reporting of the Jews.

If Fascism triumphed in Spain, France would be hemmed in on three sides by the dictatorships of Franco, Mussolini and Hitler, and her democracy menaced. Once the Fascists and Nazis were dominant in Europe, they would be in a position to isolate Britain and dominate the course of events there, exacting as the price for peace the establishing of an extreme right-wing government at Westminster. This would be Fascist in everything but name – a black jacket and striped trousers fascism, if not a Blackshirt one – which would have crushed dissent and freedom of speech as effectively as Mussolini had done in Italy.

These were not just imaginings. The formation of a government in Britain friendly to the Reich was the avowed aim of the Nazis from Munich onwards, and certainly would have been the price we would have had to pay had we done a deal with Hitler in 1940. Nor, given such external pressures, is it by any means certain that all public figures in Britain would have stood by the principles of parliamentary democracy.

Surprisingly large numbers of prominent Britons were happy to be invited to the annual Nuremberg rally. Sir Austen Chamberlain's widow – Neville Chamberlain's sister-in-law – was a personal friend of Mussolini and his family. The discipline of Nazi and Fascist youth was widely praised. Professors wrote treatises about the Fascist state and corporatism. Even if, as a newcomer from the other side of the world, I had a tendency to see the complex issues of Europe too readily in terms of black and white, there was reason enough to wish to resist the growth of Fascism in yet one more Western Europe state.

The need to take such a stand, however, was only one reason why I supported the Spanish Republic that summer of 1936. Quite as powerful was the belief that despite all the horrors and excesses committed in the name of the Republic (and offset by as many equally brutal acts by the supporters of Franco and the generals), the July revolution which resulted from resistance to the generals' coup opened the way for the ordinary people to have a better future. Suddenly a new Spain seemed possible – one where the peasants would own their land, where the people might exchange their slums for the bright sunny apartment blocks such as I had seen at Sandleiten and Lindenhof in Vienna, where they might have education and the opportunity to escape from near-feudalism into the twentieth century. Indeed it is possible that one reason why so many middle-class people in Britain rallied to the Spanish Republic was that the revolution was more of an anti-feudal uprising than an anti-capitalist one. We had been brought up to believe that, despite its excesses, the French Revolution of 1789 had been a good thing, a necessary move into the future. Spain was just across the Pyrennees and in 1936 it was easy to see events there as part of the same process, the arrival of Liberty, Equality, Fraternity one hundred and forty years later. But above all we grasped, no doubt naively, at the chance to help build in Spain that fairer society which seemed out of reach in slump-ridden Britain.

Hope for the future, quite as much as hostility to Fascism, was raised by the Spanish people's embattled resistance. In time that first gleaming vision was to be dimmed and corroded, partly by the huge human cost of the struggle and partly by the blunting, and ultimately the corruption, of the Republic's own aims, as Stalinist falsehood and terror stretched out from Moscow to influence the increasingly powerful Communist forces within the Republic. But in the early months the vision was bright indeed. *Man's Hope* was the name André Malraux gave to the book he wrote about his experiences as a volunteer fighter-pilot for the Republic, and 'Careless Rapture' was the title of its first chapter. Malraux describes his feelings in that summer of 1936 as 'hearing the voice of that which is more awe-inspiring even than the blood of men, more enigmatic even than their presence on earth – the infinite possibilities of their destiny'. His words were grander than we might have used, but they reflected what many of us felt at the time.

CHAPTER TWENTY-EIGHT

An Overseas Posting

The *News Chronicle* quickly became a most vigorous and consistent supporter of the Spanish Republicans. The *Daily Herald* also backed the Republic, but more cautiously. Anxious to keep in step with the Labour Party in Parliament, it wobbled from time to time on the question of non-intervention by other European powers. The *Daily Express* was broadly sympathetic to the Republic in its news columns, but adopted a 'plague on both your houses' stance in its editorials. The *Morning Post* and, above all, the *Daily Mail* were ardently in favour of the generals' uprising. The *Mail* in particular purveyed in great detail every item of news and every rumour about atrocities on the Republican side.

These attitudes were reflected in the choice of words to describe the combatants. To the *News Chronicle* and the *Daily Herald* the struggle was one between the Republicans, or the government, on one side and on the other the rebels or (once Fascist Italy and Nazi Germany were giving aid to Franco) the Fascists. For the *Daily Mail* it was Reds against Nationalists from the outset. *The Times* and the *Daily Telegraph*, who in their reporting strove hard for impartiality, settled for 'The Government' and 'The Insurgents'.

Events in Spain, and their reflection in international negotiations, dominated the front pages of the British press for the rest of the summer and on into the autumn of 1936. Once Mussolini and Hitler had made aircraft available to ferry across from North Africa the highly trained troops of the Foreign Legion, and of the Moorish regiments, the balance swung sharply in favour of the generals. In early September crowds on the French side of the Bidasoa River, which formed the frontier with Spain, watched the rebel forces gradually thrust their way to the sea at Irun, cutting off the Spanish Basque region. By late September four columns under General Varela were advancing on Madrid, and General Mola was boasting that a Fifth Column of their supporters was waiting within the city to rise from their hiding places when the moment came. 'Fifth Columnists' passed swiftly in common parlance as a synonym for a hidden traitor. Toledo, on the approaches to Madrid, fell on 27 September and its fortress, the Alcazar, was relieved after a siege which had lasted for two nightmare months. As October wore on the fall of Madrid – and with it the effective defeat of the government – looked imminent and inescapable.

Covering this widespread and long-running story severely strained the resources of the *News Chronicle*, and brought me my first chance to work abroad for the paper. Early in September the *News Chronicle*'s Paris office found itself denuded of staff by the demands both of Spain and of holidays. A Swiss freelance was put in charge of the office, and I was told to go to Paris and assist him.

It was an exhilarating moment when I found myself boarding at Croydon – then London's airport – one of the Imperial Airways high-winged Heracles biplanes which plied the glamorous route to Paris. It was very different from my previous departures, jammed into the corner of a crowded third-class carriage from Victoria, facing perhaps a rough sea passage and an even more crowded hard class journey on the far side of the Channel. Now I was ushered into a spacious cabin, where dinner was served as we cruised above the dark countryside until the glittering pattern of the lights of Paris showed up underneath us. There was little that was glamorous, to be sure, about the small hotel on the fringe of Montmartre into which the office had booked me. But it was Parisian through and through, even to the sounds of passion reverberating through the thin walls of my room from, it seemed, rooms on both sides and above and below. And outside the streets were redolent with the intoxicating aroma of the Paris of that day – a blend of the smells of fresh-baked bread, of freshly-brewed coffee, of freshly-ironed laundry, spiced with cheap perfume (and sometimes very costly perfume), the smoke of Gaulloises Bleus, a whiff of garlic and, alas, of petrol fumes.

When I reported for work in the cavernous old-fashioned set of rooms which the *News Chronicle* occupied, in the offices of *Le Journal*, the Swiss freelance seemed uncertain about whether I was to assist him or him me. So I widened the instructions London had given me, settled myself behind Hennessey's big desk, and took over. For the next ten days I was 'Our Own Correspondent' in Paris, moving with the boldness of half-knowledge into the midst of the complexities of the Popular Front Government of France under Leon Blum.

My task was both aided and complicated by the *News Chronicle*'s key informant, Madame Tabouis. Her link with the paper was a closely guarded secret into which I had been admitted shortly before I left London. Genevieve Tabouis was the wife of a former diplomat, and her column in the radical daily paper *L'Oeuvre* was regarded as a key source of inside information, quoted constantly by the agencies and relayed throughout the world. I was later to come to know her well, and like her greatly. But at this stage she was merely a voice on the telephone, calling punctually at three o'clock every afternoon, never introducing herself by name but merely with the unvarying greeting, '*Bonjour, cher ami*.' She would then launch into a swift, lengthy, complex tale of the manoeuvres of politicians, the thoughts of diplomats, the plans of soldiers – interspersed at intervals with '*Alors, cher ami*', or '*Vous comprenez, cher ami?*'. These calls taught me quickly one hard fact. It is a great deal more difficult to understand, and to make yourself understood, in a foreign language spoken over the telephone than face to face. You have no gestures, no signs of understanding to help you out. Yet much of a journalist's work is done on the telephone. I could read French easily, but I could not pretend to speak it fluently. Mine was like the French of Chaucer's prioress, who spoke the language

After the school of Stratford atte Bowe,
The French of Paris was to her unknowe.

Once Madame Tabouis had launched into her complicated tale, there was no interrupting her and no stopping her. I just had to glean what I could. No doubt some gems escaped me. But enough reached my notebook for me to lead the paper twice during my ten-day stint, and to provide a number of other good stories. How reliable they were I had neither the time nor the inclination to check. Tabouis was, after all, a famous columnist. Who was I to doubt her accuracy? As the days passed I noted, however, that some of the stories she had supplied me with were given much shorter shrift by the correspondents of the other papers. Only two years later, when I became a full-time correspondent in Paris, did I realise that future historians would be wise to cross-check closely many of the revelations in that celebrated column in *L'Oeuvre*.

I got out and covered other stories on my own. I tracked down a linoleum factory where the last of the stay-in strikes (a new technique at the time) which had marked the election of the Popular Front Government in June was still underway. The workers passed the time playing chess on one of the factory's products, black-and-white check oil cloth for café tables. Around the Place de la République demonstrators chanted: '*Les avions pour l'Espagne*'. At the Quai D'Orsay diplomats in tail coats and striped trousers came and went, manoeuvring for or against non-intervention in Spain. I had even a late-night fire to cover, in the screen dock at the Paris Opéra.

My Paris stint also brought one splendid perk. The Pomméry

champagne firm celebrated one hundred years of operation with a lunch in a huge warehouse above the caves, cut deep into the chalk under the city of Rheims, where their wines were fermented and bottled. The foreign press were amongst the thousand guests. Not only were five different vintage champagnes served with the Cordon Bleu meal, but a glass tube carried a constant supply of *champagne nature* along each table. You simply had to turn on the spigot opposite your place to replenish your glass. The guest list did not, alas, include their former Berlin representative, Joachim von Ribbentrop. He was too busy with his new duties as German Ambassador to Britain.

London was well enough pleased to give me a further and tougher foreign assignment. I was sent to the south-west corner of France with the instructions to try to gain access to Burgos, and become accredited to Franco's forces in their advance on Madrid. Franco's representative in London had already turned down contemptuously an application for such accreditation. The generals rightly regarded the *News Chronicle* as a foe, and were in no mood, with victory apparently close at hand, to help it in any way. But Barry thought I might be able to organise something closer to the scene of action. So I made my way by overnight sleeper to St Jean de Luz, close to the Spanish border town of Irun, which had six weeks earlier seen bitter fighting.

St Jean de Luz, set by a perfect curve of sandy bay on the Atlantic coast, was a fashionable summer resort. Now, in October, it was in the midst of a strange second season. The holidaymakers had gone and in their place were Spanish refugees, diplomats from the foreign embassies who had been at Spain's summer capital of San Sebastian when the revolt began, arms dealers and commercial agents and, no doubt, many spies. Spanish was almost as common in the streets as French. In the cafés and hotel lounges elegant women from Barcelona and Madrid, as smart as the paint on their carmine fingernails, and black-haired Spanish men with light overcoats slung over their shoulders like cloaks, read the Spanish papers and listened to the broadcasts from Seville and Burgos. Many of the women wore widows' weeds, and many of the children playing on the beach had black arm bands. The working-class areas around the railway station were packed with thousands of poorer refugees, the workers and peasants who had fled across the International Bridge from Spain when Franco's forces seized Irun.

The central trafficking point for the dealing and manoeuvring in St Jean de Luz was the Bar Basque, a small bright restaurant with vivid murals showing Basques playing pelota or dancing the rota. Here I tracked down a tall, cheerful, hard-drinking Irishman in his mid-thirties, who was reputed to be Franco's contact man. I explained my mission. He agreed to send on my letter of application to Burgos, but added, 'I doubt if they will let you in, and if they do, you had better watch your step. They detest the *News Chronicle*, and if you put one foot out of line, you could find yourself in gaol, if only as a hostage for better behaviour on the part of your paper.'

Whilst I waited for a reply, I thought I should make myself known to the British Embassy, in the temporary headquarters they had set up in Hendaye, in case these forecasts proved true and I had to appeal to them for help from a Franco prison. I found the chancellery in a former grocery shop, a small building with bare wooden floors and lines of empty shelves. Behind the counter a young well-dressed attaché sat doing *The Times* crossword puzzle. The Ambassador, Sir Henry Chilton, occupied what had been the manager's office to the rear, a small room where he sat behind a simple wooden table.

I told him of my application to Burgos, and of the Irishman's words about the risks of finding myself in prison. His reply was testy: 'I have never heard anything like this in my diplomatic experience. You come here and tell me you are about to go into a foreign country and act in a way which may land you in gaol, and then expect us to get you out. If you obey the law – and I expect a British citizen to obey the laws of any country he enters – then you will come to no harm.' He brushed aside my view that the law, in a country riven by civil war, might be applied with very rough justice to a paper deemed to be hostile: 'I know these generals. They will behave properly. If you don't, you can't expect us to help you.'

I never had to put the embassy's services to the test. Three days later a curt refusal came back from Burgos, and I returned dispiritedly to London. Any chance of my reporting the civil war in Spain seemed to have gone.

CHAPTER TWENTY-NINE

War Correspondent

Events were to determine differently. On Monday 26th October the *News Chronicle* correspondent in Madrid, Denis Weaver, was captured by Franco's Moorish troops south of the city. A car in which he and another correspondent were travelling ran into an ambush. The two Republican escorts were shot on the spot. The Moors, and an Italian officer who was with them, were all for dealing with the two journalists in the same way. But a more senior Spanish officer intervened, and Weaver and his companion were sent to Franco's headquarters at Talavera, where they were held under arrest.

The *News Chronicle* had to get another correspondent out to Madrid fast if the paper was going to be able to give a first-hand report of Franco's attack. The fall of Madrid seemed inevitable. *The Times* was already talking of 'the helpless and discredited' Madrid Government, and of facts which would make Britain 'consider with less hesitation the prospect of recognising the Government of General Franco'. Even the *New Statesman*, a vehement advocate of the Spanish Republic, believed that 'failing a miracle', Madrid must fall. Once Franco had taken the city he would almost certainly either expel or perhaps imprison any *News Chronicle* correspondent. In these circumstances, for the paper to send out one of its stars like Vernon Bartlett or Philip Jordan (a former diplomat turned journalist), looked a waste. Better to send a lesser and more expendable figure. I fitted that specification. On the afternoon of Tuesday 27 October Freddie Champion, the news editor, came to the door of the reporters' room, his face grave: 'I'm afraid you're for it, Geoffrey. We've still no word of what has happened to Denis so you are to go to Madrid right away.'

Early the next morning I was on yet one more flight to Paris. At the Spanish Embassy there I picked up a Safe Conduct, calling on the authorities of the Republic and the Militias of the Popular Front to assist this correspondent of 'the great liberal newspaper the *News Chronicle*' who was coming to Spain on 'an important mission of information'. In Paris I gained

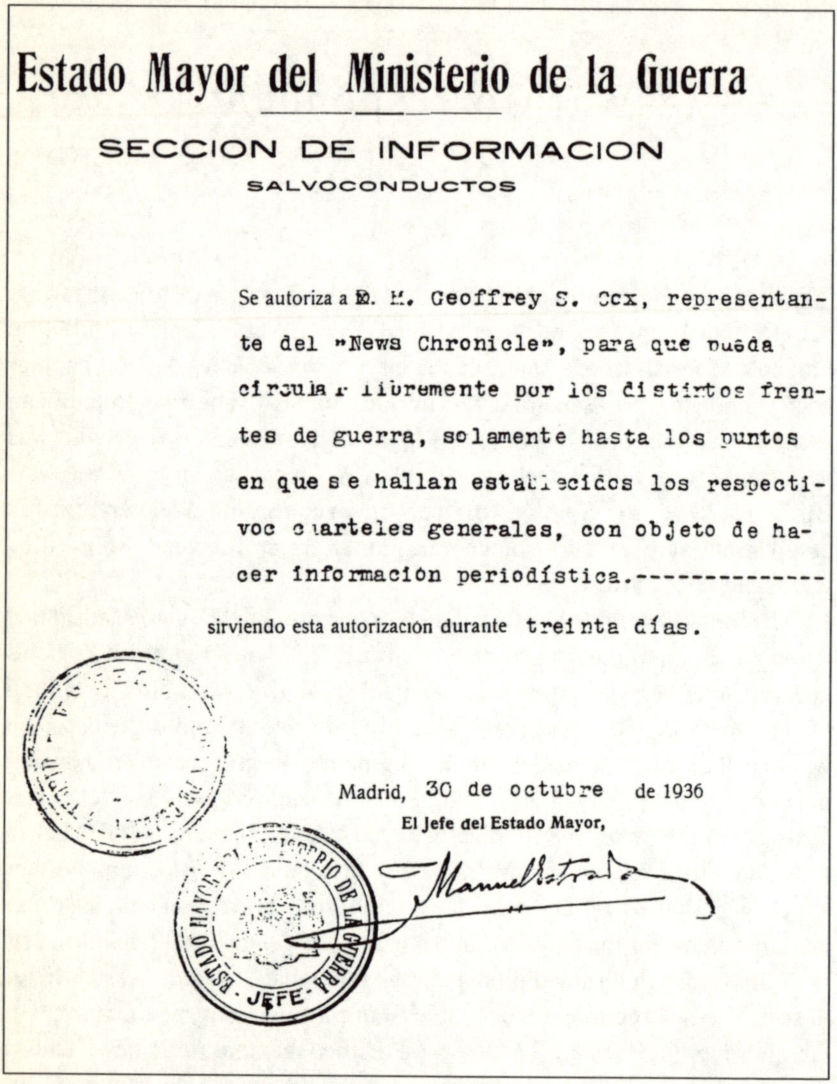

Estado Mayor del Ministerio de la Guerra

SECCION DE INFORMACION

SALVOCONDUCTOS

Se autoriza a D. M. Geoffrey S. Cox, representante del »News Chronicle», para que pueda circular libremente por los distintos frentes de guerra, solamente hasta los puntos en que se hallan establecidos los respectivos cuarteles generales, con objeto de hacer información periodística.--------------

sirviendo esta autorización durante treinta días.

Madrid, 30 de octubre de 1936

El Jefe del Estado Mayor,

Manuel Estrada

Safe Conduct issued by the Spanish Embassy.

some reassurance from Jay Allen, whose reports in the *Chicago Tribune* in August had given the world the first news of the massacres which followed the fall of Badajoz, when two thousand captured militiamen were herded into the bullring and shot. Allen surprised me by predicting that Madrid would hold out. The overnight train took me to Toulouse, and by nine the next morning I was in the sunshine of the airport of Barcelona, feeling over-dressed in my suit and collar and tie amidst a group of militiamen in overalls and espadrilles, armed with rusty rifles and very ready to teach me the skill of drinking coarse red wine from the spout of a tilted glass wine vessel.

Air France still maintained a daily service into Madrid. By early afternoon I had reached Alicante. The long wait in the airport there, until the Madrid plane left at dusk, tested my nerve. The sunshine, the blue sky and blue sea, the long empty coastline and the brown dusty plains reminded me of New Zealand. What was I doing, waiting to go to war, so far from home? But at last, in the swift autumn dusk, we were underway, flying barely a few hundred feet above the tawny hillsides, with a militiaman with a light machine gun stationed at the open door in the side of the plane as our sole defence against prowling Italian or German fighters.

Then Madrid airport in the early darkness, and a bus ride into the Gran Via in the centre of the city. There might be just time to get a brief story to London, something the paper could use to show it had filled the gap in its ranks. An unexpected force came to my aid – the comradeship of foreign correspondents in the field, a comradeship perhaps never stronger than in the thirties, when we were still few in number. As I checked in at the reception desk at the Gran Via Hotel, a small, sandy-haired man standing nearby introduced himself. He was Jan Yindrich, the Madrid correspondent of the United Press. (The next time we were to meet unexpectedly was five years later almost to the day, in a trench on the perimeter of Tobruk where he was a war correspondent and I an infantry officer.) He took me across to the press headquarters on the ninth floor of the Telefonica Building, introduced me to the censors, and showed me the message he had just put on the wires. I wrote quickly my own story from it, took my turn in the queue for the one telephone line to the outside world, and just before midnight dictated it to an astonished telephonist in Bouverie Street. Proudly next morning the *News Chronicle*'s late edition carried this message from its Special Correspondent in Madrid. Half an hour later – even in wartime, Madrid dined late – I found myself eating a huge Spanish omelette and drinking Rioja in a small Basque restaurant with Yindrich and a New Zealander from Wellington with his arm in a sling, who had been wounded in the shoulder when flying a fighter plane for the Republic. To Marichu, the young proprietress of the restaurant whose eyes seemed almost as black as her sleekly combed, shining hair, the pilot was clearly a much favoured customer, and she joined us in the intervals of attending to the other diners – mostly Republican officers in khaki uniforms and Sam Browne belts. It had been a long day, the first of many.

My first trip to a battlefield, made the next day, was nearly my last. With a young German photographer (an anti-Nazi refugee) I drove south by car along the Aranjuez road. The Republican forces had the previous day launched a counter-attack against the flank of Franco's army, using the Russian tanks and aircraft which had been landed at Spanish ports a fortnight before. The tanks made ground but the militia infantry were unable to keep up with them, and the attack– after fierce fighting in several villages – was halted by the more experienced Franco forces. This cut-and-thrust had left no clear front line. Searching for it, the photographer and I climbed a small hill close to the village of Valdemoro, to watch Italian bombers attacking positions a mile or so away. Government troops had been waiting close to the village outskirts, and in the afternoon sunshine I saw a score or so of them fan out and begin to climb the hill towards us. My first reaction was that we were in No Man's Land, and that an attack was being mounted on an unseen enemy on the far side of the hill. But it soon became clear that we were their objective. Crouching, the troops moved up the hill towards where we stood and then halted, their rifles pointing directly at us.

The photographer and I raised our hands, and the troops closed in. Then I made a mistake. I thought I should wave a white handkerchief as a clear sign of surrender, and dropped one hand to my pocket. Instantly a militiaman fired, and a bullet whistled past and hit the ground behind us. He had assumed, he explained later, that I was reaching for a pistol. A small man with a beard thrust a revolver into my ribs, and searched me for arms. I presented my passes. He could not read, but another man read them out. Then they started down the hill, leading us towards the village with the guns still in our stomachs. The German, who spoke Spanish, explained. The soldiers had thought we were spies. Who else would be standing in civilian clothes on a hilltop during an air raid, but someone signalling to planes?

At the edge of the village another wave of men came on the scene. They were not at all convinced we were not spies. Four bombers had appeared from the south, black specks in the sky heading towards the village. Obviously we had signalled to them. Better finish us off on the spot, as otherwise we might escape when they had to take cover. But the bombers passed by, a good mile away. We were taken into a house in the village square. In a shady front room a burly Spaniard, in a leather jacket and black beret, was bent over a map, side by side with a tall officer in a dark-green uniform. The Spaniard proved to be Enrique Lister, a Communist and former quarryman from Galicia, who was now Commandante of the Communist Fifth Regiment in the Republican Army. Lister had been trained in Russia and spoke French. He quickly checked our documents, dismissed the rather disappointed guards, and offered us a drink of beer. The other officer, whom I took to be a Russian adviser, stood silently in the background. The records of the period show he was Colonel Rokossovsky, who was to rise to the rank of Marshal and who led the Red Army into Poland in 1944.

On my next trip to the front I shared a car from the War Ministry with Nancy Cunard. This celebrated figure of the twenties was in Spain as a correspondent for a small avant-garde journal in Paris. With her long legs in beautifully tailored blue trousers, her small face, her thin lips a line of pillar box red, her eyes rimmed with kohl, a blue bandeau around her forehead, it was not difficult to recognise in her the original of Aldous Huxley's Mrs Viveash, in *Antic Hay,* 'the epitome of heartless elegance'. But that had been thirteen years ago. Now the fabled charm was overlaid by a brittle restlessness. We made slow progress towards the front, as every time a handsome militiaman was to be glimpsed at a barricade Nancy Cunard found some reason to stop and engage him in earnest discourse. But at Getafe, some nine miles south of Madrid, we at last caught up with the war. In the late afternoon autumn sunshine, we came face to face with the Republican Army in full retreat.

Across the brown unfenced fields stretching like a prairie towards a low ridge, over which ran the road to Toledo, were scattered hundreds upon hundreds of dark figures. Some were running, some walking. It was like a huge crowd hurrying away from a football ground. The first of them were already passing the white houses and untidy hen runs on the edge of Getafe. They wore stained khaki uniforms and espadrilles. Each had a blanket – some grey, some ordinary white ones which looked as if they had been hastily snatched from a bed – rolled across one shoulder and on the other a rifle, often with a rough sling made of cord. Their faces were unshaven, burnt a reddish brown by weeks of campaigning. There appeared to be no officers, no one giving orders, no sections in any type of formation, but just a vast crowd making its way listlessly and independently towards the village.

That morning these troops had been holding the centre of the southern front, near the village of Parla. When the line broke there, their leaders had told them to fall back and reform at Getafe. There was no panic about them. It was difficult to imagine that these men had been face to face with death all morning, and that at any moment a squadron of bombers might come over, bringing the same threat once more. In ones and twos they strolled down the pavements of the narrow main street, peering in the windows of the few shops that remained open, crowding the little bars, dodging cars with worried staff officers or buses that honked their way along in the direction of Madrid, loaded with light guns and munitions. Those who got food from the supply lorries squatted on the pavements, their backs against the white house walls, cutting slices of bread and opening tins of herrings with their bayonets. Some sat dozing in the sun in ditches lining the Madrid road. Others had taken up their positions in a line of shallow trenches just south of the town, near a wooden roadside hoarding which proclaimed: 'Stop at the Ritz when you reach Madrid.' But here too was the same slack, tired, unwarlike air. The men dozed in the sunshine or wandered about looking for food or fire wood, or read newspapers which had in some unaccountable way arrived on the scene. Amongst them were occasional militia women. Some looked even more soldierly than the men, with determined faces and rifles carried as if they meant business. But others – in neat blue overalls, with oiled, dark hair, pencilled eyebrows, vivid lips – added one more touch of unreality to the scene. Yet they too had been under fire all morning, and had, I learnt later, been amongst the last to leave the line. It was more like a waiting crowd of extras for a bandit film than an army fighting a war notorious for its complete lack of mercy.

In the church a group of refugees from Toledo crouched on an old, battered pew. One woman, a baby in her arms, clawed hysterically at my sleeve, bursting into streams of questioning. Were the Moors coming? Someone said they were just over the hill. How could she get away? She must. She must. They would kill her children; she knew it. In a cellar nearby three nuns watched over a group of children, their lips moving in prayer. What were they praying for, I wondered? The arrival of the Moors and the other Franco forces which the woman upstairs feared? Or the end of this catastrophe which tore their village apart?

Towards dusk things got better, though much confusion remained. One by one the troops shuffled up from the village street to take their places in the line. A young officer was even getting a section together to march back. Green double-decker buses, with fresh troops waving their rifles and singing out of the windows, rushed through to volleys of '*Salud! Salud*!' And a long black Cadillac, obviously bearing someone of importance – there were no trade union letters painted on its gleaming body – came to a stop outside the Commandante's headquarters in the town hall. From it stepped a tall woman with greying hair, wearing a simple black dress. Immediately the men sitting around recognised her, and one cried, 'La Pasionaria!'

Still clasping their pieces of bread and chunks of herring, they crowded around this famous woman Communist, Dolores Ibarruri, known as the Passion Flower because of her courage and her oratory, particularly during the Austrian revolt of 1934. She typified the old fire of Spain in the new setting. One sensed immediately the longing for leadership amongst these men. Shattered, retreating, dispirited, they wanted leaders who would guide their resistance.

La Pasionaria walked up the Toledo road towards the line. In the growing darkness, broken only by a fiery sunset glow on the horizon, man after man crowded after her as she turned along the line of trenches. It was spectacular – and tragic. For all her eloquence and courage, what could La Pasionaria do at this late hour to check the retreat? It seemed to me that the dying sun was like the fading glow of the Spanish Republic. On that autumn evening it appeared as if Madrid, and all Spain, must swiftly fall to Franco.

Over the next six days I was to see similar scenes of disarray at point after point, as the Republican Army fell back into the outskirts of the capital. They demonstrated two major facts about this stage of the Spanish Civil War – the power of attack from the air, and the Republic's need not only for arms, but for the organisation to use them.

Throughout October the Nationalists had clear air superiority on the Madrid front, particularly after they had caught and destroyed on the ground many Republican aircraft at the two military aerodromes of the capital, at Getafe and Cuatro Vientos. They used their planes to bomb and machine gun at low level the continuous trench lines which were then, in the tradition of World War I, seen as the essential technique of defence. Since the Republican units had few proper entrenching tools, these were often no more than shallow ditches, scraped in the hard Castilian soil, providing cover from ground-level fire, but making a clear target for attacks from the air. Under such attacks the Republican forces often broke and retreated, even though casualties were usually light. In this these raw Spanish troops were not exceptional. The campaigns in Western Europe in 1940 and Greece and Crete in 1941 were to demonstrate that even well-trained and well-disciplined troops could become disorganised and at least temporarily demoralised under air attack, particularly from an enemy with complete command of the air.

The Republican forces before Madrid were, moreover, lacking in both organisation and discipline. The revolution which had followed the defeat in Madrid and Barcelona of the generals' uprising had produced a multitude of militia units organised by the Socialists, Anarchists and Communists of both of the orthodox Stalinist and Trotskyist-Poum varieties. Such army units as had stayed loyal to the Republic had been disorganised by purges of officers whose loyalty was deemed suspect, or their ranks swollen by half-trained volunteers. Only at the end of September, as Franco began his final thrust towards Madrid, did Largo Caballero, the Socialist leader who had become Prime Minister three weeks earlier, decree that all militia units be reorganised as part of a new Republican Army. This was composed of brigades, rather than of larger, more unwieldy divisions. Political commissars were attached to these brigades not so much to indoctrinate them with a political attitude as to persuade them to sink their political differences and accept a common military discipline in the name of the Republic. Only later, when the Communist Party became the dominant force in the Republican Government did the role of the commissars change to that of preaching Stalinist orthodoxy and identifying and rooting out any variant of it.

This stiffened and reorganised Republican Army had, by late October, available to it formidable quantities of modern Soviet arms, which had been shipped through the Black Sea and the Mediterranean and loaded at Cartagena and Valencia. The day after I had witnessed the retreat at Getafe I was driving with Louis Fischer along the Aranjuez road. Close to the isolated conical hill, the Cerro de los Angeles, which is said to be the geographical centre of Spain, we saw in an olive grove by the roadside twenty tanks, their greenish-brown bodies skilfully hidden under the thickly branched trees. Fischer spoke in Russian to the young Soviet officer in charge of them. To my untrained eye the tanks looked formidable. Each had a light cannon as well as a machine gun, and their turrets could swing round in an arc. They were, I learned later, T-26 tanks, forerunner to the T-34, the great work-horse of the Red Army in World War II, and were superior to the Italian C3 tanquettes, which were all Franco had available at that time, though he was soon to gain the strong German Mark II tank. These Soviet tanks did not in themselves constitute a decisive force on the Republican side, but they were strong enough to safeguard the flanks of Madrid, preventing Franco from cutting off the capital's lifeline to Valencia – a line which was to remain intact to the war's end.

CHAPTER THIRTY

A City at Bay

Madrid, as Franco's forces came ever closer, remained surprisingly calm. Throughout the next week, I drove back to the city each evening from the front (or more exactly from the several fronts on the roads along which Franco's columns were advancing). With its crowds hurrying homewards through the dusk, its lighted shops and cafés, it seemed a world away from the plains where crumpled bodies lay in the brown fields and under the roadside trees.

The cafés were crowded with militiamen 'on excessive guard duty', as the papers termed it, talking, drinking, playing dominoes. The wide pavements of the Gran Via were thronged with strollers – men in uniforms ranging from the blue, crimson-lined cloaks of the regular cavalry to the rough overalls of the militia, and neat senoritas in black, with little red or yellow or green combs in their shining black hair. In the Puerta del Sol the old women still sold tickets for the state lotteries, though the crucifixes and rosaries they had hawked in former days were now replaced by cards of hammer-and-sickle badges or red-and-black anarchist caps.

A huge poster in Atocha Square warned: 'At Badajoz the Fascists shot 2,000 people; if they capture Madrid they will shoot half the city.' Yet the placards that turned the lamp posts in the Gran Via into a column of red were not about the defence of the city, but were advertising the Soviet film *The Sailors of Kronstadt*. On the radio and in cafés 'The Girl with the Dreamy Eyes' and 'You are my Lucky Star' competed with the *Internationale*.

The British journalists who reported what the world – and we – assumed to be the dying days of Republican Madrid were a small band, never numbering more than half a dozen. One of them, William Forrest of the *Daily Express*, was to be – though he was unaware of it at the time –a most valuable tutor to me in the art of popular journalism. Forrest was a small, open-faced Glaswegian, with a quiet, wry manner. He was widely believed in Fleet Street to be a member of the Communist Party. If this was so, he did not show it in the wording of his copy, which was punctiliously objective, though it may have been reflected in the stance from which he approached his stories. Forrest had a remarkable gift not only for descriptive writing, but for establishing a link with his readers. I learnt a great deal from him during the ten days when our paths overlapped in Madrid. Since there were only two telephone lines from the capital to the outside world, we read our stories over the line to our London offices from the censors' large open office, covering half of the ninth floor of the Telefonica skyscraper. Our voices carried inescapably to the other journalists in the room. So it was that, after reading my own piece, I would hear Forrest's treatment of the same events. His capacity to render major events into terms which would interest the most casual of readers came home to me forcibly the day Franco's forces arrived at the suburbs of Leganes. I reported that they had reached the tram terminal there, only seven miles from the city centre. Forrest began his despatch with the words: 'I took a two-penny tramride to the front this afternoon.'

Forrest had also an eye for significant detail, that essential element in painting a word picture. I had acquired some feel for this in the feature articles I had written for New Zealand papers during my years at Oxford. Now I trained myself not merely to rely on details which struck my mind, but deliberately to seek them out and note them down. I came to learn, too, the great value of simile and metaphor in illuminating a scene or an issue. Another aspect of descriptive writing I learnt later. This was the curious fact that I could convey a clearer and better-proportioned picture of a scene or an event twenty-four hours later, rather than when I had to write it up – as in daily journalism – immediately on the heels of the event. But if you waited longer than twenty-four hours the sharpness of what you had observed and what you had thought and felt at the time began to fade. Samuel Johnson, I was later to discover, had set all this out a hundred and sixty years before, when he advised Boswell to keep a diary. 'The great thing to be recorded,' he said, 'is the state of your mind; and you should write down everything that you remember, for you cannot judge at first what is good or bad; and write immediately, while the impression is fresh, for it will not be the same a week later.'

Another of the correspondents in Madrid offered a model of superb war reporting for a more learned public. *The Times* correspondent in Madrid was a quietly spoken Frenchman, de Caux, who had a loose grey moustache of the type favoured by Marshal Foch. He wrote beautiful English, as in this passage from an article on Madrid on 23 December, 1936:

> The Manzanares marks the line between anti-Fascism and Fascism – what a fateful burden for the sandy little stream which Philip II dreamt of connecting

by canal with the Tagus to carry galleons from the New World, but which has never carried anything larger than minnows.

And this brave comment on the atrocities which sullied the government's record during the defence of the city:

> It is pitiable that a strife, which in proportion to the tremendous issues at stake for society at large, is an epic on its own, should be marred by such shameless butchery. To the west and south of Madrid brave men fall fighting for a high and generous idea: to the north and east each morning lie the huddled corpses, women as well as men, old as well as young, victims of hate.

We had a good deal more freedom in covering Franco's drive on Madrid than war correspondents were to have in World War II. We were free to go where we would – or where we dared. There was no supervision by conducting officers – those combinations of guide and guardian which became, from an early stage in World War I, part of the apparatus for both helping journalists to learn what was happening, and controlling what they did with the information. In Madrid we had passes entitling us to visit the battle zones, and were provided with a car and a driver from the War Ministry. But where we went, and what we tried to see, was up to us. Official guidance was, too, in short supply. The government issued regular communiqués but news briefings, even of an elementary kind, were rare. There was, however, strict censorship of what we sent out. We had to submit our copy to official censors, and then telephone the censored message to our offices with a censor sitting beside us, his hand on a switch, ready to cut us off if we deviated by one word from the approved text.

As a latecomer to the scene, I did not form a working link with any of my English colleagues and rivals until the battle got right into the suburbs of Madrid. Instead, since the War Ministry required correspondents to share the few cars available, I found myself working with a Swedish correspondent, Barbro Alving, of the *Stockholm Dagens Nyheter*. A stocky woman in her mid-twenties, with an open, eager face, and hair cut short in what in those days was called an Eton crop, she had unhesitating courage. On one occasion we nearly met the same fate as had befallen Denis Weaver when we confidently approached a village into which trucks were moving from the south. We thought they were the trucks of the Republican rearguard, only to realise that they were full of turbaned troops – unmistakably Franco's dreaded Moors. We turned the car round on the outskirts of the village and made a very hasty retreat.

When the fighting had reached the outskirts of the city, Barbro Alving and I had with us the German photographer who had shared my experience on my first day in the field. I was keen to be photographed in a trench, alongside troops of the militia, in order to give the paper a picture they could use on their posters. The *News Chronicle* had made great play in this way of a photograph of their Paris correspondent, Jocelyn Hennessy, crouching behind a barricade of sandbags on the bridge of Irun, covering the fighting on the riverbank.

Just beyond the last line of houses on the road to Castlejon we came upon militiamen digging what seemed to be a line of reserve trenches. It looked a good place for me to be portrayed peering out from a trench, flanked by militiamen with rifles at the ready. Even if it was a reserve line, not the battle line, that seemed to me the type of 'fakery in allegiance to the truth' which the leading film series of the day, *The March of Time*, deemed justifiable. Barbro Alving explained to the officer what we wanted to do, and the cameraman got into position on the parapet. 'No time, no time,' reported the officer impatiently. Why not? 'Because this is the front line, not the reserve line,' he said. At that moment an incoming shell burst about a hundred yards to our right. 'Get out, get out!' the officer shouted. 'Your car is attracting their fire!' So I never did get my chance to appear on a *News Chronicle* poster.

These shared experiences were to profit me not only in Spain, but also three years later in Finland, where my path and that of Barbro Alving crossed once again. We renewed our collaboration there, scooping the rest of the press by several days with the first eyewitness accounts of the fighting in the snow in the forests of the Arctic Circle.

Reuters were represented in Madrid that autumn by Henry Buckley, a small, quietly spoken, highly able man who showed himself remarkably resistant to propaganda pressures from all sides. His brave reporting did much to make known the nightly political murders which had been the hideous accompaniment to the front-line fighting of these critical days.

Only when, in the first week of November, Franco's troops advanced into the outskirts of Madrid did the city's mood abruptly change. Barricades of paving stones and sandbags were hastily built between the Manzanares River and the southern and western districts. The mocking notice on a café table in the Puerto del Sol 'Reserved for General Mola' (he had boasted he would take coffee in Madrid by 12 October) was still there, but its irony looked very thin. The trade union lettering which had marked the sides of requisitioned cars began to be painted over. Even the weather changed, as if symbolically. Blue skies gave way to grey clouds and cold winds. By early evening on Friday 6 November the cafés were half empty. Few among the crowds hurrying into the underground station in the Puerta del Sol paused to listen to a Communist speaker haranguing them from the back of a propaganda draped lorry. Everyone wanted to get home to people they knew and could trust, to walls offering some slight protection against the danger which seemed to lurk everywhere in the growing darkness.

It was in this setting that I learnt the government had that afternoon fled to Valencia, leaving the defence of the city to a military junta under General José Miaja, a portly career officer who had stayed loyal to the Republic. Censorship forbade us to send out the story, but in the ill-lit lobby of the Gran Via Hotel with its bare dark walls, this sign that the end of Republican Madrid was near produced an almost palpable sense of strain. Journalists who were due to leave in a convoy for Valencia the next day paid their bills or conferred with the chief censor, who was going with them. He showed me the flat automatic pistol he carried in the pocket of his well-cut suit. There was a sudden flurry when one man came downstairs with his bags, flung them into the hall, and called frantically for the porter. He had passed through the lounge a few minutes earlier. By chance no journalist had been sitting there. He thought we had all gone and he had been left alone, with the Moors and the Foreign Legionnaires no doubt moving up the street.

William Forrest was amongst those who left for Valencia. He did so for an excellent motive. He had been persuaded to return to London to try to organise a group of MPs to come to Madrid in order to limit the slaughter which, it was assumed, would follow the fall of the city. Should I go too? That question posed itself sharply that Saturday morning, when a place became available in one of the cars leaving for Valencia. I had to make a decision then and there, on the pavement outside the hotel. I could validly argue that my work could now be better done from Valencia, that even if I witnessed the fall of the city Franco's censors would never allow me to send out the story, that I might find myself for several weeks in a Franco gaol. But I opted to stay. I did so less from a journalistic desire to cover the big story than from the feeling that history was about to be made, and I had the chance to witness it. It proved a wiser decision than I knew, for the city was not to fall, and I was to find myself one of only three British journalists who were on the spot to confront what was to be the biggest story in the world that weekend.

Henry Buckley and I had an indication early that Saturday afternoon that Madrid was going to prove a much tougher proposition than imagined. We had set out for the front line in Carabanchel, on the Toledo road along which the main Franco thrust was expected. We had to go on foot as cars were no longer available for correspondents. We were crossing the Toledo bridge from the city centre when we heard overhead the unmistakable whine and slither of shells. We lay down for cover against the stone sides of the bridge – they stank of every dog in the city – and waited for the shell bursts. These came, not in the government-held areas behind us, but way ahead in Carabanchel. Gradually it dawned on us that these were government guns, not those of Franco's forces. They were, we learnt later, Soviet-made field guns which had been deployed in the Retiro Park. A bit shamefacedly we picked ourselves up and went, encouraged, across the bridge to where half a dozen government tanks and a force of infantry were massed. A mile and a half further on we reached the front line – a barricade of sandbags, paving stones and wine barrels filled with sand, linking up with a row of houses from which militiamen were firing at Moorish troops in the nearby bullring. Beyond the houses shallow trenches had been dug in open ground. Bullets sang overhead, cutting the telephone wires, cracking against the brickwork. Along the line the firing was continuous, like the crackle of an enormous blaze of sticks. Many of the men manning this line were Communists. One, at an observation post on the roof of a small house, insisted on pouring out to me the Party line against non-intervention, only desisting reluctantly when he had to deal with four enemy tanks which suddenly appeared, moving across broken ground in the dusk.

Firing was still heavy in Carabanchel as we made our way back to central Madrid. Even more ominous were the sounds of gunfire from the Casa del Campo, further west, the great park which provided an open route to the edge of the city centre. It was clear that attacks were coming in there as well. That night there were no more than half a dozen diners at Marichu's, and Marichu herself was pale with anxiety. She could expect a rough time from the Francoists, for her Republican sympathies were well known. The streets outside, completely blacked out, rang with rifle shots, whether from nervous sentries or from fifth columnists we could not tell. We decided the safest place to walk was not on the pavement, but in the middle of the road. It seemed a very long way up the wide Paseo del Castellana to the British Embassy, where we had been offered beds for the night. I was thankful when the big iron gates of the embassy, guarded by a couple of old policemen armed with equally old rifles, closed behind us, and we could stretch out on mattresses in the ballroom, watched by portraits of King George V and Queen Mary.

CHAPTER THIRTY-ONE

The International Brigade

During the night of 7–8 November the Republican leaders in Madrid took a decision which was to save the city. They moved troops who had been placed to the city's south-east, ready to guard the vital road to Valencia, and – if possible – to counter-attack Franco's forces on the flank, across Madrid to the Casa del Campo and the area where the half-built buildings of the new university opened a way to the northern streets. This shift was undertaken because on the Saturday afternoon a map showing the plan of attack of Franco's commander on the Madrid front, General Varela, had been found on the body of a Fascist tank commander killed in the Casa del Campo. It showed that the main attack was due to come through the Casa del Campo and the university city. Colonel Vicente Rojo, General Miaja's Chief of Staff in Madrid, acted quickly on this information, in what was a classic example of the value in battle of the right intelligence rightly assessed. He gave orders for the XI Brigade of the recently reorganised Republican Army to be moved during the night by train from Vallecas, close to the Valencia road, to reinforce the Republican troops in the Casa del Campo.

The XI Brigade, a newly formed force, less than a month old, was to pass into history as the first of the legendary International Brigades. During October the Communist International – the Comintern – had organised two formations – the XI and XII International Brigades – composed of foreign volunteers. Ever since the start of the Civil War individual foreigners, like the New Zealand pilot Captain Eric Griffiths, had come to Spain, either to fight Fascism or to seek adventure. Only in the autumn, with the Republic's military position desperate, did Prime Minister Largo Caballero agree to the organisation of what was in effect a left-wing Foreign Legion to fight for the Republic. The International Brigades came into being at Albacete, midway between Valencia and Madrid. They formed part of the Republican Army, and included many non-Communists in their ranks, but were recruited, organised and staffed from the outset by the

Comintern, with the assistance of some Red Army officers seconded for the purpose. Altogether five International Brigades were to serve the Republic during the next two years. Of these the first two, the XI and XII International Brigades, were to have a special character, containing as they did a mixture of young idealistic anti-Fascists and of veteran European Communists who had known civil war – and in some cases brief periods of Communist rule – in the turbulent period after World War I, in countries like Poland, Hungary, Italy, Germany and Austria.

These veterans were very different from the wary, set-faced Party *apparatchiks* of post-war Communism, waiting in serried ranks in their epauletted uniforms or their square cut civilian suits to applaud on signal their equally robot-looking leaders on the Party platform. The men who were drawn to fight in Spain in 1936 had not grown up in the faith, but had come into it either because of intellectual conviction, or by hard experience. They were mostly strong, forthright individuals – which may have been one reason why Stalin was glad to see some 600 of them who had taken refuge in the Soviet Union, depart to join this highly dangerous venture. In the rough corduroy trousers and floppy berets of these first International Brigades were ranged men like Ludwig Renn, author of the pacifist novel *Krieg*; the French poet Louis Aragon; the dashing, gallant Hungarian writer Mata Zalka, who commanded the XII Brigade under the *nom de guerre* of General Lukacz; Ralph Fox, the Magdalen don from Oxford; and John Cornford, the Cambridge poet.

Almost every man in these first two brigades – and I was to come to know them well in the weeks ahead – had a tale to tell about why he was caught up in this anti-Fascist struggle in someone else's country. There was the French officer who had refused an order to fire on German workers during the occupation of the Ruhr – he had been cashiered and had turned Communist. There was a German Social Democrat who had been tortured in Dachau, had escaped to England, and had given up a job teaching in a Suffolk school to come to Spain; there was George Nathan, former Company Sergeant Major in the English Brigade of Guards, who as Captain Nathan in Spain was to show outstanding coolness in battle. There were hardline Stalinists as well – men like Gottwald, who was to lead Czechoslovakia in 1948 into its second – and more durable – bondage; and Ulbricht, who was to become boss of Communist East Germany after the war. But there was a cavalier touch about at least the first two International Brigades which was very different from the grim visage of later communism. This was reflected in the jaunty, amused manner of the first commander of the XI Brigade, who went under the name of Emilio Kleber. He was a

Hungarian Jew, whose true name was Lazar Stern, who had been taken prisoner by the Russians during the 1914–18 war, and had become a colonel in the Red Army. In the XI and XII Brigades on the edge of Madrid I was to encounter for the first time that confident, jesting camaraderie which is one of the signs of a good fighting unit – and one of the rewards for those who serve in it.

Early on Sunday 8 November the XI International Brigade marched through the centre of the city from the railway station towards the Casa del Campo. Their route took them along the Gran Via. Moving in a trained, disciplined formation armed with modern weapons, many of them with the bearing of experienced soldiers, they were very different from the straggling columns of the militia – so different that the Madrilenos, hearing orders shouted in foreign tongues, took them for Soviet troops, and shouted '*Viva los Russos!*' They marched towards the sound of gunfire, for Varela's artillery had opened up its barrage for what he hoped was the final assault on the city. Close up behind the Fascist line the British and American correspondents with Franco's forces waited, ready to file their first accounts of the fall of Madrid.

But as that long grey day unfolded, we in Madrid began to realise that perhaps this was not going to happen – or it was going to take much longer than the outside world assumed. That night I was able to report, in the story I telephoned as the gunfire rattled the windows of the Telefonica, that after a day of intense fighting 'The Loyal troops have kept the rebels at bay.' The *News Chronicle* printed this on its front page, and did so triumphantly not only because it wanted the Republic to win, but also because, within the intense rivalries of Fleet Street, it had its own man on the spot whilst the great *Daily Express*, that paper which above all loved a scoop, had to rely on agency copy. It was to be several days before the *Express* could get another correspondent out to Madrid to replace Forrest. On Monday morning, however, the *Chronicle* printed my name in bold black type above a Madrid dateline, giving full scope to what I had witnessed in Carabanchel – an air raid on the heart of the city, the fighting to the west, and the march through the Gran Via of what I called 'the International Column of Anti-Fascists' – the first reference in print to the International Brigade. My reports were to lead the paper throughout the week that followed, transforming me from an unknown reporter to the full – and then glamorous status – of a foreign correspondent.

CHAPTER THIRTY-TWO

Grandstand View of War

We had a grandstand view of much of the fighting of this first week of Franco's attack. The Telefonica was the tallest building in Madrid, and from its eleventh floor we could survey the outskirts of the city from the Hill of the Angels to the south in a great arc round to the north, where the masts of the Quatro Vientos wireless station were outlined against the distant, brown grey mass of the Guaderrama mountains. Through field-glasses we followed the dark zigzag lines of trenches dug across open fields, and across the parkland of the Casa del Campo, and we watched, as if from a spotter aeroplane, small dark figures which were men crouching there, as the earth spouted in black fountains under shellfire and bursts of shrapnel formed sudden, small white clouds above them. Trees in the parkland splintered under the shell fire, and the flashes of the rebel batteries would show up, like giant electric torches switched on and off, on the western outskirts.

From the Telefonica we watched, too, the war in the air. Franco's Savoia and Junker 52 bombers, gleaming silver shapes against the blue sky, with the small, dark figures of their Fiat fighter escort above them, would move in apparently leisurely procession above the barricades of Carabanchel and the trenches of the Casa del Campo. Flashes of flame and clouds of white smoke and dust would appear suddenly below them, and a moment later the thunder of the explosions would reach our ears. Then, unexpectedly, one afternoon the air behind the Telefonica was filled with sound. At rooftop level half-a-dozen snub-nosed Soviet fighter planes, the red stars clear on their fuselage, swept across, and the sky was filled with them – whirling, diving, roaring. Though we had no inkling of it at the time, that afternoon marked a turning point in the battle for Madrid, for in it Franco lost the control of the air. Though daylight raids continued, they were now likely to be hurried affairs, needing substantial fighter escort – and even that often proved inadequate, for these Soviet Polikarpov fighters – a copy of the American Curtis plane – proved themselves a match even for the new German

Messerschmitts deployed on Franco's side.

For a closer view of the fighting we went to the barricades in Carabanchel, where the front line had been stabilised close to where Buckley and I had visited it, or to other barricades guarding the south side of the salient which the rebel forces had thrust from the Casa del Campo into the university city area. In the university city I had my first experience of coming under aimed fire. Henry Buckley and I were chased along the high, brick front of the newly built School of Philosophy by a light field gun which fired half-a-dozen shots at us as we ran. One shell burst just ahead of me, throwing me to the ground. My legs for the moment were numb with shock, and I felt them anxiously for signs of blood. But there were none, and I completed the last fifty yards to the corner – and shelter – as if I were on a rugby field with the entire All Black pack after me. The commander of the Polish company in the philosophy building was not concerned at our experience. What worried him was that Franco's forces had apparently enough ammunition to expend several rounds in this way.

As the week wore on, and Varela's forces had still not got across the narrow but important barrier of the Manzanares River, our hopes grew that the capital might be held. The Republicans even launched a counter-attack against Franco's right flank, with Russian tanks and the XII International Brigade. But it was a failure. The War Ministry in Madrid claimed that Getafe airfield had been recaptured, but this proved untrue – one of the very few false claims made by the Madrid High Command at this stage. With this attack held, Franco's General Varela made one more major thrust to the north of the city. This time they got across the Manzanares River, seized many buildings in the university city, and even drove the Anarchists in disarray towards the Plaza de Espana, well within the built-up area of the city. But that attack, on Tuesday 17 November, marked the limits of Franco's advance towards the city centre. From then on his forces were to become bogged down in close-quarter fighting in the bare spaces and new high-rise blocks of the half-completed university, a long bitter struggle fought from room to room, floor to floor, building to building, in which the superior training and skill of Franco's troops was of little avail against the larger numbers, and the considerable guerrilla skills of the Republicans.

Whilst this fighting on the ground continued, the outside world waited to see if the German and Italian air forces on the Nationalist side would launch a mass attack against the civilian areas of Madrid. There had been localised, sporadic, and at times intense bombing of parts of the capital ever since the last week of October, but these had been aimed at specific targets like railway stations, road junctions and gun positions. No large-scale attack designed to break civilian morale had been launched, even though conventional military wisdom had long declared that this would be a major feature of any new war. What this might entail had been envisaged in the film of H.G. Wells' *Shape of Things to Come*, which had packed the cinemas in 1935. In one particularly realistic sequence, crowds in Piccadilly Circus had stampeded down into the Underground when London was attacked by bombers at night.

Franco resisted pressure from his German and Italian advisers for any such attack on Madrid, no doubt because he had no wish to wreak destruction on a city which he hoped would soon be his. But on Tuesday 17 November, he yielded. For much of that day and the previous one, the Telefonica and the Gran Via had been heavily shelled – a legitimate enough action, given that the Republican Army used the roof of the Telefonica as an observation post for directing their artillery fire. Early on the Tuesday evening rebel aircraft launched a series of raids with incendiary bombs on the city – perhaps to act as markers for later attacks. In one of these the Palace de Liria, the home of the Duke of Alba, Franco's representative in London, was set on fire. The Duke was later to write indignantly to *The Times* protesting that inadequate care had been taken by the government in rescuing his art treasures from this blaze, started by the bombers of his own side.

We were busy at our typewriters in the Telefonica, setting out the story of these raids, when the attack with high explosive bombs began. The building rocked like a ship struck by a heavy wave. Explosion followed explosion. Outside flares lit up the Gran Via, so that the buildings seemed to dance in a mad greenish haze. A girl, earphones still on her head, ran shrieking from the switchboard room and flung herself into the arms of her supervisor. *Roar, roar, roar*. Three more bombs had struck close by. Again the building lurched, as if uprooted. There was an acrid smell of smoke. All the way up the staircase came the sound of sobbing. One telephone girl near me was weeping unrestrainedly in the arms of another. Outside the windows flames flickered.

Half-way along the Gran Via a car blazed. Dark figures – the wounded – were being picked up from the pavement and carried off in cars. Men shovelled earth onto flames licking at a pile of broken beams. Up the Calle Montera people were streaming, their arms filled with blankets, books, a canary in a cage, buckets of precious coal – anything they had been able to snatch from their burning homes. Ghostly figures against the flames were trying to beat out fires with shovels, mats, some even with their hands. From the doorways where people crouched came the sound of sobbing. In the Puerta del Sol gaped two holes, twenty feet across, in which lay a tangled mass of paving stones, piping, twisted iron, broken balustrades from the underground entrance, plaster from ruined walls. Two trams, with windows smashed, lay on their sides.

By later standards this was a small raid. But its impact throughout the world was profound. Here at last was the reality of the spectre everyone had dreaded since the early thirties, when it had become accepted that the next war would be largely a war from and in the air. 'The bomber will always get through' was an unchallenged truth – so much so that London and Paris were, three years later, to go into World War II expecting to face devastation within hours of hostilities breaking out. The people who read our reports about the bombing of Madrid did so not only to learn what was happening in Spain, but what was likely to happen to them. The British Government were sufficiently concerned about the impact of our stories on public opinion that they made sure that the delegation of British MPs who visited the Spanish capital early in December included an ex-Air Force officer who could play matters down. This Wing Commander Archibald James (later Sir Archibald), Conservative MP for Wellingborough, proceeded to do with relish. On his return to England he said, 'The correspondents in Madrid are brave men. But they are young men – one of them is even a Colonial. They are too young to have been in the Great War, and do not know what a heavy bombardment is really like.'

I savoured being singled out as a Colonial. His attack showed that our reports had attracted public attention.

The Wing Commander was not comparing like with like. He was setting our reports of the bombing of a civilian population alongside the World War I front-line bombardments of military positions. Nor did we exaggerate. What we reported from Madrid on the first night attack on 17 November, we experienced, and we saw.

By that evening the *Daily Express* was once again represented in Madrid. Their star correspondent, Sefton Delmer, had come out to replace William Forrest. Tom Delmer, as he was known to his colleagues and friends, was then one of the half-dozen best-known figures in British journalism. A big, stout man in his early thirties, he was a blend of Friar Tuck and Prince Hal, with a commanding presence, a sharp eye for his own (and his paper's) advantage, and yet with a merry, boyish manner in which there was even a hint of diffidence under a tough outward assertiveness. The son of an Australian-born professor of English in Berlin, he had spent World War I as a schoolboy partly at a German gymnasium and partly at St Paul's in London, at both of which he had suffered because he did not fit the accepted norm. He spoke perfect German, a quality which had made him an outstanding correspondent in Berlin for the *Daily Express* – he had walked through the burning Reichstag with Hitler – and was to make him a formidable head of Black Propaganda in World War II. He ran, from London, a radio station broadcasting in perfect German, which purported to be a dissident station operating from within Germany. It gave news which the Nazis were hiding from their own people, and sardonic and subversive comments.

Delmer had courage in abundance, and he needed it to come to Madrid at this stage, for he was known to have been a friend of several top Nazis during the years of their struggle for power, when his reporting of Nazism had done much to present a sympathetic picture of Hitler to the British public. He had also reported the Spanish Civil War briefly from the Nationalist side. But Delmer met these suspicions head on, emphasising that he was above all a reporter, and he was to become one of the longest-serving correspondents on the government side during the remaining seventeen months of the war.

One factor which helped Delmer to win trust was his manifest interest in people as individuals. This was clear when, on the morning of his arrival in Madrid during the second week of Franco's attack, I took him to the headquarters of the Ministry of War to secure the necessary passes. What caught his attention in the gilt drawing room in the mansion of the armaments millionaire Juan March, which the Ministry had taken over, was less the political complexion of the junta (though he wrote about that in due course) than that the quiet, grey-haired woman who stamped his documents wore a leather bracelet containing live .22 ammunition. And though Comrade Maria, as we all knew her, protested that what mattered was the people's struggle, not her bracelet, her cheeks glowed pink with pleasure at Delmer's interest.

My relationship with Delmer was later to become strained because he liked to surround himself with acolytes, a role I was certainly not going to fill, but in these autumn days in Madrid we – or at least I – enjoyed an easy friendship.

The presence in Madrid of the six-man team of British MPs, including Wing Commander James, enabled us to meet for the first time the Soviet officer commanding the International Brigades. Until then he had been kept well out of sight of the press. General Emilio Kleber, as Lazar Stern was presented to the MPs, proved to be a solidly built man of middle height with thick greying hair *en brosse*, dark eyebrows, and keen, slightly ironical brown eyes. In the suburban villa which formed his headquarters he wore no badges of rank, but merely a grey lumber jacket, khaki riding breeches and blue puttees – those strips of cloth wound round the calves which were then part of military uniforms in most countries. Kleber admitted readily to having been in the Red Army, but covered his true Hungarian origins by claiming to have been a Canadian who had gone over to the Bolsheviks from one of the armies of intervention fighting in Russia. With him, as Chief Commissar of the Brigade, was an Italian with a shock of black hair who called himself Nicolleti, but who later emerged as Giuseppe di Vittorio, a colleague of Mussolini in the days when the Italian dictator had been a socialist. After World War II di Vittorio was to become head of the Italian Communist Trade Unions.

Kleber-Stern told the British delegation that Franco's first attack was now definitely halted, and that provided the Nationalists did not get further Italian and German reinforcements he could throw them back from Madrid by Christmas. The proviso was important, for Kleber must have known that an organised force of German ground troops and airmen, the Condor Legion under General von Sperle and Colonel Richtofen, was already in Seville, tipping the balance once again strongly in Franco's favour. To questions by the MPs, Kleber gave easy, bantering replies. Asked whether he thought the presence of the delegation had been the reason why Madrid had not been bombed or shelled in recent days, he replied, 'I had put it down to the fact that I have a Mexican artillery officer who can shoot straight.' And he seemed to savour the irony when the soldierly instincts of Colonel Crawford-Green, a true blue Conservative MP, proved too strong for his politics, and led him to point out eagerly to Kleber on his wall map just where he could usefully mount a counter-attack.

The first International Brigade to reach Madrid, the XI, which we had seen fight so stubbornly in the Casa del Campo, had been composed principally of Germans, Poles, Hungarians and Italians. The second Brigade, the XII, which had by now arrived, included a unit of twelve Britons in its ranks, as members of the Thaelmann Battalion, commanded by the pacifist writer and World War I veteran, Ludwig Renn. Among the Britons was Esmond Romilly, Winston Churchill's eighteen-year-old nephew, who was a few months later to marry Jessica Mitford and, during World War II, to die as an RAF pilot. Handsome, upright, with fair hair and open features, he fitted, in this very different context, Frances Cornford's line about Rupert Brooke: 'a young Apollo on the edge of strife'.

Esmond Romilly and his older brother Giles had had a widely publicised reputation as rebels ever since they had been expelled from Wellington for publishing a pamphlet attacking public schools. Indeed my first impression of Esmond Romilly – his open face, with its wide set eyes, grey with fatigue and unshaven, his khaki jacket crumpled and stained as he stood in the street of the small village of Fuencarral where his unit of the XII International

Brigade had been in action – was of an exhausted schoolboy. I saw him again a few days later, when he had an afternoon's leave from the front, in a basement bar in the Gran Via. He and a couple of other British volunteers were being bought beer by a visiting British Communist dignitary, Ivor Montagu, who was in Spain making a propaganda film. Montagu, the heir to Lord Swaythling, was to remain a staunch Party member despite all the twists and turns of Communist policy in the years ahead. Romilly, clean shaven and rested now, his khaki jacket and grey flannel trousers well brushed, was in this setting very much the self-possessed and reticent Englishman, spurning irritatedly my queries about his motives for fighting in Spain. 'Isn't it enough that I am here?' he retorted. He listened in cold sardonic silence as Montagu, a fleshy, sleek figure in his mid-thirties, looking – despite his studiously simple clothes – every inch a very rich man, set out in a Mayfair accent the importance of the International Brigade in the anti-Fascist struggle. Romilly was indeed much more forthcoming in talking to Delmer.

As I was watching Esmond Romilly and his two colleagues clamber aboard the truck which was to take them back to the front, and saw Montagu make his way into the lounge of the Gran Via Hotel, Delmer said to me with sudden intensity, 'I hate men like that, ready to send decent British boys into a battle he takes damn good care to keep well away from himself.' And indeed within a month of that meeting ten of the twelve Britons in the Thaelmann battalion were dead in fighting around the hamlet of Boadilla. Only Romilly and Bert Ovenden, a Communist from Stockport, survived.

Esmond Romilly left Spain soon after the battle of Boadilla, but meanwhile his brother Giles had joined in his stead. I came to know Giles well in 1940 when we were both correspondents in Finland. Shorter, and lacking the striking good looks of Esmond, Giles had at least three of the qualities of his famous uncle – a puckish humour, a skilled use of English, and instinctive bravery. By the time he joined the International Brigades, they were a much bigger force – less Communist in composition, but more harshly Communist in ideology – as their commissars carried out in Spain the same Stalinist purges as were being so terribly undertaken in Russia. Giles Romilly served throughout the hard fighting of the Brunete offensive of July 1937, and was wounded. But this did not prevent him being arrested as a suspect British spy and suspect anarchist (he was certainly not the former, and only in the vaguest way the latter). He was held in prison in Alicante until, after questions had been asked in Parliament, he was released and put across the border into France. The Romilly brothers' exploits had brought so many references to them as the nephews of Mr Winston Churchill that

Churchill himself had once protested to the House of Commons, 'I hope that I have some other claim on the attention of this House than as the uncle of the Messrs Romilly.'

By the second week of December the fighting in and around Madrid had reached a stalemate. It was clear that Franco's first attempt to capture the city by a swift, direct thrust to its heart had failed. Several reasons for that failure were apparent. The courage and tenacity of the Spanish Republican army and militia had proved doubly effective when the battle moved to the narrow streets and barricades of the city, where the superior organisation and training of Franco's forces mattered much less than had been the case in the open field. Soviet weapons and Soviet technicians had arrived just in time, providing tanks and aircraft superior in quality to those on Franco's side. The International Brigades had provided a shock force not only because of the many seasoned soldiers in their ranks, but because they were made up of volunteers prepared to die for their beliefs, as very many of them did. In military parlance, they were a force prepared to accept an exceptionally high level of casualties.

So, in that cold grey autumn on the high Castilian plain, the seemingly impossible happened. Madrid did not fall. Instead for the first time Fascism was halted. Men and women had shown that it could be stopped, and in doing so gave heart to those outside Spain who felt that it must be stopped.

In Britain, news of a very different kind was now making headlines. King Edward VIII's desire to marry the divorced Mrs Simpson was now swamping the newspapers and the radio bulletins. The *News Chronicle* decided it was time for me to come back to London for a spell of leave. I paid my bills for the accommodation the British Embassy had extended to correspondents since the siege began – a mattress in the corner of the embassy ballroom and coffee and brown bread for breakfast – and got a ride in a volunteer Scottish ambulance to Alicante.

I had known in these weeks in Madrid, if not the comradeship of battle, the comradeship of shared danger. And I had tasted something more. I had sensed and felt at first hand the hopes of those millions of Spaniards who had been presented, suddenly and unexpectedly through the failure of the generals' uprising in the big cities, with a chance to take their destiny into their own hands, to build a fuller and richer life. Though the fears and strain of war obscured the future in Madrid, hope was still strong. It was to be seen in the new schools, opened in requisitioned villas of the rich; in the People's Restaurants, the most celebrated of which was in the Ritz; in the hospital and orphans' home in the Palace Hotel; in the peasants, on those brown wide plains around the city, owning for the first time the land on which they and their ancestors had laboured for generations.

The cost of all this to those who had stood in its path was also plain: in the shells of burnt-out churches; in the white faces and haunted eyes of prisoners, each with a blanket slung over his shoulder, waiting in the courtyard of the Model Prison, whilst the guns of their would-be rescuers thundered nearby. Soon they would board the double-decker buses which were to take them not to other prisons, but to their death. It was a cost that both sides were still paying in the battlelines around Madrid every hour of the day. But the gains were there, clear to see, above all in the bearing and pride of the militiamen and women, crouching at the barricades or moving in single file by the roadside towards yet another battle.

The long months of war ahead; the curbing – in the name of the survival of the Republic – of many of the liberties for which the people were fighting; and above all the sense that the rest of Europe would not let the Republic win: all were to blunt and sadden this spirit of hope. But in Madrid in those autumn and winter months of 1936 it was still unmistakable and, even across the years, unforgettable.

In the ambulance by which I travelled from Madrid was a wounded English volunteer who had been shot in the hand during the fighting in the Casa del Campo. His wound had turned gangrenous and arrangements had been made for him to get specialist treatment at the British hospital in Paris. I undertook to escort him there. In the Air France plane the odour from his bandaged arm was nauseating; in the two-berth sleeper I secured for us on the train from Toulouse it was almost intolerable. I was thankful when, after a bitter argument with the hospital authorities about who would pay the bills, I saw him at last into a ward, and could escape into the streets of Paris. The leaves had gone from the trees in the Champs Elysées, the cars were sleek in the streets, the dark furs of the women gleamed in the cafés. The papers carried the farewell message which the former King, Edward VIII now the Duke of Windsor, had the night before broadcast from Windsor Castle. I barely glanced at it. It seemed monumentally irrelevant to that struggle where I felt our future was at that very moment being shaped, in the cold drab trench lines and shattered buildings where the Castilian plain stretched away under leaden winter skies towards the Guardarramas, their ridges already whitened by the first snows.

PART IV

Onto the International Stage

CHAPTER THIRTY-THREE

Crossing The Street

I had expected to be back in Spain within a few weeks, but that was not to be. More senior journalists, like Philip Jordan and Denis Weaver, who had been expelled from Franco's Spain forty-eight hours after his capture, now took over the story. Even more significantly, William Forrest had left the *Daily Express* and joined the *News Chronicle*. It might well be six months before I got another chance to report the Civil War. I found myself back on day-to-day reporting duties, with intermittent spells of chasing fire engines and ambulances on night shift.

I offset my frustration by writing a short book about the blunting of Franco's first onslaught on Madrid, utilising my own experiences as part – but only part – of the evidence of the events which had unfolded on those autumn days and nights on the Castilian plain. It was an attempt at a contemporary history, and had the disadvantages but also the considerable advantages of such a method. The story was inevitably incomplete. But it was at first hand, and if I could not establish all the facts, I could ensure that the atmosphere and the detail I had observed were faithfully recorded.

I took the manuscript to the one publisher who I thought would bring it out quickly – for there was always the chance that the city would fall, and my account seem superfluous, within a matter of weeks. Within twenty-four hours of my delivering the manuscript to Victor Gollancz he called me to his office in the stylish but surprisingly cramped premises of his publishing firm in Henrietta Street. He would publish the book, but he asked for three changes. One concerned the British volunteers in the International Brigade. I had described how I had expected them to be like the stunted, gaunt men, with faces pale and graven by malnutrition and fatigue, who had formed the main element in the Hunger March of 1932. Instead I had found that many of them might have stepped – as some had – out of the ranks of a public school OTC. He thought this offensive to the British workers. I did not, but since no question of historical fact was involved, I removed the passage. His second point was more delicate. In my opening chapter I had, in describing La Pasionaria rallying the militia outside Getafe, said the scene must have resembled those when Trotsky rallied the Red Army outside Leningrad. The reference to Trotsky, Gollancz said, was perhaps unfortunate. Would he prefer me to change it to Stalin, I asked? My irony was wasted on him. Yes, that would indeed be preferable. So I deleted it altogether.

His third request was more fundamental. The book contained a chapter on atrocities, stating that many had been committed on the Republican side as well as by Franco's forces. Gollancz wanted this chapter out altogether. Any admission of Republican atrocities in a book published by such a prominent supporter of Spain as Victor Gollancz would be greeted by Franco's supporters in Britain as clear proof that such happenings were true. This was for me a sticking point. The darker side of the revolution was undoubtedly true, and unless I stated it, I threw doubt on the validity of everything else I had recorded. We parted company, and I walked round to the office of Dick Campbell, to tell him my first attempt at authorship had foundered. But a day later Gollancz agreed to accept the book with this chapter still in. Two months later, in a vivid yellow and black dust jacket which was Gollancz's hallmark, *Defence of Madrid*, 221 pages, price 2s 6d, was in the shops and on the bookstalls. It sold well. It was widely and for the most part favourably reviewed. *Harpers* magazine in the United States ran an extensive segment of it as an article. *Time* magazine devoted a column to excerpts from it, and to somewhat patronising praise of it, as their main foreign story of the week. A Danish publishing house brought out a Danish version. And I experienced the joy of opening for the first time a book one had written, to see one's words hammered out so laboriously on a typewriter in the early morning hours – for I had retained from my student days a pleasure in getting in a couple of hours work before breakfast – set out now in confident black print upon white paper.

My book gave the Soviet Union full credit for the key role it played in the defence of Madrid. I had not changed my view that communism, whatever economic advantages it might bring, demanded too high a price in individual freedom. But that was not the issue at that time. What mattered most then was that Hitler should be stopped before he was so powerful that he could either crush liberty in Britain, or embark on war. In the autumn of 1936 the Soviet Union was a major element on the side of the anti-Nazi and anti-Fascist forces in the West. I recorded its role in Spain, just as, three years later, I was to record its brutal and unprovoked attack on Finland in my book *The Red Army Moves** – and to gain, as a consequence, the obloquy of British Communists.

---

* Gollancz, 1941

My experience in Madrid had also set me – though I did not know it at the time – firmly on the road to a lifelong career in journalism. It had given me, as someone who loved history, the unexpected and deep satisfaction of witnessing history in the making. The night the bombs fell around the Telefonica, I had known not only the excitement of covering a big story. I had been there as a page of history was turned. I relished the opportunity, and the privilege, of being able to record this great event

In early April 1937 Franco launched a major offensive against the Basque provinces of northern Spain. This second front offered a chance for me to get back to Spain, and I asked Gerald Barry to send me to Bilbao. But he assigned Philip Jordan to the task. However, before Jordan could get to the Basque front there occurred, on 26 April, the event which was to imprint the name of Guernica into the consciousness of the world. Heinkel and Junker bombers destroyed the centre of this small but historic Basque town in a series of bombing raids spread over three hours. *The Times*, the *Daily Telegraph*, Reuters and the *Daily Express* all carried stories the next day from their own correspondents on the spot, some of whom had picked up bomb fragments that proved the attack had indeed come from the air (so giving the lie to Franco's claim that the Basques had blown it up themselves). The *News Chronicle*, however, had to rely – and that a day late – on the evidence of the daughter of the captain of a British merchant ship which had been in Bilbao at the time. She was, as events have later shown, a careful and reliable witness, but she was not a trained journalist, and her name – Fifi Roberts – sounded more like that of a can-can dancer than a war correspondent. Against the reports in the other papers, the *News Chronicle*'s contribution on this historic event looked meagre and lacking in authority. I studied the papers that day in a small café behind Waterloo Station, where I had been sent to track down yet one more suicide in yet one more street of long, drab terraced houses, where a boy – shown at the inquest to be mentally deficient – had put his head in a gas oven. I decided then and there to wait no longer in the *News Chronicle*'s queue of foreign correspondents, but to take the first good opening abroad which was offered on another paper.

A very good opening soon came my way. One of my fellow reporters, Richard Greenhough, arrived back in the *Chronicle*'s reporters' room one afternoon from a late lunch, in an aroma of cigar smoke and claret. He announced with relish, 'I've just been lunching with Charlie Sutton, the *Express* foreign editor. Denis Clarke is giving up their Vienna job, and Charlie has assured me that the job is as good as in my pocket.'

Presented with this information, I did not delay. I wrote that evening to

Arthur Christiansen, and applied for the post. Letters were delivered swiftly in those times, and the next day I was summoned to Christiansen's office, behind the gleaming, black-glass façade of the *Daily Express* building on the other side of Fleet Street. I found myself facing someone who, at first glance, might have been cast as Mr Pickwick when young: a sturdy, erect figure with black curly hair beginning to thin, and a round boyish face – for Arthur Christiansen was then still only thirty-two. But there was nothing Pickwickian about the sharp, searching eyes behind the horn-rimmed spectacles. His manner was both friendly and combative, the bearing of a clever boy who had learnt not only to protect himself but assert himself in bare asphalted playgrounds and drab state schoolrooms. He eyed me hard and questioned me hard. Then he offered me the job at a salary nearly double that which I was receiving from the *News Chronicle*, on condition that I said 'Yes' or 'No' on the spot.

I accepted. Yet even as I walked from the building, through the lofty hallway where a bronze bust of Lord Beaverbrook looked sceptically at his employees scurrying up and down the stairway, qualms assailed me. Was I going to find myself dealing with trivia, rather than with news that mattered? Above all, was I hiring out my pen to write news, not as I saw it, but as the paper's powerful proprietor saw it? I had been aware of these dangers before I had applied for the Vienna post, but only now did they seem real. They were indeed to prove real. But I managed to keep them at bay, and to work to my own standards, until the war came two years later, changing all our lives and cutting even newspaper proprietors down to size.

Arthur Christiansen was then well on his way to becoming a legendary figure. There had been no journalism in his background. He came from a shipbuilding family of Danish stock, and had been born at Wallasey on Merseyside. He began as a reporter on the local paper at the age of sixteen, and by the time he was twenty-two had become news editor of the *Sunday Express* in London. Two years later, as assistant editor, he attracted fame – and the attention of his proprietor, Lord Beaverbrook – by bringing out a special edition of the *Sunday Express* which, alone amongst the Sundays, gave news of the crash of the R101 airship near Beauvais. A brief spell as northern editor of the *Daily Express* was followed by a year as assistant editor of the paper in London.

Christiansen judged – rightly – that he would be a much better editor than Beverley Baxter, a Canadian and a friend of Beaverbrook, who then held the post. Christiansen set about demonstrating this in a series of memos to Baxter about how the paper could have better handled the news – and sending copies of these to Beaverbrook. Within a few months Beaverbrook had taken the point, and made Christiansen editor of the *Daily Express* at the age of twenty-nine.

Christiansen wisely insisted that I should do a stint on the sub-editors' desk in London before I left for Vienna, so that I could learn the methods and the style of the *Express*. The paper was then reaching the peak of its reputation, claiming as it did on its front page next day the world's largest net sale; it was a mass circulation newspaper which was also read, albeit disdainfully, by people of power. So I spent a month as an assistant sub-editor, helping Charles Foley, the chief foreign sub-editor. The foreign subs desk was set at right angles to the celebrated back bench, where the shaping of the paper was determined each night, giving me a chance to see Arthur Christiansen in action, exercising his now legendary skills of editorship.

Christiansen would usually arrive in the newsroom about ten in the evening, just when the first edition was due up from the presses, which could be heard thundering distantly in the basement like the engines of a great liner. By then the big open-plan newsroom was at its busiest, thronged with shirt-sleeved sub-editors working at serried desks under brilliant strip lighting, whilst in the background dark-suited reporters hurried in with late copy, telephone lights flashed above booths to indicate a foreign correspondent was on the line, office boys hurried – and at times ran – with galley proofs or pages of agency tape.

Chris, as everyone on the paper referred to him, and as he was addressed by all the senior editorial staff, would often be wearing a dinner jacket, having come from the first night of a film, or from a dinner at the Savoy Grill or the Café Royal. He would hang his jacket over the back of the chair kept vacant for him at the back desk, roll up his sleeves, scrutinise – and often redesign – the layout of the front and the centre pages. By expanding the size of a picture here, modifying a headline there, seeing virtue in a story buried away at the foot of a page and promoting it to vary the appearance and the content of an otherwise heavy slab of copy, he could turn a good front page – for his night editor and chief sub were themselves masters of layout – into an excellent one calculated to arrest attention on the news stands, and convey excitement, interest and glamour.

Under Arthur Christiansen the *Daily Express* had style. At a time when high fashion demanded of women a bandbox smartness with every hair in place, every accessory neat and gleaming, when the leaders of fashion were, in J.B. Priestley's words 'so chic that it hurts', the *Express* outshone its competitors. Alongside it the *News Chronicle* seemed demure, the *Daily Herald* clumsy, the *Daily Mail* dark and harsh, the *Daily Telegraph* portentous. Only *The Times*, its typeface chosen by the gifted Stanley

Morison, could make a parallel claim to style. But the impact of its clear layout and typography was offset by having its front page filled, not with news, but with classified advertisements.

Christiansen's fame as a great sub-editor is firmly part of Fleet Street's story. But it was only part of his editorship. He also had an eye for good writing and nurtured new writing talent. Alan Moorehead and James Cameron were two of his friends. J.P.W. Mallalieu and Alan Wood were others. In the mid-thirties the *Express* interwove a strong element of sophistication with its quest for hard news and sensation. Osbert Lancaster's pocket cartoons not only served a valuable technical task of enlivening the appearance of the front page. They ensured that even the testiest of senior civil servants or the most reactionary of club men would at least glance at the paper. 'William Hickey's Diary', contributed by Tom Driberg, was far from being the society's gossip column of today's populars. Though it appeared under the title 'These Names Make News' (lifted by Beaverbrook from a comparable feature in *Time* magazine), and though it contained items of social and political gossip, it was for the most part an account of events witnessed or experienced by Driberg, under the name of William Hickey, comprising meticulous observation and shrewd reflection presented in clear, scholarly (and at times pedantic) prose.

John Rayner, the very able features editor, looked like an important figure in the Foreign Office – which he was later to become. Lucy Milner, who was to marry Alan Moorehead, presided over a woman's page free of the patronising sentimentality which marked much writing for women at the time. It had, in Robb, a fashion artist of real quality.

Christiansen was an editor who led from the front – who believed that a newspaper editor must constantly make clear his values and his standards to his staff. 'I praise when I can and I kick when I have to,' he once said – as good a summary of the art of editing as I know. Much of this praise, and some of the kicks, were delivered in the bulletins which he issued about the paper, and which were pinned on office noticeboards. These seldom amounted to more than a score or so of typed lines, and would single out a story in which the paper had done well, or one in which it had faltered, analysing a particular bit of writing or the quality of a picture. It was a technique of editorial leadership not easy to use. I tried it in my early days as editor of Independent Television News, but quickly gave it up, as I found that with a small staff criticism delivered publicly in this way could be so painful as to defeat its object, which was not to reprove a reporter or sub-editor, but to use their mistakes as a text upon which to preach improvement. In broadcasting I found it best to praise publicly and blame privately. But I valued those of Christiansen's bulletins which assessed my work, and kept them in my files.

His other key instrument for injecting his vitality into the paper was the daily news conference. This was 'conducted with high spirited, shirt sleeved exuberance which not only expressed his own jovial, generous nature but also set the tone for the next day's paper. Dullness was banished, optimism shone through'.*

Christiansen was not a political animal – his personal politics were mildly Tory – and he was content to steer the paper along bearings laid down by Lord Beaverbrook. 'The policies were Lord Beaverbrook's job, the presentation mine' Christiansen readily admitted.† The policy line of the day – or the hour – reached Christiansen either by telephone (Beaverbrook very rarely came into the *Express* office) or in memoranda dictated onto round dictaphone cylinders, like those of the earliest gramophones.

The main interpreter of this policy, in that summer of 1937, was Frank Owen. As Liberal MP for Hereford, Owen had been, at twenty-four years of age, the youngest member in the 1929–31 Parliament. When he lost his seat in the National Party landslide of 1931, he joined Beaverbrook, readily paying the price which Beaverbrook demanded – that of becoming a member of his personal entourage as well as of expressing his policies in the leader columns and feature articles. Frank Owen had given my book on Madrid a warm review in the *Express*, but treated me coolly when he found me at work a couple of desks away from his post at Christiansen's elbow. One evening, waiting for copy to sub, I began to read that week's *New Statesman*, which was lying on Owen's desk. When he came in he took it abruptly from me. 'I'll deal with anything that arises from the weeklies,' he said curtly. I realised later that he foresaw something I never then dreamt of – that I might attract Beaverbrook's attention and become a potential recruit to his inner circle.

---

* Sir Edward Pickering in the *Dictionary of National Biography*, (Oxford University Press)
† *Headlines All My Life*, Arthur Christiansen (Heinemann, 1961), p. 44

CHAPTER THIRTY-FOUR

Posting to Vienna

I went to Vienna in mid-June 1937 by a roundabout route. Charles Sutton had a hunch that the Nazis were about to mount a *putsch* in Danzig, then an International Free State on the northern edge of the Polish corridor, which separated East Prussia from the rest of Germany. Any such move seemed to me highly improbable – and it proved to be the case – but at least I gained a glimpse of this old Hanseatic port with its high-gabled, red brick houses, whose fate was to be one element in precipitating, two years later, the outbreak of war. It offered a rich mix of nationalities. I found myself dining with Monseigneur O'Rourke (a Pole), the Roman Catholic bishop of the area; an English timber merchant with a White Russian refugee wife who dressed in pre-1914 style with wasp waist and puffed sleeves, and who hated Hitler and the Jews with equal fervour; and her daughter of the second of her three marriages, who was Canadian by birth (and accent) and the local Reuters correspondent. We played bridge, and I lost one guilder – about ten pence.

Back in Berlin a tougher assignment awaited me. Mrs Bruno Hauptmann, the wife of the German-born carpenter who had been executed in New Jersey after being found guilty – on very tenuous evidence – of the kidnapping and murder of the Lindbergh baby, had come back to Germany with her own small son. The *Express* stringer in Bremen had missed her when the ship she was travelling on had docked there, and there was no trace of her whereabouts. It was now Thursday and Sutton desperately wanted her tracked down and interviewed before the Sunday papers got to her.

Selkirk Panton, the *Express* man in Berlin, told me the lead could come from Hauptmann's mother, a very old woman living in Zittau, a village in Silesia on the Czech border, three hours away from Berlin by train. Before I set off, Panton consulted me on another problem. A young Englishman was going the rounds of the foreign correspondents in Berlin claiming to be a former volunteer pilot with the Spanish Republican Air Force, and asking for donations to a fund to help Spanish orphans. Was he to be trusted?

The man who entered the room a few minutes later I had last seen in the Gran Via in Madrid in December. He received great publicity in the summer of 1936 as one of the first Britons to volunteer for the Republic. The *Daily Mirror* had devoted the whole of its front page to the story of an Oxford undergraduate who had put the training he had received from the University Air Squadron at the service of the Republic. Here, it seemed, was one Englishman prepared to back the Republic with deeds, not just sympathy. When I first encountered him in Madrid he more than looked the part in a black leather jacket with two sets of airman's wings on the breast, another set on each shoulder, and a further set for good measure on the thigh of his trousers. Strapped round his waist was a huge revolver in a holster, and a sheath knife. The foreign press in Spain had long since nicknamed him Wings. When I asked which was his Oxford College, he replied, 'Oriel.' That surprised me, as the Air Squadron men at Oriel had been a small and noticeable band. Which quad did he have rooms in? 'Oh, I did not live in Oxford. I came over by bus from St Albans every day.'

Wings may have detected my scepticism at this manifest absurdity, for he hurried on to tell me of the leg wound he had sustained during one of his first sorties with the Republican Air Force. We never could find out, however, which unit he had been attached to, or any action in which he had fought. Certainly by then most of his service seemed to be in or around the Gran Via Hotel, or in the Miami Bar. He had produced near panic in the dining room of the Gran Via when, on the day after the first heavy night air raid on the city, he had produced two unexploded incendiary bombs. Holding one up at the full extent of his arm, he had demonstrated how it worked by allowing it to drop towards the floor, catching it just a moment before it would have landed and set the whole room ablaze. It took much patient persuasion to get him to hand the bombs over to the waiter, who put them in the ice box for the duration of the meal. When his constant companion, a little Spanish bar-girl called Conchita was arrested, Wings had arrived in a state of great agitation in the Telefonica press room and had suddenly collapsed, writhing, on the floor, moaning about 'pools of blood, pools of blood'.

Wings was now wearing a neat grey suit, but still had his aggressively distant air. He was clearly not pleased to see me, for he left quickly, after only the most cursory appeal to Panton for money. It was a strange, surrealist incident to occur in the heart of Nazi Germany, with swastika flags hanging from the buildings outside the office window, and somewhere in the distance the sound of a military band. Was there a sinister interpretation of the way in which this ex-volunteer for Republican Spain could move so freely about the Reich? Not necessarily. There were many gaps in the Gestapo's net, and no visa was needed for Britons to visit Germany. I never discovered the answer, for I had to begin my search for Frau Hauptmann, and our paths never crossed again.

In Zittau a hotel porter led me to the home of Hauptmann's mother, a shrivelled, white-haired figure sitting inert in an armchair. Her brief periods of lucidity alternated with the long silences of the very old. Patiently the porter, who knew her well, asked her for her daughter-in-law's address. Nearly half an hour passed before she muttered the word 'Stuttgart'. After another agonising hour of long silences and occasional mumbling she suddenly produced the name of a street in Stuttgart. I wrote it down hastily, left a bundle of Lord Beaverbrook's marks on the table, gave another bundle to the porter, and sprinted for the night train to Berlin. Stuttgart was right on the other side of Germany. But the Reich had a good internal air service, and late the next afternoon a small Lufthansa Junker plane, buffeted twice by huge thunderstorms, got me there a couple of hours before the deadline for Saturday's paper. I took the first taxi – a gleaming, black, very conspicuous Mercedes Benz. The street on my precious scrap of paper proved to be in an area of new, two-storeyed red brick council houses. The driver asked a youth in brown Storm Trooper uniform if he knew where Mrs Hauptmann was staying. When the SA man learnt I was a British journalist he grew nasty. 'We want none of your dirty Jewish press tricks here,' he said. 'Isn't it enough that you and your kind have sent a good German to his death for a crime he didn't commit?'

He shouted to another Storm Trooper clipping grass in front of a nearby house. Within minutes a squad of them had gathered, one with a rubber truncheon and another with a thick stick. But the taxi driver, perhaps fearing for his car and mindful of his as yet unpaid fare, took my side. 'At least let Frau Hauptmann decide whether she wants to see him,' he suggested. So I was escorted up the street to a semi-detached house. The group, now swollen by half the children on the block, waited at the gate as I made my way up the short concrete path. A middle-aged woman, her face hostile, answered my ring on the bell. In the hallway behind her I glimpsed a red-headed woman in a black skirt and black jersey which looked American in style. I addressed this second figure in English, 'Mrs Hauptmann?' 'Yes?' 'I am from the London press,' I said. 'May I speak to you for a moment? I'm sorry to disturb you in this way.' 'That's all right,' she replied, in nasal Bronx tones. 'Don't you worry. That's your woik. We've all got our woik to do. You come right in.'

My sigh of relief could have been heard on the far side of the Rhine. The gang at the gateway dispersed sadly, robbed of their chance to strike a blow for the Fatherland. Half an hour later I emerged with Mrs Hauptmann's tale of her journey on the boat, shunned by American passengers, cosseted by the Germans, but with her three-year-old son treated with absolute fairness, she stressed, in the liner's crèche. It was, by any standards, a moving human story, and I phoned it from an hotel in Stuttgart in time for it to make the deadline and give the *Express* an exclusive. It had cost the *Express* a packet in fares, car hire and payments, but that did not concern me. What mattered was that I had got the story on this, my first real assignment for these tough new masters in the black-glass building on Fleet Street.

CHAPTER THIRTY-FIVE

Vienna Revisited

I inherited from my predecessor in Vienna, Denis Clarke, a flat on a small leafy square, the Modenaplatz, just round the corner from the British and German embassies. It was close to the Landstrasse Hauptstrasse, the historic road leading from Vienna towards Bratislava and Budapest – the highway at which Metternich had declared 'the Balkans begin'. The flat was on the fourth floor of a modern building, and its spare bedroom, just by the front door, had been converted into an office. Here we settled in, I to learn on the job how to be a foreign correspondent, and Cecily to await the birth of our first child, due in September.

With the flat I inherited an assistant, a refugee from the Reich called Roland Bochow. He had been on the staff of von Papen, Vice-Chancellor in Hitler's Government until, with the death of Hindenburg, Hitler had in August 1934 made himself the absolute ruler of Germany. Bochow had been an important contact when Tom Delmer was *Express* correspondent in Berlin. He spoke almost flawless English, liked to wear a bowler hat (then considered a very English thing to do) and was delighted when, on a holiday in Britain, people on buses and trains had taken him for English. He had been born in India of German parents, who had been interned – and, he claimed, badly treated – in the Far East during World War I. Bochow had worked for some years as a planter in Malaya, until driven back to Berlin by the slump. He was a big man, similar in bulk and bearing to Delmer.

Only his quick wits had saved him from being shot by the SS on 30 June 1934, when Hitler had widened his purge of Ernst Roehm and the brownshirt Storm Trooper leaders to include the former Chancellor, General von Schleicher, and those on von Papen's staff whom the Nazis mistrusted. Bochow and his colleague von Bose were on this list. Von Bose was shot in his office by the SS, and Bochow, who worked in an adjoining office, escaped only by taking down his hat from the hat stand and sitting, hat on knee, in the waiting room as if he were a visitor. This deceived the head of the SS execution squad when he appeared, smoking revolver in hand, as von Bose's dead body was being rolled up in his office carpet.

Bochow was allowed to leave the office, and got his family away safely to Switzerland. He then crossed into Czechoslovakia through woods which he knew from an earlier vacation.

On Delmer's recommendation Bochow had been taken on as assistant in the *Express* office in Vienna. He had found himself a flat next door, where he lived with his wife Hansi and his two sons, aged six and nine. He was just round the corner from his old boss, von Papen, whom Hitler had rusticated to the post of German Ambassador to Austria. Bochow re-established his links with von Papen, but discreetly, as both men assumed they were under the surveillance of Gestapo agents. Bochow was also in close touch with another member of von Papen's entourage, the Baron von Keppler, who had been on the SS's death list in 1934, but had got away to Switzerland, and now held a post in the Vienna Embassy under his old chief. A third trusted figure in this group was Keppler's secretary, a small, dark-haired girl in her twenties, whose first name was Rosa and who had a flat opposite ours in the Modenaplatz.

I found myself in a sadder, drabber Vienna than the city I had known four years earlier. Then both the Socialists and the old Imperial Nationalists had retained their pride, and some faith in the future. Now the Socialist Party had been driven underground, and even the coats of new paint on the walls of Sandleiten and the Karl Marx Hof could not hide the scars of the artillery bombardment of 1934. The Fatherland Front had put its own Storm Troopers into a black uniform on Nazi lines, and its red, white and black flags hung everywhere. But the menace of Anschluss, of an enforced union with Germany, hung like a thundercloud over the city. Only Mussolini, by moving troops up to the Brenner Pass, had prevented this happening when Dollfuss was assassinated in 1935. But now he and Hitler were moving closer. In every aspect of Austrian life the Nazis – though illegal – muttered and glowered and bided their time.

Hitler had already struck one harsh blow, which exacerbated Austria's greatest problem – unemployment. He had banned German tourists from Austria, crippling its tourist industry. Signs of unemployment were everywhere, even though I now looked at the city from the other side of the tracks, with an expense allowance that enabled me to travel by taxi rather than tram, and to eat at Sachers or the Drei Hussaren rather than amidst the austerity of WOK. Thin, grey-faced people in threadbare clothes eyed you in every street. It was impossible to sit on a bench in the Stadtpark or the gardens of the Belvedere without being constantly approached by beggars. Our flat doorbell would ring three or four times a day and you would find a child outside, hand outstretched, whilst lurking halfway down the stairway would be an adult, waiting to gather in his takings. If you gave nothing you were liable to find your doormat drenched in urine, or worse.

One hot summer evening we dined in a restaurant on the Ringstrasse which set its tables out on the pavement, walled in by large wooden boxes and tubs of flowers. Out of the corner of her eye Cecily saw a child's thin, brown arm move between the flower boxes and then, with the swiftness of a snake striking, seize the bread roll from the plate. Out on the pavement there was a scuffle, and a small boy darted round the corner with his booty.

There were pleasant tennis courts in a park near us, but playing there was always spoilt for me because you were expected to engage, as a ballboy, a grown man, his figure blackened by constant exposure to the sun, who ran round scooping up the balls with a sort of wire ladle. For carrying out this undignified task, he got the equivalent of sixpence an hour.

Those in work saw it as a duty to sustain, by one means or another, as many relatives or friends as they could. We acquired a maid, Rosa, a resolute, robust girl from the Burgenland whose red hair hinted at Hungarian blood. She slept in a maid's room on the top floor of the building – each flat was allocated one. Despite strict regulations to the contrary, her boyfriend slept there too. He was in the Fatherland Front's employ, and wore always his black Storm Trooper uniform because it was the only decent set of clothes he had. Rosa carefully preserved the tea leaves from our teapot, dried them in the oven, and shared them out with her family and friends. Nothing left over from any of our meals ever found its way into the ice box. Sisters or brothers or friends were always at hand, slipping into the kitchen to finish anything spare. I once emerged from the bathroom to find a complete stranger, a worried looking middle-aged woman with greying hair, polishing the outside handle on the bathroom door. Rosa, challenged to account for this stranger's presence, explained that it was 'die honnete Frau von der Molkerei', who kept the small dairy on the corner, and who urgently needed to earn a few extra shillings. I opened the door to the kitchen one day to find half-a-dozen people round the table enjoying my – or Lord Beaverbrook's – hospitality. However strenuously Cecily, who had quickly acquired a grasp of fluent household German, stressed to Rosa the need for economy, and however strenuously Rosa – concern for her job and concern for her relatives competing in her expression – would promise that no one except herself would ever cross the kitchen threshold again, we knew that within a few days everything would be as before.

Offsetting this was the happy-go-lucky friendliness of the working-class Viennese, very like the Cockney cheerfulness of the time. When, on 19

September, Cecily had our first child, Peter, not only Rosa but the whole neighbourhood treated him like a prince. Only the porter of our block of flats reacted differently. He was, we later discovered, an ardent Nazi. When he saw Jews among our guests at Peter's christening party on a very cold night in December, he switched off the central heating to our flat – a move we countered by moving to a night-club, something which in those days of a strong pound and generous newspaper expenses we could afford.

CHAPTER THIRTY-SIX

Foreign Correspondent

In Vienna I found myself admitted to another charmed journalistic circle, the tight-knit fellowship of the foreign correspondents. The thirties were the heyday of the foreign correspondent, certainly of those of the British and American press. Not only were British newspapermen abroad free of competition from radio and television, but they were the main source of foreign news for newspapers, and these mattered in a country which mattered – indeed mattered greatly. Britain was then still very much Great Britain, a worldwide authority and power, able not merely to influence but to determine issues of peace and war. It is a role which, since 1945, we have held only in localised conflicts like Suez and the Falklands. But in the thirties, particularly on the key issue of whether to stand up to Hitler or to appease him, Britain's position was decisive. It was an issue resolved by two governments, those of Britain and France. But France was much of the time politically in such a continuing state of muddle that the ministers in its frequently changing Cabinets were prepared to leave the initiative to the British, particularly once Neville Chamberlain, with his singleminded, firm (if disastrous) policy, came to power.

This made the work of a foreign correspondent not only exciting, but significant. We felt that what we wrote was important, that it could not only interest people, but influence them – and through them influence events.

Foreign correspondents were fewer on the ground then, not part of the great phalanx of reporters and cameramen, producers and recordists, engineers and back-up staff who descend upon the scene of any big news story today. This gave us our own esprit de corps. No one had put this better than Douglas Reed, who was *The Times* correspondent in Vienna in 1937.

> The House of Commons is called the best club in London. The confraternity of journalism is the best club in the world. It is the most comradely of crafts. You have friends wherever you go. There are no barriers of race or creed. You fly on some mission and when you land you find men you know. You speak several languages, and the hopes and fears of Croats and Ruthenians

and Walloons and Basques become as familiar to you as those of your own countrymen.

You speak with kings and dictators and statesmen in the full pride of power, and you see them sitting miserably in exile in a dingy coffee house in Prague. You see a man, the almost forgotten ex-ruler of a Balkan country, dining quietly in a London hotel, and then you see him as King George of Greece in his palace in Athens. You see vast crowds thronging to acclaim King Edward VIII of England as he drives to the Abbey, you eat your schnitzel in a half empty Vienna restaurant while the Duke of Windsor eats his at a neighbouring table.*

The significance of our role was enhanced by the fact that the leading figures on the world stage were more remote, more mysterious then. Television did not bring their faces, night after night, into the sitting rooms of the land. People gained their impression of those who shaped, or sought to shape, events from still pictures – or from a glimpse in a newsreel – images too scanty to convey knowledge of what the man or woman in the news was really like. For that they depended to a considerable degree upon the correspondents in the field. The same was true of foreign places. Travel was, in the thirties, still to a considerable degree the privilege of relatively few people. Mass tourism was two decades away. Indeed in France even mass vacationing (set in train by the paid holidays the Popular Front secured in 1936) did not come about until a year or two before the war when, for the first time, the Riviera beaches were packed with summer holiday makers. It was part of the foreign correspondent's task, therefore, to portray the scene in which events took place, as well as to record and recount those events; this added an agreeable element of the travelogue to the routine work of giving the news.

The British and American correspondents in Vienna in 1937 were, by modern standards, an odd lot. There were few university graduates amongst us – except for the Americans – and certainly no one who had been near a school of journalism. Two of the most important of my colleagues had made their way into journalism after being uprooted from their backgrounds by the Great War. Douglas Reed of *The Times* had been a bank clerk from Brondesbury in 1914, and had ended the war as an officer in the Royal Flying Corps. Eric Gedye of the *Daily Telegraph*, small, fierce and indomitable, had in 1914 gone from being a student at London University to a subaltern in the trenches in France within a matter of weeks.

Reed had gained his first footing on *The Times* as a copytaker, taking

---

* *Insanity Fair*, Douglas Reed (Random House, 1938), p. 209

down over the telephone the copy of foreign correspondents – a route also followed by William Haley. Gedye had begun writing articles when serving on the Inter-Allied Commission in the Rhineland after the war. Both, by that summer of 1937, were deeply concerned at the way in which, in their view, Britain was betraying those who had fought in World War I by now appeasing Hitler.

Marcel Fodor, the *Manchester Guardian* correspondent, was by contrast Viennese to his fingertips. A small, benevolent, balding man, he came of a family of Jewish industrialists. He had been sent to Sheffield as a young man to learn steel manufacture. He recalled how, so intense was the heat and so constant the perspiration induced in the steel mill, that he and his fellow trainees used to consume a bottle of whisky a day, mixed in small quantities to give some taste to the huge volume of water they had to drink to keep going.

Fodor held court in a small café, the Café Louvre, in the northern part of the inner city, at a Stammtisch where Austrian writers, civil servants and a constantly changing series of minor informants would gather. It was here that I had my only meeting with Negley Farson, one of the most celebrated of roving American correspondents of the time, whose book *Way of Transgressor* was then a best-seller. In it he had described the wartime injuries which had partially lamed him. With this in mind Denis Clarke had commented, 'I had half expected to see you carried in here.' 'Don't worry,' was Farson's reply, as he called for a bottle of whisky. 'If you wait around long enough you'll probably see me carried out.' He shared one passion with Gedye. Both were fanatical fly fishermen, a sport which could then be practised on some excellent trout streams in Lower Austria. In *Going Fishing*, perhaps the best book ever written describing trout and salmon fishing, Farson has left a work which is likely to long outlive his more political writings.

Fodor was extremely knowledgeable about the complex national and racial elements which made the politics of all Balkan states at the time a seemingly inextricable tangle. Through him I became friendly with the quiet, charming Jew who headed the Austrian Foreign Office, Dr Kleinwachter. He used to talk to me not only in the same room as Metternich had occupied on the Ballhausplatz, but from behind Metternich's own elegant writing table.

The *News Chronicle* correspondent was the small, shy but determined John Seagrue, who came originally from Liverpool. As one of the first British correspondents in post-war Russia, he had covered Lenin's funeral. He was to show great bravery when the Nazis seized Austria in 1938 in reporting their atrocities against the Jews. On one occasion an SS officer, mistaking him for a Jew, thrust a rag into his hand and set him to work helping a large group of Jewish men and women, many of them old, who were being forced to wash the cars of the SS – and being kicked and beaten in the process. Seagrue did the work, then produced his British passport and said, 'I could not believe the stories about your brutality were true. I wanted to see for myself. I have seen. Good day,' and stalked away. But in 1941 he was captured in Belgrade when the Nazis attacked Yugoslavia and died eighteen months later in a Nazi internment camp.

The pressures of the next few years affected us all in different ways. An occasional visitor to the journalists' table at the Café Louvre was a big, quiet American called Richard Best, who worked for the American news agency the United Press. He had been a doughboy in the Great War (at what point, I wonder, did American slang substitute the term GI for doughboy?), and had stayed on in Europe afterwards. Reserved yet friendly, accompanied sometimes by an equally reserved, fair-haired Austrian countess who was his mistress, he seemed the prototype of the expatriate yet patriotic American. Yet when America was drawn into war with Germany after Pearl Harbor, Best opted to remain in Vienna, and became a broadcaster of Nazi propaganda. Occasionally, in the later stages of the war in Italy in 1945, I used to catch, through the crackle of static, his appeals to the American troops in Italy to give up the struggle.

Schuschnigg's Fatherland Front dictatorship was a ramshackle affair, more akin to the inefficient authoritarianism of the old Habsburg Empire than the new, all-pervasive totalitarianism then evolving in Soviet Russia and Nazi Germany. Illegal newspapers and broadsheets from the banned Socialist and Communist parties, and the banned Austrian Nazis, circulated with surprising freedom. The left-wing newspapers were mostly printed just over the Czechoslovak border, in Brunn. They were often miniature copies of banned papers like the *Arbeiter Zeitung*, excellently printed on the very thin paper then used for airmail editions of papers like the London *Times*. Small and lightweight, they could be smuggled across the border by car or lorry in substantial quantities. They reached me regularly, thrust through my letterbox by unseen couriers. The banned Nazi *Osterreichischer Beobachter* was a cruder job, cyclostyled in typescript, each page ending in a slogan attacking either Schuschnigg or the parties to the Left.

This Nazi material, like other information about the banned Nazis, reached me through a Czech-born informant called Novak. I had inherited him, as I had Bochow, from my predecessor. Novak would call two or three times a week. A small, furtive middle-aged man, his fingers stained a deep yellow from the cigarettes he smoked incessantly, he brought items of gossip about demonstrations which were likely to occur, about changes in the government hierarchy, or of arrests. His material was seldom useful, and I proposed to have done with his services, even though they cost us only a few schillings a week. But Bochow persuaded me to let him stay. 'He's almost certainly a police spy,' was Bochow's case. 'If we get rid of him they will simply assign some other to the task of watching you – and the next man might be more efficient and more troublesome.'

Some of the socialist propaganda was subtle and skilful. One effective item posed as a booklet in English for tourists called *Beautiful Austria*. Purporting to describe a tour of the main public buildings of Vienna, it gave in, terms of heavy irony, an account of the dictatorship which now dominated all parts of Austrian life, detailing examples of the police brutality in the prisons and the police headquarters on the Scottenring.

Also in Vienna was George Lansbury, who had been ousted from the leadership of the British Labour Party because his pacifist views were too extreme – and too impractical – for Ernest Bevin and the main union leaders. He arrived in early December as part of a tour of European capitals, in which he was urging pacifism on the Continent's leaders. A member of the Viennese socialist underground asked me to help smuggle into Lansbury's press conference a representative of their party, who wanted to enlist Lansbury's aid in getting help for imprisoned Socialists who were seriously ill. I did so by the simple process of shepherding the young man into the press conference as if he were my assistant, handing him my briefcase and papers as I showed my press pass. The officials allowed him in without query. When the conference ended he was able to speak briefly to Lansbury, and give him a letter with details about the Socialist prisoners. He got away before the plain-clothes police present realised what was happening. The letter was all the more effective for being clumsily translated, appealing for a Christmas amnesty so that 'these poors may once again see their families'. Lansbury took up some of the cases with Schuschnigg the next day, and at least two prisoners, one a woman suffering from tuberculosis and another in danger of going blind, were released.

I never heard any more about the matter but Novak warned me that the police suspected that I had a part in it. I realised that however worthy my aims, I had not only acted rashly, perhaps putting my rights to work in Austria at risk, but wrongly. Such actions, however right in themselves, are not open to journalists. We are given access to people and places of importance in order to write about them, and if we utilise that access for other purposes we put at risk the freedom of action essential if we are to carry out our central task of informing the public. To be an observer or an onlooker, rather than a participant in events, can seem a secondary or even ignoble role, until you realise the great power – and great responsibility – which rests with those whose task is to try to tell things as they are. Your report of an event can rival the importance of the event itself – and that was never more important than when the dictators of the thirties were moving forward behind a smokescreen of lies and deceptions.

CHAPTER THIRTY-SEVEN

Balkan Newsbeat

In hard news terms, the Balkans in the latter part of 1937 were relatively quiet. There were few action stories of the kind the *Daily Express* relished. We had, it was true, one spectacular riot in the streets of Belgrade, when a tall, black-bearded Orthodox priest led a procession of protest against a treaty with Mussolini which gave Catholics in Yugoslavia more freedom. He held aloft a heavy gilt crucifix as he marched towards a police cordon. A police officer stepped forward and told the priest to stop. When he refused to do so, the police officer wrestled the crucifix from his grasp, and then struck him heavily on the head with it, knocking him to the pavement. It took troops an hour to check the fighting which followed.

But human interest stories too kept us busy. The recently married Duke and Duchess of Windsor came through Vienna on their way to their first home in exile, a villa in Carinthia. No member of the Austrian aristocracy offered them hospitality overnight. Instead they stayed, like any other well-heeled traveller of those days, in the Hotel Bristol in the Ringstrasse. The next morning they left through a bowing concourse of managers, porters, bellboys and excited American tourists, looking much smaller than their photographs made them appear. The Duchess, her eyes moving swiftly in an otherwise set, meticulously made-up face, had an aura of almost metallic elegance, every black hair in place, her suit free of the least wrinkle, her shoes gleaming. They settled into a large, nondescript house above Lake Carinthia, where they were – at their request – left untroubled by the press to a degree that certainly would not prevail today. No paparazzi lurked in the woods nearby to photograph them. Only an occasional visitor came from London, and to get a game of tennis the Duke used to invite up the baker from the nearby village. The *Daily Express* carried only a very occasional story about their activities, whilst the other London dailies left them entirely alone.

That same September a twenty-four-year-old German princess came suddenly into the news. Princess Frederika of Brunswick became engaged to Prince Paul, brother of the recently restored King George of Greece and heir to the Greek throne. I interviewed her in a hunting lodge owned by her family in the Salzkammergut, set amid broad, carefully tended plantations of oaks and beech and pine. It was a cool September morning, with the grass and leaves gleaming from an overnight shower. Huntsmen in lederhosen, with wide-lapelled green jackets, black retrievers at heel, gathered in the forecourt. The Princess, eager-faced with thick, waved bronze hair, spoke in excellent English of her delight in her engagement. She showed no trace of anxiety about the fact that she was linking her fate to one of the most unstable regimes in Europe, a fate which was very soon to bring her to exile, and then to civil war and long years of political turmoil. I put her confidence down to lack of awareness of the world outside this rich and privileged enclave. But events were to show that if this was true, it was only partly so. For as Queen Frederike of the Hellenes, she displayed in abundance one quality essential for a monarch – bravery. 'The first duty of a king is to show courage,' Winston Churchill told King Carol of Rumania, when that monarch sought advice soon after the war as whether to stay and resist the Communists on the spot, or go abroad and set up a government in exile.

One reminder of the dangers lurking around the apparently tranquil Vienna had come to me a few days earlier. I had been visited by a young Cambridge graduate, whom I shall call Rex Andrews. He had what seemed to me the most glamorous of jobs, that of being a talent spotter in the Balkans for Alexander Korda, then at the peak of his film-making fame. Andrews and I had mutual friends in England, and had played tennis a few times together, but I was astonished when he announced that he was a member of the British Secret Service, and that he needed my help. There was always a chance, he explained, that his cover might be blown, and that the Austrian police, heavily penetrated by the Nazis, might run him in on some pretext, and then allow the Gestapo to grill him clandestinely. He needed someone to whom he could turn in such an emergency. He could not demand to see his boss, who was a consular official, without his cover being blown. Could he, if arrested, give my name as a friend whom he wished to contact, so that I could set in train a demand for his release, and also tip off his superior officer?

I agreed readily. It seemed to me right to do so, both as a human being and as a Briton. I was interested, and indeed excited, to find myself in contact with someone from the then mythically efficient British Secret Service. I also admired the nerve of this slim, sandy-haired youngster plying this dangerous trade on the edge of Nazi Germany. But I made plain my contact must be on a personal basis. I wanted no link, formal or informal, with the secret service. Common sense told me that if there were two masters whom no man could serve at the same time, they were journalism – the essence of which was open inquiry – and intelligence gathering, the essence of which was covert inquiry.

In October, with little news coming to the fore in Austria, I persuaded the *Express* to let me do a stint in Rome, where the paper maintained no regular correspondent. It brought me a further clash with a British diplomat, this time the press attaché at the embassy. From the American military attaché I learnt that the Italian forces in Spain, which Mussolini insisted were all volunteers, now numbered 46,000 – a figure far higher than previously admitted. This would, I knew, be unpalatable news to the British Government, who were busy playing down the Fascist and Nazi intervention in Spain. Before sending the story, I thought I should check with the British Embassy to see if they had any such information. Not only was none available, but I met an angry tirade from the press attaché for sending out unfounded rumours which could only harm relations between Italy and Britain.

I sent off the story – just in time. A couple of days later the Italian press was full of stories proclaiming that there were now some 46,000 Italians serving in Spain, and listing the Italian Army divisions in which many of them were grouped. The Fascist Government, it was clear, had decided that the British and French were unlikely to give any real help to Madrid, and that they could therefore safely boast of their support for Franco. When I triumphantly showed the Italian newspapers to the British press attaché, he saw no inconsistency in his earlier stance. 'If the Italian Government wishes to make such matters public, that changes the situation,' was his comment.

My visit to Rome brought me my one glimpse of Mussolini. A small, white-uniformed figure, he strutted out amidst an escort of Blackshirt guards from a ministry building at the lower end of the Via Veneto. A handful of onlookers cheered, but most of the other people nearby, hurrying home during the rush hour, barely glanced at him. Mussolini, like Hitler, was lying low, digesting the empire he had seized in Abyssinia, and coping with the high cost of a Spanish Civil War which dragged on and on.

My dealings with the British Embassy had not been helped by the fact that I had developed an infection in the middle ear passage of my right ear. It became increasingly painful. Antibiotics were then unknown, and as it got steadily worse I had no choice but to face a mastoid operation. I went into the American hospital on the Via Nomentana, where the doctor decided that my condition was so serious that my wife should be sent for at once. She came down by the Italian airline from Vienna – a nightmare flight in fog over the Alps. Fortune favoured me. The night before I was due to undergo what was in those days a dangerous operation, I woke to find my pillow soaked with pus. The abscess in my ear had burst, fortunately breaking open the ear drum, and clearing away the infection. I felt immediately much better. No operation was needed. 'You were lucky,' the Scottish nurse confided to me. 'The last time I worked with the Italian surgeon who was to do the job he smoked right through the operation, and got furious when I complained at his resting his cigarette on the edge of the operating table.'

The infection gone, I made a quick recovery and a fortnight later I was back in Vienna. In December, with Austrian news still scarce, I persuaded Christiansen to let me tour the Sudetenland, the border area of Czechoslovakia where the population was largely of German stock. It seemed highly likely that if Hitler succeeded in gobbling up Austria, the Sudeten Germans would be the next group he would try to incorporate into the Reich. The *Express* did not favour situationers – reporters of situations which might develop into news. It liked hard news – what was happening rather than what might happen. And though Beaverbrook had not yet embarked on his campaign to assure the British public that there would be 'no war this year or next year either', he did not like gloomy articles forecasting trouble. But Christiansen yielded to my urging that I should get to know this potential trouble spot.

Konrad Henlein, the leader of the Nazi-style Sudeten German Party, was, on Hitler's orders, lying low. Hitler needed to have Austria firmly in his grasp before he stirred up rebellion in the Sudetenland. But the ground was being prepared. In Reichenberg, the biggest industrial city in the region, I attended a meeting of Henlein's party. A big hall was hung with red, black and white banners looking just like Nazi flags, except that the swastika was replaced by the initials of the party – SDA. A short, bald man, looking every inch a Nazi despite his grey civilian suit, was speaking to an audience sipping beer at trestle tables. A police officer sat by the platform making notes. When the speaker criticised President Benes, the officer was on his feet at once, insisting that the meeting be closed, as it was illegal to attack or speak against the president. The SDP press officer, a tall man with duelling scars, could hardly disguise his pleasure that this should have happened when a foreign journalist was present – the first, I discovered, to have visited Reichenberg for many months.

I sat until late in the night with the leaders of the local SDP, pressing them as to whether they really wanted only home rule, and not union with Germany. But they were well drilled, insisting that all they wanted was the right to rule themselves within the Czechoslovakian state.

But the choice was not theirs to make. For not only were they of German stock, natural recruits for Hitler's Greater Germany, but the mountains they occupied were of great strategic importance. 'He who is master of Bohemia is master of Europe,' Bismarck had said. On the hillside near Reichenberg I found a reminder of this. A stone cross bore on its plinth the words: 'Here Austrian troops engaged the Unlans of Prussia in 1866.' These were the fields of Sadowa, where Bismarck's troops, equipped with the new breech loading Mauser rifles, had defeated the Austrian Army, whose Habsburg commander still placed his faith in the old smooth bore-muzzle loaders. Despite the victory, the time was not then ripe for Bismarck to attach these Bohemian mountains to the German Empire. His successor as Reich Chancellor was, within ten months of the time I stood by these snow-covered fields of Sadowa, to complete that task.

It was indeed easy to have a sense of foreboding amongst these pine-clad hills under the grey, brooding skies. Prague in the winter was, by contrast, a city of compact beauty, with the snow gleaming white on the high roofs of the Hradčany Castle and on the statues of Christ along the Charles Bridge, which spanned the swift, dark Moldau River. Budapest, that other great city of my varied bailiwick, was equally grand in winter, with the wide Danube sweeping eastwards under the fine bridges which linked the old city of Buda and the new city of Pest. But it was at its best in the summer, bathed not only in sunshine but in the serene light of the great Hungarian plain. A fast modern train ran from Vienna to the Hungarian capital, and it was possible to travel down in three hours on a Friday evening, spend the weekend by a swimming pool or on a cafė terrace on the Margaretan Island, or – once the weather closed in – walking by the riverside where the royal palace, topped by its strange, crooked cross, was outlined in gilt against the wide arching Danubian sky. We became knowledgeable about the spiced Hungarian dishes, and the subtly different types of Tokay, and in the art of sitting without embarrassment at a restaurant table as the violinist played a Ziguener serenade for you and your partner for what could seem, under the scrutiny of your fellow diners, a very long five minutes.

In Vienna itself there were the Sunday morning concerts of the Singerknaben, and open-air skating on the tennis courts near the Stadtpark, flooded now to make a rink where you could take an hour's exercise before going off to lunch at a Ringstrasse café, its tables enclosed by wooden and glass partitions against the cold. The ghosts of bygone Hussar officers still hovered over the tables at the Hotel Sacher, where the dark chocolate sachertorte was still served amid all the old baroque glitter. Less romantically, three of today's cavalry officers, now demobilised, ran the Zu Den Drei Hussaren restaurant further up the Karntnerstrasse. Lesser scions of the deposed Habsburgs could be glimpsed in the nearby Eden Bar, where a pianist alternated Strauss waltzes with George Gershwin themes at cocktail time. In the Burg Theatre Claire Booth's *The Women* was staged in German with a dazzling cast, and an even more dazzling audience of modish Viennese, many of them Jews who seemed superbly – indeed perhaps blindly – indifferent to the dangers awaiting them. In the Spanische Reitschule the Lippizaner horses – their white hides gleaming, their tails plaited with gold ribbons – reared and pirouetted as, guided by the riders in brown tailcoats and cocked hats, they paced through the gavotte and the slow waltz. I became friendly with an attaché at the Yugoslav Embassy, a tall, dark Serbian who took us to dine on kebabs and stuffed paprikas on the steamer which plied between Belgrade and Vienna, and whose cook was so celebrated that people queued to eat in its stateroom when the vessel docked in Vienna. We drank toasts in slivovitz to the Triple Entente and to France and to Britain, and the Serbian paid outrageous court to every woman at the table, under the amused scrutiny of his beautiful Montenegrin wife. '*Faute de mieux, on se couche avec sa femme*' he said to me once, but in tones which made it clear that such better alternatives seldom, if ever, presented themselves.

One of the Habsburgs in the Eden Bar, the Archduke Leopold, a cousin of Prince Otto, who was the claimant to the Austrian throne, provided me with a story which delighted Arthur Christiansen. Though his title was formidable – he was His Imperial Highness Archduke Leopold Salvator of Habsburg Toscana, Knight of the Order of the Golden Fleece of the Holy Roman Empire – he was in fact a small, balding middle-aged man with a dark moustache, whose most recent job had been bicycling films – carrying the print of a feature film from one Vienna cinema to another by motor cycle. In November 1937 he sued his mother for an increase in the allowance she made him of seven Austrian schillings a day – worth about five shillings in British money. His cramped flat in an outbuilding of Schonbrunn Palace had only an oil-stove and a pantry shelf as its kitchen. He showed it to me with indignation: 'You see what my mother brings me to. It is because she is a Bourbon, and has all the Bourbon iron will. She will not give me more, even though she has huge estates in Austria, a vineyard in Italy, jewels of great value.'

It was indeed a full life, yet it was vitiated by the knowledge that we led it amongst people whose own lives were darkened and numbed by fear – fear of unemployment; fear of a Nazi takeover; fear, ultimately, of war. Though a British passport seemed a sure enough protection against any upheaval (short of war itself) we could not escape from – nor did we seek to escape from – the constant uncertainty, the sense of living on the slopes of a rumbling volcano, which characterised Vienna in the autumn and winter of 1937. During our first few months there I had a strong sense that I ought to be back in Spain, where Madrid continued to resist all onslaughts – as it was to do until defeat for the Republic on other fronts forced its surrender in March 1939. I felt strongly that our future was being fought for on the bare dusty battlefields of Brunete or in the mountains around Santander, rather than in this cushy billet on the Danube. But as the autumn went by and I came to sense that struggles even more significant for our future might soon be staged in Austria and Czechoslovakia, this feeling gradually weakened – though it never quite left me.

Shortly before Christmas 1937 Arthur Christiansen told me he wanted me to take over the post of *Daily Express* correspondent in Paris. It was promotion – rapid promotion, for Paris at that time ranked with New York as the paper's most important overseas post – but I was dismayed. It meant giving up a field in which the main flow of news was political. As Sefton Delmer had put it when, five years earlier, he had been moved from Berlin to Paris: 'I was required to report the parties of Woolworth heiress Barbara Hutton, chase eloped British couples, follow up the Paris end of British crime stories, and keep a watch on tourists and trippers.' It also meant leaving Central Europe just when, I sensed, truly historic events were about to occur there. It meant, too, breaking up one home and establishing another with a three-month-old baby. But I knew that I had no real choice, so on New Year's Eve we completed our packing, handed over the office to my successor, Bill Morrell, and set off for Paris from Vienna's West Bahnhof. Rosa and her young man had seemed genuinely sad to see us go, and even the gnädige Frau von der Molkerei and others from the neighbourhood had appeared that morning to see our bags safely downstairs and into the taxi. As the train drew out through the now leafless valleys of the Vienna Woods I felt moved by this display of affection. 'They may be an inefficient people, but they are a lovable one,' I said to Cecily. Her comment was less favourable. She had just opened her suitcase to find that most of her underwear and her stockings and her nightdress had disappeared. Some of the willing helpers of the last few days had clearly had other motives than those of simple friendliness.

CHAPTER THIRTY-EIGHT

Paris

The *Daily Express* office in Paris was an altogether grander affair than that in Vienna. It was housed in two large rooms in the modern seven-storeyed building of the leading French popular paper of the day, the *Paris Soir*, in the Rue due Louvre. Its setting was a mixed *quartier* of tall, grey-stuccoed, wooden-shuttered buildings where finance, newspapers, small workshops and good restaurants jostled one another. The Paris Bourse, a grey-columned building like a discoloured Greek temple, was close by, and during dealing hours the clamour of its dealers bargaining on the wide steps of the building brought echoes of penned animals in distant stockyards. The Bank of France, the National Library, and the colonnades and garden of the Palais Royale were at our back. So too were several of the most celebrated *maisons closes* of Paris – one, the House of Nations, offering its delights in bedrooms each decorated in the style of a different country.

Paris Soir was an evening paper, owned by a millionaire textile magnate turned newspaper proprietor, M. Jean Prouvost, and edited by Pierre Lazareff, a small, eager Jew, with thick, pebble-lensed spectacles, whose family stemmed from Poland. Lazareff was a genius in news presentation – quite the equal, in French terms, of Arthur Christiansen. He used his front page largely as a billboard for the contents of the inside pages, with huge headlines dramatising the main story, and a lavish use of pictures. His wife, dark and good looking, was an equally successful editor in her own right and under her own name of Hélène Gordon. She had built up the women's weekly *Marie Claire* into part of the fabric of French life. Under them the *Paris Soir* building, jutting like the rounded prow of an ocean liner onto the small Place D'Aboukir, pulsated with life, as motor cyclists dashed up with the latest copy or cans of film, as elegantly dressed reporters, overcoats slung like cloaks over their shoulders, moved gravely towards the lift. I relished the vitality of it all, enjoyed being greeted as '*Cher colleague*' by Pierre Lazareff as, in his high-pitched, confident voice, he would call me into his office, ostensibly to tell me some item of political gossip, but really to share with me his pleasure in the pattern of a page or the use of a photograph.

I inherited a substantial staff of three assistant correspondents and a secretary: a White Russian, Princess Mara Scherbatoff. Tall, dark, calm with a rounded, Slavonic face, she glided rather than walked, moving with an erect, easy dignity no doubt acquired by generations of her forebears on the parquet floors of lofty palace rooms in St Petersburg and Moscow. She moved '*comme la Reine Elizabeth*' the commissionaire in the hallway of the *Paris Soir* building would comment admiringly, going on to explain that the Queen he had in mind was not the recently crowned Queen of England but the new great liner portrayed in newsreels of the time making its way serenely across the seas.

Mara Scherbatoff was the oldest of four equally beautiful sisters, one of whom was the head *mannequin* at Balenciaga. They lived with their old Swiss governess in a flat in Passy. Scherb, as Mara was called by everyone, had no shorthand and her typing was slow, but she spoke English, French and Russian perfectly, and provided an admirably steady as well as glamorous centre to the swirl of a newspaper office.

I did not share Delmer's delight in having an entourage, and saw no need for three assistants. I advised London that I thought the one Frenchman among them, Robert Chasseuil, and one Briton would be enough. Charles Sutton reorganised matters and sent me as my one British assistant a young Australian who had worked for the *Daily Express* as a freelance, Alan Moorehead. It was a mistake. For though Moorehead and I became good friends, and for a time worked well together, our journalistic qualities were too similar for us to form a balanced team. We were both essentially descriptive writers – he in time to emerge as the greatest of his generation – each at his best on a big story where an eye for significant detail could be deployed. But what I wanted was an assistant who not only could handle the gossip and crime and scandal stories the sub-editors delighted in, but enjoyed doing so. That would leave me to deal with the big, and above all the political, stories. Only when Moorehead was moved on to Rome, and a crime reporter, Donald Robertson, took his place, did I have a set-up which worked without strain. In the early days of the war in September 1939 this human interest dross would lose its news value, and when George Millar was added to our team I found myself working with a man who became, and has remained, one of my closest friends. The Paris post then became fulfilling indeed.

But in the early weeks of 1938 I found it far from satisfying. I was homesick for Vienna, or rather for the type of news Vienna had offered – news which became all the more significant as it became clear Hitler was moving towards a showdown with Schuschnigg. Paris proved, too, to have many snags for anyone setting up a family home. We had a flat in the elegant district of Passy, but it was a dark, gloomy place with a minute, badly equipped kitchen. TB-tested milk fit for a small baby was difficult to buy. I found a supply only by tramping round the outskirts of the Auteuil racecourse in the Bois de Boulogne to a dairy farm which pastured its cows in the centre of the racetrack. Ultimately we discovered a further source from a firm called Necessary Luxuries, which supplied bottled and tested milk to the big American colony in Paris.

Much of the work was discouraging. Every day there seemed to be yet another member of the aristocracy who had eloped to Paris with someone else's wife, about whom the news desk was frantic for a story ('The Beaver's especially interested, old boy: he knows them both well').

Other stories were less troublesome. At the opening of the first Surrealist Exhibition, held in Paris, a young actress, chains swathed round her nude body, leapt from a luxurious bed of yellow satin into a pool of water fringed by pampas grass. There she splashed muddy water not only over herself but over the *haute couture* gowns of the onlookers. Screams of horror and anguished cries came from a hidden gramophone. Salvador Dali's main contribution was *Raining Taxi Cab*. In a car wreathed with ivy, a blonde wax model in evening dress, with a snail over her left eye, was drenched by jets of water pouring from holes in the roof.

The French Riviera, hard hit by the slump, decided to publicise itself as a summer resort and laid on a sumptuous press trip. I told the organiser that the *Daily Express* never guaranteed, if it accepted a publicity trip, to write anything favourable – or indeed anything at all – but he told me to come along anyway. Cecily and I had three days at the best hotels in Nice, Cannes and Monte Carlo, with meals of unbelievable excellence. That at the Hotel Negresco in Nice ran to twenty-three courses – though to be fair several of these were sorbets served to freshen our palates between dishes. We bathed in the clear waters of the pool at Eden Rock, and underwater in the sea off Cannes where untreated sewage bobbed around us and caused us to retreat hastily to the shower bath on the beach. I also met for the first time a legendary figure of the Côte d'Azur, a freelance American journalist who did occasional work under the name of Jean Martin. We invited him to join us for a drink on the terrace of the Hotel Carlton in Cannes. Martin hesitated. He had arranged to lunch with his girlfriend. 'Bring her too,' I suggested. He somewhat warily agreed. He turned up accompanied by a fleshy, sunburnt, dark-haired woman in her thirties, quietly dressed in a black suit and white blouse, but wearing a good deal of expensive jewellery. She had a reserved, enigmatic manner. Her arrival caused a stir. People at two nearby tables turned to study us. A man at the bar abruptly swallowed his drink and left. Another man, I noted, hurried his party into the dining room, and away from the terrace. It was only that evening that the barman explained the mystery: 'Did you know that your guest at lunch time is the Madame of the leading *maison de rendezvous* in Cannes?'

Jean Martin was a good correspondent and helped me with many stories. Protected by his American passport, he was to remain on the Riviera, later moving to Berlin when France fell in 1940. After the war began I heard his voice only once again. During the fighting at Thermopolyae the New Zealand Divisional Headquarters was dive-bombed. As I took shelter in a slit trench, the radio in the nearby cooks' truck continued to carry an American short-wave news broadcast from Berlin. Above the drone of the planes the voice was unmistakable. It was Jean Martin, reporting to New York about German elation at their victorious thrust in Greece. On that April morning on a Greek hillside, the Carlton Bar at Cannes seemed very far away.

CHAPTER THIRTY-NINE

Anschluss

In early March the avalanche began to move in Central Europe. Schuschnigg was summoned to Hitler's mountain retreat at Berchtesgarten to be bullied and threatened by Hitler – the first of the melancholy procession of European statesmen to face this treatment. He responded by calling a plebiscite on the question as to whether Austria should stay independent. Hitler moved his troops to the frontier and called the Austrian Nazis into the streets, producing an extraordinary spectacle on the Ringstrasse and the Karntnerstrasse, with one pavement packed with clamorous Nazis and the other with equally clamorous Socialists and Fatherland Front supporters, shouting defiance at one another. I was determined to be in on this story. The plebiscite was fixed for Sunday 13 March. I persuaded Charles Sutton to let me go by overnight train from Paris to Innsbruck. I could cover the story there over the weekend, and take the train back on Sunday evening. By eight o'clock on the Friday evening, I was on my way by the *Arlberg Express*.

Many leading American correspondents were on the train, among them John Whitaker of the *Chicago Daily News* and the famed H.R. Knickerbocker, of the Hearst Press. There was also a young reporter from the *New York Herald Tribune*, Walter Kerr, with whom I was to share many assignments in the next few years, and who was to become one of my closest friends. It was a moment to savour as I sat with them round a table in the wagon-lit dining car late into the night, the pundits swapping reminiscences and arguing about the future of Europe.

I was to work closely, and easily, with American correspondents in this run-up to the war – more easily than with the correspondents for British papers. I felt myself linked by background and attitude to 'that small swarm of young American journalists who, however deficient in scholarly background, infested foreign capitals, boldly bearded their great men, pugnaciously investigated their political movements, demanded the unornamented truth at a thousand press meetings'.*

* *Not So Wild A Dream,* Eric Sevareid (Knopf, 1946), p. 9

Many of the Americans came, as I did, from small, remote towns, and had grown up with a sense of being out of things – and a longing to be in the midst of them – which provided a powerful impetus towards daily journalism. 'The people who live remote from cities inherit the earth,' wrote Katherine Mansfield. By that she meant, I am sure, not only that they frequently inherit a healthy and probably beautiful environment, but that they are also possessed of an eager sense of wonder, a desire to explore the older, thickly populated and highly developed centres of the world depicted in the books and magazines and newspapers they read, and which seemed constantly to beckon from beyond the distant, quiet horizon. In those days journalism offered not only the best but almost the only way to carry out such explorations, for travel was costly and difficult, scholarships and grants and fellowships few and hard to come by, and business opportunities scanty. So from the main streets of small towns in the back-blocks of New Zealand, Australia, Canada and above all middle America, a determined or lucky few of us battled our way towards the bright lights and the centres of power. We were well fitted for the rootless trade of the foreign correspondent because our deepest roots had already been wrenched up. It was no coincidence that many of the leading American correspondents of this period were from remote places in the United States – Ed Murrow from North Carolina, Eric Sevareid from North Dakota and, in his turn, Walter Cronkite from Missouri. And though Walter Kerr was an Easterner from New York State, he was not from New York City, but from Syracuse way up north close to Lake Ontario.

We woke the next morning, in the brilliant light reflected from the snow-covered mountainsides, to astonishing news. Hitler had denounced the plebiscite, and was moving his troops into Austria. In the train corridor I was approached by a well-dressed, extremely agitated Austrian Jew, appalled at finding himself returning into the jaws of the avowed enemies of his race. Was it true, he asked me, that the great H.R. Knickerbocker was on the train? When I told him this was so, relief spread over his face. 'With the foreign press here they won't dare do anything wrong, will they?' he kept asking. 'We will be all right with you there.'

It was an impressive reminder of the power the press possessed in those days – or had possessed. I wished I could have shared in his confidence, though maybe there was more wishfulness than real hope in his words. But I knew in my bones that we were a very fragile defence indeed against the forces even then being unleased upon the people of Austria.

At St Anton Station in the Tyrol, American voices rang loud and confident on the clear, frosty air as a group in vividly coloured ski clothes greeted friends who had travelled on our train. 'Yes, the Germans moved in at dawn,' one man proclaimed. 'And as you see, everything is quiet and normal – though no doubt the press fellows will soon be telling a pack of lies about trouble and all that. But everything is peaceful and just fine.'

In Innsbruck Kerr and I hired a car and set off up the road towards the German border. In the hall of the hotel the Jew who had spoken to me on the train, his face grey with fear, was frantically trying to get through on the telephone to Switzerland, whilst in the corner the radio blared out the cheers of the crowds waiting in Linz for Hitler's arrival.

The snow, still heavy on the mountainsides, lay in streaks across the black earth of the fields. The road wound alongside the River Inn. At one bend a peasant boy in lederhosen, a tiny swastika flag in his hand, rushed to the roadside shouting, 'The German Army is coming – the German Army is coming!' We had just time to pull on to the road edge as, round the corner, came a dozen or so steel-helmeted motor cyclists, rifles slung on their backs. Behind them came a line of swiftly moving, camouflage-bedaubed military trucks filled with grey-green uniformed troops sitting bolt upright, rifles between their knees. In some trucks a heavy machine-gun barrel pointed skywards; others hauled anti-tank guns, their barrels covered with canvas. Then came the sound of drums, and a long column of infantry marching three-abreast, following behind a regimental band. Then came a line of staff cars, some with skis piled on top.

It was a thrilling, chilling sight. Here in the bright spring sunshine were the machines of war rolling across frontiers, like the first falling rocks and shifting earth of a great landslide which could engulf us all. That morning, on that cold mountain road, I was sure not only that war would come, but that it had already made its remorseless beginning.

Scene after scene was etched into my mind as the day wore on. As the Reichswehr columns approached Innsbruck, from a side road a yellow sports car appeared and halted. A bronzed woman in an expensive coat jumped out and flung her arms round the neck of the nearest German officer. At the Brenner Pass a German mechanised army unit and a straddling column of Austrian Nazi Storm Troopers in white shirts, black trousers and swastika armbands halted a few yards from the Italian frontier post. A Reichswehr colonel, clicking the heels of his shiny, high leather boots together, saluted the Austrian customs official and assured him of the 'comradely feelings of the Germans'. The late afternoon sun glowed on the snowy slopes of the Dolomites as the swastika flag was raised on the Austrian customs post. In fields near Kitzbuehl children ploughed knee deep through snow to pick up yellow leaflets scattered from German planes, welcoming Austria into the Reich. The road behind was jammed with horse-drawn field kitchens and horse-drawn machine guns. And in the streets of Innsbruck, as the foremost German units marched into the town, I found myself standing next to a grey-haired Jewish woman tremblingly holding out her hand in the Nazi salute whilst the crowd roared out the 'Horst Wessel' Nazi hymn, the words of which she tried with her mouth, but clearly did not know.

By evening I had telephoned a story to the *Sunday Express*, and another to *Paris Soir*, who proclaimed me as 'Notre Envoyé Special, M. Sandford Cox'. The Paris train was due to leave in half an hour. But I was determined to see this turning point of the history of our times come to its fulfilment, and to be in Vienna when Hitler entered the city. I decided, even at the risk of getting myself into trouble with the *Express*, to reinterpret my instructions and go on to Vienna rather than back to Paris. I got as far as Strasbourg by midnight, passing the lake at Zell am See gleaming in the moonlight. I got a bed in an hotel in Strasbourg which had Reichswehr sentries on the door, and the names of twenty-seven German officers – among them a major-general – in the register. By midday on Sunday I was back at the Modenaplatz, having made my way through streets where units of the Reichswehr rumbled past, moving on towards the Czech and Hungarian frontiers.

Bill Morrell had left for Prague that morning. His wife was pregnant, and he wanted her to be in safety. Bochow was alone in the office. I telephoned Sutton. Far from him being angry at my breach of instructions, he was delighted. 'Thank God you are in Vienna!' he said. 'I did not know how I was going to face Chris and tell him we had no one there at this moment. Take over as correspondent until Morrell gets back next week.'

Bochow had another cause for worry which was sharply personal. He was awaiting a call to present himself at the headquarters the Gestapo had set up in the Hotel Metropole. When the call came he looked suddenly grey and thin with strain, as he had on the morning when he had been telephoned by Herr Baumgarten. I watched him drive off in a taxi, and then settled down to write my story of what I had seen the day before. Half an hour later Bochow was back. He came into the room glowing, looking physically bigger – almost as if his whole body had been inflated. His tone was confident to the point of arrogance. 'I'm in the clear,' he said. 'I thought I would be all right, as the life insurance people renewed my policy only a month ago, and these insurance companies keep close contact with the Gestapo as to who is in trouble and who isn't. Now I have it officially.'

'This is a great day for the Reich,' he continued, warming to his theme. 'There was a time after the war when I thought Germany was done for, and I even thought of trying to get British citizenship. But I'm glad I didn't. We are a great country again.'

I never knew what price Bochow had paid for this rehabilitation. But he was the only member of von Papen's entourage to escape retribution. Papen himself retired to his estates in East Prussia, there to sit out the war until he was tried at Nuremberg. Von Keppler, whom Bochow had always spoken of as a close friend, disappeared on the day of the Anschluss. His body was picked up in the Danube a week later. Fräulein Rosa met a similar fate. I noted on that Sunday morning that a swastika flag hung from the window of her flat on the Modenaplatz. When I commented on this to Bochow he shrugged his shoulders: 'It is a bit late for her to make such gestures. She has been very foolish, I fear, poor dear.' Within a week she too was dead.

That evening the press were summoned to the Federal Chancellery, where we were informed that the new Austrian Chancellor, the Nazi lawyer Seyss-Inquart, and his Cabinet had declared that Austria had become a state of the German Reich. A monocled official, Dr Mazar, read the announcement to us in a room just down the corridor from that in which Chancellor Dollfuss had been shot dead by the Nazis three-and-a-half years before. Through the windows came the shouts of the crowds, cheering the Reichswehr as they drove along the Ringstrasse. On my way out I looked into the room where Kleinwachter had worked. His desk was deserted. He had been arrested, and was already on his way to the concentration camp at Dachau.

The next day ecstatic crowds lined the streets to see Adolf Hitler drive in triumph into the city which had rejected him as a failed artist and casual labourer twenty-five years earlier. A huge crowd packed the space in front of the Imperial Hotel. When Hitler appeared on the balcony – a triumphant, smiling figure in the same type of brown shirt uniform he had worn at Nuremberg – every arm went out in salute. I raised my own with them. To have done anything else would have been suicide, for no passport, no claim to be a foreigner could have stood against the hysteria which filled the air.

Already the mass arrests of Jews and Socialists and other opponents of Nazism had begun. On the Sunday evening, after I had filed my story to London, I visited a Jewish family in the Mariahilfestrasse, one member of which, a lawyer, had often joined Fodor's table in the Louvre. Seventeen of them were gathered together to discuss whether they should try to leave at once, or stay and face it out. They sought my advice and my help. Already two cousins, both journalists, had been arrested. In the street outside sirens wailed as the Nazis in cars and vans careered up and down making arrests. The family were anxious to get word to relatives in France who could help them emigrate and did not dare trust the telephone or the mail. I undertook to carry their messages for them.

Earlier that evening I had had a visit from the English writer John Lehmann, whose name I knew, but whom I had never met. He sought me out in the Modenaplatz in a state of high agitation. Could I persuade the British Embassy to give some help to a young German, an emigré, who was working as his secretary and whose life would now be in danger? He took me round to his flat, where a neat, slim young German sat – his eyes wide with fear, his arms hanging despairingly by his side. It was clear at a glance that he was more than just a secretary. He was the prototype of the young German working-class boy for whom unemployment, hopelessness and homosexual relationships had become a way of life. 'They will kill me if they find me,' he said in tones of sullen despair. 'I left Germany to avoid military service.' I undertook to ring one of the Embassy staff – which I did – but I warned Lehmann, as we stood by ourselves on the stairway outside the flat, that I could see no grounds upon which the Embassy were likely to intervene. He was furious, and shouted at me as I descended the stairs, 'Callous – that's what you all are. Callous!'

That afternoon I had a more direct reminder of Nazi methods. I was looking out from the office window across the Modenaplatz when I saw a khaki-clad squad straggling across the grass of the square. At the front was a tall, gangling Storm Trooper in what was clearly a brand new khaki uniform. Behind him came a dozen or so other Storm Troopers in a variety of garb. Some had khaki shirts and black trousers; others khaki shirts and lederhosen; others the white shirt, black trousers and swastika armband which was the most easily adopted version of the Nazi uniform. Their leader was trying to get them into some form of marching formation, but they looked a sorry lot. I called Bochow to the window and taunted him with the bearing of his new allies. 'You'll never get Austrian Nazis even to march in step,' I said – and then paused, for I realised the squad were crossing the road towards the doorway of our flats. A few minutes later we could hear the clang of heavy boots on the stairs, and the doorbell rang. Bochow said quickly, 'I will see to this.' I could hear voices raised when he opened the door, then argument, and suddenly Bochow's voice, in sharp Prussian tones, ordered them away. He came back into the room, aggressive but also a little shaken. 'These Austrian fools,' he said. 'That bloody janitor who turned off the heat on the night of your party was responsible for this. He had denounced you as an enemy of the Nazis and a friend of the Jews, and persuaded the local SA to come round and teach you a lesson. They were going to wreck the flat and beat you up. I gave them a piece of my mind, I can tell you – and as for that bloody janitor, I will see he is out of his job before the week is out.' From the window we watched the squad file sadly away. They halted in the middle of the square, and gathered round arguing. One man clearly wanted to return, and kept trying to get others to follow him. But in the end they dispersed.

Later that evening Morrell returned, eager to resume his duties – the more so since my story had not only led the paper that morning, but had filled three columns of it. I took the night train back to Paris, carrying in my pocket a story of incidents of Nazi brutality which Morrell and I had gathered, and which we thought wiser not to try to put over the telephone. It was the first of a number of such reports which Morrell, with great courage, sent out of Austria during the next few weeks when the Nazi terror there was at its height.

I saw Bochow for the last time in his flat, just before I left for the train. His two young sons, wearing Hitler Youth uniforms, their faces white and drawn with exhaustion, were back from a day of marching and demonstrating which had begun at seven that morning. It was clear that Bochow's family, as well as the man himself, had to take every chance to make clear their devotion to the new regime. It seems likely that Bochow did not survive the war. One report was that he was shot by the Russians in East Berlin in 1945. Certainly he never crossed the path of any of us again. During the war I used sometimes to wonder whether I might encounter him in a London street, for he would have been well fitted to be parachuted into England as a spy. I also used to wonder, when it seemed likely in Greece or Crete or the Western Desert that I might be taken prisoner, whether the Nazi system would be efficient enough to identify a New Zealand infantry officer with the former *Daily Express* correspondent in Vienna, and single me out for special interrogation, for I think Bochow assumed that I was in the British Secret Service – the more so because Rex Andrews was a frequent visitor to my flat. Bochow took a keen interest in him – and he in Bochow – and I suspect Bochow saw through Andrews' fairly thin cover quite easily. I would not like to have been on the receiving end of a Bochow investigation in a Gestapo cell, for in his heart he hated as well as envied the British. But fortunately the matter was never put to the test.

My journey back to Paris provided a strange postscript to this first Nazi conquest. On the train, on a hard wooden seat in an open-plan third-class carriage, was a girl in her late teens, manifestly British, with a swathe of blonde hair across her forehead, a delicate complexion, and cheeks which seemed to have still the fullness of adolescence. On her dress was pinned a swastika badge. I recognised her as Unity Mitford, friend and ardent admirer of Hitler. One of her sisters had married Sir Oswald Mosley, and another Esmond Romilly. She answered my questions angrily and disdainfully.

'I was heartbroken when I did not see Hitler when he arrived at his birthplace at Linz,' she said. 'Another English friend, who was with him there, said it was the most wonderful experience of his life.

'But I saw his entry into Vienna, and perhaps after all that was best. Afterwards I saw him for a few minutes in his hotel. He was tired, but seemed very moved by it all. I think it was wonderful.'

The other friend who had been with Hitler in Linz was G. Ward Price of the *Daily Mail*, the most prominent apologist in the British press for Hitler and Mussolini. At Linz he had stood on the balcony alongside Hitler, watching the Reichswehr march in, and had broadcast in English over the German radio's live transmission of the scene his delight at it all. With men like that writing in powerful newspapers, I felt double grounds for deep concern. With Hitler now openly on the move, war in Europe seemed not only bound to come, but it could come with Britain lulled into a false belief in Hitler's character and his aims.

The Anschluss marked for me the end of the first phase of my overseas experience. As the train carried me back to Paris, I knew that war was now inevitable. I sensed that the grey-uniformed marching troops I had seen on that March morning in the valley of the Inn would be the first of many, many German columns which would spread out from the Reich, treading down the freedoms in other lands that had already been crushed in their own. In time that could only mean war.

Two more years of reporting lay ahead of me in Europe. In that summer of 1938 I covered the Munich crisis from Prague, and saw Czechoslovakia sacrificed in Chamberlain's vain bid to win peace for our time. But all he achieved was to hand over to Hitler the great natural defences of the Sudeten mountains, and the formidable man-made defences the Czechs had erected in their midst. This opened the way for Hitler to seize, early in 1939, the rest of the Czechoslovak state.

That action brought me back to the Balkans once again, to report from Hungary and Romania and Yugoslavia, now open in their turn to German pressure. Then it was back to Paris to cover the steady drift to war, which came to Britain and France on 3 September 1939. On the first night of it we waited in a blacked-out Paris for the mass bomber raids to begin. But the bombers did not come – then. Instead we had the months in Europe of the Phoney War, when you had to strain your ears on the Western Front to hear the sound of a rifle shot from a distant patrol. But there was real war for me to report from the snow and the forests of Finland.

In November 1939 the Soviet Union, suddenly and without warning, attacked Finland. Stalin was angered by the reluctance of the Finnish

Government to lease him two naval bases, which he considered essential to protect Leningrad from an enemy who might advance through Finland. Without even presenting an ultimatum – to which the Finns might have yielded – Soviet airplanes bombed the centre of Helsinki, and the Red Army advanced across the border at more than a score of places.

It was to prove a costly blunder. The Finns fought back tenaciously, helped by unusually early falls of heavy snow. This blocked the forest roads, immobilising the Soviet tanks and guns, but enabling the élite Finnish ski troops, equipped with white camouflage uniforms and lightweight weapons, to move swiftly on their skis. On road after road Red Army columns were cut off, and then destroyed in the bitter cold, against which the Soviet troops were ill equipped.

For three miraculous months the Finns held the Red Army at bay, inflicting on them such heavy casualties that Stalin never again allowed his troops to get seriously embroiled with the Finnish forces. Finally the Russians regrouped, and broke through in the south with massive forces – and by a bold strategic move in which they sent tanks across the frozen Baltic Sea to outflank the Finnish defence line.

I covered the war from start to finish. My despatches helped to bring home the extent of the early Russian losses, particularly where extreme cold turned the dead on the battlefields into scenes which resembled vast waxworks displays. And I became a key witness on the attitude of the Finnish people. Soviet propagandists, and their supporters in the Communist parties in Britain and America, claimed that the Soviet intervention had been justified to release the Finnish people from the oppressive right-wing government of President Mannerheim. This was untrue. The Finns fought the war heart and soul.

My reporting from Finland, and the book I wrote a year later, *The Red Army Moves* brought me under fierce attack from Communist and fellow-travellers in Britain. But I did not mind. I knew my work would stand the test of time – as it has.

By May 1940 I was in Brussels to cover the launching of Hitler's blitzkrieg against the West. With Belgium overrun, and the panzers racing across northern France, I moved back to Paris for that city's last month of freedom for four long years. German tanks were already on its outskirts, and I followed the French Government to Tours, and then to Bordeaux. When the French sued for an armistice I got aboard the last English ship to sail from Bordeaux, back to a Britain girding itself for invasion.

Just over eight years had passed since that grey, rainy day on which I had sailed from Wellington, on the first stage of my journey overseas. Those years had brought me a range of experience of people, places and events far wider than I had ever thought possible. Now it was time for a new phase.

As we waited to disembark in Falmouth at the end of our hazardous voyage from Bordeaux, I heard on the BBC radio news that a New Zealand Brigade had arrived in the United Kingdom, diverted there from the Middle East. That decided me. Six weeks later I was in battledress, camped under pine trees in Surrey, a private in the 23rd Battalion of the Fifth New Zealand Brigade. I had rejoined my fellow countrymen, to share in that profound form of overseas experience which faced our generation – active service in war.

Postscript

At the end of 1940 the New Zealand troops in Britain, the Fifth Brigade, were sent by sea, round the Cape of Good Hope, to join up with the rest of 2 NZ Division in Egypt. I served with the Division in the campaigns of Greece and Crete, and in the Sidi Resegh campaign in the Western Desert.

In May 1942, when the Division was doing garrison duties in Syria, I was transferred from the Army to the New Zealand Diplomatic Service, to the post of first secretary at the newly established New Zealand Legation in Washington. The legation (the title at the time, now abolished, for the diplomatic missions of smaller countries) had been hastily set up when Japan came into the war. Since New Zealand was directly threatened by the Japanese thrust into the South-West Pacific, the government rightly believed it was essential for us to be directly represented in Washington, as the very existence of our country could be at stake. Except for the high commissions in London, and in Australia, and a trade commissioner in Brussels, New Zealand had until then had no diplomatic service. The government widened recruitment outside the ranks of the home civil service, and decided that I had qualifications they needed. During my years at Oxford and in Fleet Street I had established close links with the High Commission in London, and in 1936 had been invited to become press secretary to the New Zealand delegation at a meeting of the League of Nations in Geneva. My Fleet Street commitments prevented me taking up the post, and John Mulgan went in my stead. Another reason for my selection for Washington was that I had close links with the American press and broadcasting. These stemmed from my working with the small but highly influential band of American foreign correspondents in Europe, and from my own work – which I had doubled with my work for British papers – as the first European correspondent of *Newsweek*.

My role in Washington turned out to be more significant that I had anticipated. To give New Zealand a powerful voice in the United States, Walter Nash, one of the leading figures in the New Zealand War Cabinet, was appointed as Minister to the United States. But he also retained the post of Minister of Finance in Wellington, requiring him to spend a good part of each year in New Zealand. In his absence I was left, as chargé d'affaires, as head of the legation for eleven of the twenty-one months I was to serve in the United States. This involved me, on eight occasions, in representing my country on the supreme political body overseeing the war in the Pacific, the Pacific War Council; in taking part in the early planning for a future United Nations; and on one occasion signing a treaty on behalf of New Zealand.

The government wanted me to remain in the diplomatic service and urged me to go to Moscow in 1944, with the rank of counsellor, to set up the New Zealand Legation there. But I was determined to go back to the Army, and early in 1944 rejoined the Division, then in the final stages of the battle of Cassino. I served for the rest of the European war with the Division, becoming the Chief Intelligence Officer on General Freyberg's staff.

When I was demobilised late in 1945 I rejoined the *News Chronicle*, instead of returning to the *Daily Express*. The *Express* were anxious to have me back, and offered me a substantially larger salary than did the *News Chronicle*. But the *News Chronicle*'s left of centre stance was much more in accord with my own political views than was the maverick conservatism of Beaverbrook.

For the next nine years I was political correspondent of the *News Chronicle*, reporting at first hand the profound changes in British society brought about by the post-war Labour Government. I had voted Labour in the British 1945 General Election, and exulted in their victory. I greeted it as a chance to see the evils of the slump redressed, and for the social ownership of major sectors of the economy to be brought about. I reported eagerly the various measures of nationalisation which were introduced, and also the setting up of the National Health Service and the establishment of the welfare state.

On the foreign front I was at first reluctant to accept the reality of the Cold War, despite the foretaste of it that we had had in Trieste. I strongly opposed proposals to hand Trieste over to Yugloslavia, and put those views to the New Zealand delegation to the Paris Conference on peace with Italy, to which I was attached for a time as an adviser. But at that stage I saw the Trieste issue as one primarily between Yugoslavia and Italy – as indeed it was – rather than as an aspect of the wider Cold War.

During the closing months of 1945 I hoped against hope that the tension between the Soviet Union and the Western Allies would ease; that Stalin would allow an element of democracy in the Eastern European countries, would call off the civil war in Greece, and would respond to the desire for co-operation which undoubtedly existed at that time in Britain, and to a considerable degree within the United States.

But by the early months of 1946 it was clear that the Cold War was inescapable. The Russians were determined to impose their regimes on the countries behind the Iron Curtain, and were answering a chilly '*Niet*' to every proposal of co-operation. In Western Europe they were utilising the local Communist parties to make trouble for the Western democracies, and to support Soviet aims. This latter fact was apparent within the British Parliament. Though only two MPs had been elected as open Communist Party members, there was no doubt that at least six others in the Labour Party slavishly followed the Communist Party line, and who were probably Party members. Perhaps up to thirty more were fellow travellers, always ready to see good in the Soviet Union and bad in those who opposed her. These were facts generally accepted by most lobby correspondents at the time. This duplicity was, to me, very wrong. It cut at the basis of democracy when MPs who had stood for one set of views, and had signed up to one Party's proposals, were in truth pursuing the aims of another. By early 1946 it was clear that the Cold War was on, and I supported the West wholeheartedly in it.

Western Europe in those immediate post-war years was vulnerable to Communist influence. Communist parties in France and Italy were large, and powerful. Only astute work by British officials and British Labour MPs, loyal to democracy, prevented a fusion of the Communist and Social Democrats in West Germany – a fusion which would have given the Communists control of the German Left on the west as well as the east of the Iron Curtain. When the Soviets showed their hand to the full in 1948 by crushing out the last vestiges of democracy in Czechoslovakia, it seemed as if all Western Europe might turn Communist. I certainly remember thinking at the time that, if that happened, the best I could hope for in Britain would be to find work on a farm, as journalism would certainly be barred to me. But the Marshall Plan saved the European economy from collapse, and after the defeat of the Russians by the Berlin airlift the danger receded – and now no doubt looks quite unreal.

I supported all the Labour Party's nationalisation plans up to the point when in 1949 they proposed to nationalise steel. Lord Layton, Chairman of the *News Chronicle*, was an expert on the steel industry and adamantly opposed its nationalisation on purely practical grounds. I accepted his expert view, an action which started my disillusionment with public ownership. It soon became clear that in practice there was a major snag in nationalisation. It meant monopoly – and monopoly conferred great power not only on those who ran the monopoly, but on the trade unions who represented the workers in that monopoly. And in the 1950s the British trade unions proceeded vigorously to abuse that monopoly. Instead of helping their industries to operate more efficiently, they used the great powers trade union legislation gave them not merely to exploit their position to gain advantages in wages and conditions for their employees, but to push their demands to a where the general interest of the country, and the very viability of their own industry were at stake. This owed much to the fact that by the 1950s some key unions were under virtual Communist control. Thwarted at the ballot box by the British voter, the British Communist Party, with great skill, set about getting its members – and its stooges – into key positions in the unions. They had no hesitation about pushing their demands to a point which damaged the industries concerned, and called strikes wherever possible, on the Marxist ground that since capitalism was bound to collapse, helping it to do so simply speeded up the inevitable march of history. In short they sabotaged British industry, and did so with relish. This process sickened me – as did the failure of major parts of the media to bring these facts home to the British public. At the same time, under the same Communist influence – whether exercised directly or indirectly – the key unions, by backing unilateral disarmament, endangered the safety of Britain.

These developments had, by the end of the 1950s, disillusioned me with socialism and the Labour Party. I voted Labour in 1950, 1951 and 1955. But in 1959 I broke what had until then been the pattern of a lifetime – and an expression of my political beliefs over the previous thirty years. In my home area of Hampstead the Labour candidate put out a manifesto taking a completely fellow-travelling line – indeed advocating a foreign policy virtually the same as that of the Communists. I told Hugh Gaitskell, the Leader of the Labour Party, who had by then become my friend (as he records in his diaries) that I could not vote for the Labour candidate but would vote Liberal. He argued that given his own firm stand against unilateralism and Soviet expansionism, it was the Labour Party's policy, not the candidate's, which I should vote for. But in fact I was also at odds with the nationalisation policies Gaitskell still stood for.

I voted Liberal in that 1959 General Election. But the Liberals were no answer. They were either would-be Labour men and women, unwilling to admit the fact, or futile figures. So in 1964 I voted Tory, and continued to vote Tory from then on – reluctantly until Margaret Thatcher came on the scene, but enthusiastically so long as she was the Tory leader.

We who became socialists in response to the slump in the 1930s were proved wrong so far as the nationalisation of ownership of key areas of the economy was concerned. But socialism was, at the time, a route worth testing. Indeed in Britain in 1945, such was the revulsion against the waste and squalor of the slump, and the waste and horror of the war, that the public demanded fundamental change. In purely economic terms, too, the huge capital investment needed for the coalmines to supply the energy Britain needed – and coal, in those days, was the only major energy source available within the United Kingdom – could only have been provided by the state. Furthermore, had the law not given British trade unions a position of privilege that put them in some respects above the law, nationalisation might have been much more successful. But even if it is deemed to have failed, we who advocated it insisted as well on another, more fundamental, condition – that the process of democracy was the only way that nationalisation should come about. It should be achieved only by the ballot box, and would have to operate within the law, so that the way would be open for the experiment to be cancelled should it fail. We did not advocate, or try to achieve, a victory for public ownership on the basis of a 'sacred' dogma, a dogma within which the people of the countries where communism gained power were to be imprisoned for over half a century.

In 1954 I moved from the post of political correspondent of the *News Chronicle* to that of assistant editor. But my eye was already on a new form of journalism, then in its infancy – television. When in 1956 the chance arose of editing the news service of the newly established commercial television network, I seized it with both hands.

I carried into my new post of editor of ITN a political position forged by the experiences of the previous twenty-five years, a position which has remained virtually unchanged ever since. I defined my position at the time as that of an unaligned radical. I still believed there was need for change, particularly in improving state education and doing away with class shibboleths, in improving housing and in opportunities for better sport and leisure. But my thinking was dominated – as it had been in the thirties – by the need to sustain democracy and the rule of law. Those principles were under powerful threat in the international field from the Soviet Union, still pursuing a policy of belief in the inevitability of communism, and within Britain by the Marxists and fellow travellers still active and influential in politics, in the trade unions, and in teaching and the media. Within the remit of impartiality – indeed by making that impartiality into a positive force – I set ITN on the course of protecting democracy and the rule of law by trying to tell the truth about public issues – knowing that part of that truth was to ensure the public was not conned by Marxist pressure abroad and at home.

The survival of Marxist ideas in British intellectual life between the mid 1950s and the fall of communism in the Soviet Union at the end of the 1980s is a curious phenomenon. The Cold War, and the seizure of power in

Czechoslovakia, together with the siege of Berlin, had so thoroughly discredited communism in the West, even amongst ardent fellow travellers, that in 1950 Richard Crossman could gather together, in his book *The God That Failed*, the disavowals of their former faith by six former Western Communists and fellow travellers. The crushing of the Hungarian rising in 1956 drove a further group of one-time hard-liners out of the British Communist Party. Yet by the early 1960s Marxism, even if in a somewhat watered-down variety, was a fashionable, indeed dominant creed in British universities and in sections of the media – particularly in television current affairs. Its proponents showed no sign of having ever read anything by Marx, but they accepted as gospel a number of basic elements of Marxism – that capitalism was bad and unfair; that truth was not an absolute, but reflected one's class position and class bias; that the authority of the contemporary state – falsely depicted as a coherent right-wing Establishment – should be challenged and undermined. They believed that in international affairs we should give up nuclear weapons, even if that meant yielding to the Soviet Union – and indeed that we should give the Communist bloc countries the benefit of the doubt on contentious issues. In particular in Vietnam – the one area of open conflict with a Communist regime – they believed we should disregard the proven horrors which awaited the South Vietnamese once the Gulags of the North could be put in place, and see only the Nationalist, and not the Communist, element in the North Vietnamese state.

In Britain, strikes were seen as part of a struggle against an unfair and unjust Establishment. Any suggestion that the strikes might be led by Communists with long-term political rather than short-term economic aims was dismissed as 'Reds Under the Bed' scaremongering. All of this became the orthodoxy of the universities and the media, and found its way into parts of the civil service, until the reality of the collapse of Soviet power brought the whole phoney intellectual structure crashing down. For an indication of how far this rot had spread, one had only to compare the picture of the Soviet Union as portrayed in the BBC series *The Comrades*, broadcast in the mid-1980s, with the reality of Soviet life as exposed when communism fell.

There were valiant fighters in the British media and in the universities against this trendy leftism – foremost among them being Bernard Levin. I ensured that ITN was not tainted by this modish leftism. It is interesting that a leading broadcast journalist of that era, Julian Pettifer, has since declared that he and his colleagues gave a one-sided picture of the war in Vietnam, playing up the scenes of horror of the fighting, without any indication of the type of regime which would follow a Communist victory. That those horrors have been of shorter duration than might have been expected owes nothing to North Vietnamese generosity, but is due to the collapse of communism in the Soviet Union, the Communist great power of which North Vietnam was a client state.

The great new power of television did very little indeed to defeat communism, and a great deal to protect and further its influence in the West. Programmes which told the truth about Communist activity and about the Soviet Union were very few. Woodrow Wyatt's exposure of Communist vote-rigging in the Electrical Trades Union, and a BBC programme pinning the Katyn massacre onto the Soviets rather than the Nazis, were amongst that few. In *See It Happen* and *Pioneering Television News* I have set out how the documentary and current affairs programmers failed in their task not only to protect democracy but to record the truth.

Since ITN had only limited access to current affairs programming, and that access itself was limited by a shortage of money, there was little I could do outside the news to correct this imbalance. But within the news – above all by adhering to a strict impartiality at a time when that concept was under strong attack from the media intelligentsia in Glasgow and Leicester universities – we did what we could. I have told the tale of that in *See It Happen*. An important element was that I left in ITN a team of journalists dedicated to impartial journalism. This tradition and its practice has continued to this day. The same is true in the international news agency I helped to found – at first called UPITN, now Associated Press. Through it we made the fruits of this fair and impartial journalism available to countries throughout the world.

Seventy years have now passed since Jim Gallagher and I forked hay alongside the Waikato River, and he urged me to 'get out into the world and tell us the truth'. I have tried to do so.

Index

Abbott, John 157
Abyssinia 171, 174, 257, 193
Alba, Duke of 223
Alexandra, Queen 47
Allen, Jay 205
Alving, Barbro 213-14
Amery, L.S. 96-7, 121
Anschluss 104, 188, 246, 267-74
Aosta, Duke of 193
Aragon, Louis 218
Arbeitsdienst *see* German Youth Labour Service
Arrow, John 178
Associated Press 283
Ataturk, Kemal 112

Baker, Philip Noel 174
Baldwin, Stanley 152, 174, 187
Bareau, Paul 177
Barry, Gerald 177, 179, 181, 182, 183-4, 200, 235
Bartlett, Vernon 161, 171, 177, 203
Baxter, Beverley 236
BBC 188
Beachcomber (J.B. Morton) 184
Bean, Atherton 115
Beaverbrook, Lord 39, 156, 183, 184, 236, 238, 239, 258, 265
Bedermann, Karl 100
Bennett, Tiwha 21
Berlin *see* Germany
Bertram, James 12, 115, 128
Best, Richard 252
Beveridge, Sir William 97
Bevin, Ernest 253
Beyer, Lynn 88, 93, 115
Bledisloe, Viscount 11
Blum, Leon 198
Blunt, Sir Anthony 15, 147
Bochow, Roland 245-6, 252-3, 270-1, 272, 273
Books, Collin 178
Bowles, Sally 68
Brand, Rev. Dr 89
Brown, John 109-11
Buchan, Charles 182
Buchenwald 151
Buckley, Henry 214, 215-16, 222
Butler, Samuel 15

Caballero, Largo 210, 217
Cadbury family 182
Cadbury, George 162
Cameron, James 238
Campbell, Colonel 27-8, 29, 93
Campbell, R.M. (Dick) 172-4, 234
Capone, Al 39
Carol, King of Rumania 256
Cecil, Lord 120
Chamberlain, Sir Austen 62, 194
Chamberlain, Neville 97, 188, 194, 249, 274
Chamberlain, W.H. 149
Champion, Freddie 165, 203
Chasseuil, Robert 264
Chilton, Sir Henry 201
Chisholm, Helen 178
Christiansen, Arthur 161, 165, 184, 236-9, 258, 260, 261, 263
Churchill, Winston 28, 112, 162, 186, 226, 228, 256
Clarke, Denis 39, 235, 245, 251
Clarke, Tom 39, 162-3,167, 191
Coates, J.G. 172
Cold War 278-9, 281-2
Cole, G.D.H. 91, 148-9, 156
Copeman, Fred 96
Cornford, Frances 226
Cornford, John 218
Coster, Ian 156
Cox, Cecily (née Turner; GC's wife) 169, 193, 247-8, 261, 265
Cox, Charles Percy (GC's grandfather) 15-16
Cox, Geoffrey
LIFE AND CAREER: family background 15-18; high school 18-19; farming experience 11-14, 22; Rhodes Scholar 11-12, 21, 88; Otago University 19-24; first articles published 21-2; to England 25-31; Oxford University 28, 38-40; learns German 71-2, 99; reads Marx and Freud 90-2; Nazi youth labour camp 127, 129, 135-8; encounters Storm Troopers 132-3; contributor: *New York Times* 147, 155, 158; NZ

papers 147, 148; *Spectator* 147, 151, 155; decides on journalism 148, 155; marriage 169-70; *News Chronicle* : freelance 159-60, 163-9; reporter 180, 189-91; Paris correspondent 198-201; war correspondent, Madrid 203-10, 211-16; foreign correspondent 217-19, 221-9; *Daily Express*: 236-7; Vienna correspondent 241-4, 245-8, 249-54, 255-61; Rome 257; Sudetenland 258-9; Prague 259; Budapest 259; Paris correspondent 261, 263-6, 267, 270-4; covers the Anschluss 270-4; covers Munich crisis 274; war correspondent, Finland 214, 227, 234, 274-5; New Zealand Army 20, 116, 276, 277-8; *Crete News* 153; diplomat, Washington 277-8; political correspondent, *News Chronicle* 278; assistant editor 281; editor, ITN 238, 281-3; joint founder, Associated Press 283

IMPRESSIONS OF PLACES lived in or visited *see also* Denmark, France, Germany, Invercargill, London, Ongaroto, Oxford, Russia, Vienna

VIEWS/OBSERVATIONS: love of history 20, 235; being British 27; right-wing private armies, 1930s 28; class differences in Britain 36-8; education 82-3; forebodings of war 62-3, 66, 88, 92-3, 259, 260 1, 269, 274; state intervention 23-4; communism 61-2; 91-2, 112, 151, 234, 279-83; intellectual Left, mid-30s 125, 148-51; attitudes to Fascism in 1930s Britain 193-4, 257; Spanish Republic 194-5; nationalisation 278, 279; monopolies 279-80; democracy 281-3; political stance 92-3, 278, 279-81; Fleet Street, 1930s 161-2, 189-91; foreign correspondents 249-54; American journalists 267-8, 277; journalist's role 253-4, 283

BOOKS: *Defence of Madrid* 223-4; *The Red Army Moves* 234, 275; *See It Happen* 283; *Pioneering Television News* 283

Cox, Mary (née MacGregor, GC's mother) 16, 18
Cox, Peter (GC's son) 248
Cox, Samuel Fortnum (GC's great-grandfather) 15
Cox, Sandford (GC's father) 16

Crawford-Green, Colonel 226
Croall, Jonathan 81
Cronkite, Walter 268
Crossman, Richard 282
Cummings, Arthur 161, 178
Cunard, Nancy 207

Dachau 131, 151, 271
Daily Express 39, 156, 161, 183, 197, 233, 235-9, 241, 244, 255, 258, 261, 263, 265
Dakin, James 27
Dali, Salvador 147, 265
Davis, John 179, 184
Dawson, Geoffrey 194
de la Roque, Colonel 28
Delmer, Sefton (Tom) 161, 224-5, 227, 245, 246, 261, 264
Denmark 65-6
Depression (the slump) 13, 22-3, 26, 35-6, 39, 61, 92, 95, 112, 148, 157-8, 186, 195, 233, 246-7, 265, 280-1
di Vittorio, Giuseppe 226
Dimbleby, Richard 188
Doidge, Frederick 156, 159
Dollfuss, Engelbert 28, 102, 105,106, 128, 246, 271
Driberg, Tom 238
Duranty, Walter 149

Eden, Sir Anthony 175
Edward VIII 228, 229, 255
Einstein, Albert 38
Elder, J.R. 20
Eritrea 171
Ewer, W.N. 161

Fairbridge, Kingsley 121
Farson, Negley 251
Fischer, Bram 43, 50
Fischer, Louis 149, 210
Fodor, Marcel 251
Foley, Charles 237
Forrest, William 211-12, 215, 219, 224, 223
Fox, Ralph 218
France: Marseilles 30-1, Paris 93-4, 263-5
Franco, General Francisco 194, 197, 200, 203, 206, 209-10, 211-14 *passim*, 217, 219, 221-8 *passim*, 235, 257
Franz Josef, Emperor 102, 107
Frederika, Princess 255-6
Freyberg, General Bernard 278

Gaitskell, Hugh 128, 280
Gallagher, Jim 156, 283
Gallipoli 22

Gandhi, Mahatma 30
Gardiner, A.G. 177
Gedye, G.E.R. 161, 250, 251
George V, death of 185-6
George, King of Greece 256
German Youth Labour Service 127, 135-8
Germany: Berlin 66-9, 128-33; Heidelberg 71-2; Kiel 65; Nuremberg 128, 132, 139-43
Gibbs, Philip 163
Goebbels, P.J. 114, 128, 140-2, 188
Goering, Hermann 140, 141
Gollancz, Victor 233-4
Gordon, Hélène 263
Gosse, Sir Edmund 178
Gottwald, Klement 218
Greenhough, Richard 191, 235
Grey, Ralph 27
Griffiths, Eric 217
Gunther, John 99

Haile Selassie, Emperor 174, 193
Haldane, J.B.S. 149
Hale, Lionel 177
Haley, William 251
Hamilton, Lord Douglas 152
Harper, Arthur 121
Harper, Bishop (GC's great-grandfather) 15, 18
Harper, Sarah 15 (GC's grandmother)
Hauptmann, Mrs Bruno 241, 243-4
Henderson, Arthur 122
Henlein, Konrad 258
Hennessy, Jocelyn 214
Hess, Rudolf 140-2, 152-3
Hickey, William *see* Driberg, Tom
Hill 60 22, 73, 74
Himmler, Heinrich 140
Hindenberg, Field Marshal von 128, 130
Hindenburg Line 73
Hindus, Maurice 41, 58
Hitch, Charles 114-15
Hitler, Adolf 61, 66, 69, 72, 93, 103, 107, 109, 112, 128, 130-1, 139-43, 148, 151, 152, 187, 194, 197, 225, 234, 245, 246, 246, 251, 258, 265, 267, 268, 269, 271, 273, 274, 274; attitudes in 1930s Britain to 148, 193-4, 225, 274
Hoare, Sir Samuel 174
Hobson, Oscar 177
Hoover, Herbert 61
hunger marchers *see* Depression
Huxley, Aldous 207
Huxley, Julian 149

Ibarruri, Dolores 209
International Brigades 217-18, 228
Invercargill 19
Isaacs, Sir Isaac 122
Isherwood, Christopher 68, 69, 71

James, Sir Archibald 224, 225
Jarman, Tom 43,49
Johnson, Marvin 164-5
Jordan, Philip 203, 233, 235
Joseph, Noel 184

Kaltenborn, H.V. 188
Keir, David 159
Kennedy, John F. 21, 114
Keppler, Baron von 246
Kerr, Walter 267, 268
Keynes, J.M. 92, 172
Kleber, Emilio 218-19, 225-6
Kleinwachter, Dr 251, 271
Knickerbocker, H.R. 68, 267, 268
Krupskaya, Nadezhda 45
Kuhn, Ferdinand Jnr 158

labour camp *see* German Youth Labour Service
Lancaster, Osbert 238
Lang, John 27-8
Lansbury, George 253
Laski, Harold 122, 149
Laval, Pierre 174
Lawence, Frieda 112-13
Lawrence D.H. 29, 112, 113
Layton, Sir Walter 159, 162-3, 178, 179, 279
Lazareff, Pierre 263-4
Lean, Tangye 177
Lehmann, John 272
Lenin, Vladmir 42, 45-6, 50
Leningrad *see* Russia
Leopold, Archduke 260
Levin, Bernard 282
Lindbergh baby 241
Lindbergh, Charles 39
Lindemann, Prof. 38
Lins, Mrs 78, 79-80
Lister, Enrique 207
Lloyd George, David 162
Loftus, Colonel 158
London 33-6
Lothian, Lord 148, 156
Low, David 149, 173-4
Lynd, Robert 177

MacDonald, Ramsay 52
MacGregor clan 74-5

MacGregor, Duncan 16-18, 23, 88
MacGregor, Mary (GC's mother) *see* Cox, Mary
Mackay, Ian 177, 179
Mackay, Jessie 20
Mackenzie, Robert 166-9, 179-80
McNamara, Robert 114
Madrid 197, 199-201 *see also* Spanish Civil War
Mallalieu, J.P.W. 238
Malraux, André 195
Mandela, Nelson 43
Mansfield, Katherine 15, 34, 96, 268
Mao Tse Tung 115
March, Juan 225
Martin, Jean 265-6
Martin, Kingsley 92, 97, 149
Messines Ridge 22, 73
Miaja, José 215, 217
Millar, Geoge 264
Milner, Lucy 238
Minns, Percy 27
Mitford, Jessica 226
Mitford, Unity 273
Mola, General 197, 214
Montagu, Ivor 227
Moorehead, Alan 238, 264
Morrell, Bill 261, 270, 273
Morison, Stanley 237-8
Moscow *see* Russia
Mosley, Sir Oswald 28, 109-16, 120, 182, 194, 273
Muggeridge, Malcolm 150-1
Mulgan, John 12, 115, 157, 159, 277
Murray, Gilbert 120
Murrow, Edward R. 189, 268
Murry, J. Middleton 96
Mussolini, Benito 112, 171, 174, 175, 194, 197, 226, 246, 255, 257

Nash, Walter 277-8
Nathan, George 218
Needham, Joseph 149
Neill, A.S. 77-83, 88, 99, 131
New Zealand Army: 2 NZ Division 116, 187, 266, 277, 278; Fifth Brigade 20, 276, 277; 23 Battalion 276; Maori Battalion 138
News Chronicle 156-7, 159, 161-9 *passim*, 171-80 *passim*, 181-4, 190-1, 197, 198-201, 203, 205, 214, 219, 228, 233, 235, 237, 251, 278-81
Nicholas II, Czar 47

Ongaroto (Waikato farm) 11-14, 22, 23, 41, 93
Oppen, Baron von 127
Otago Witness 21
Ovenden, Bert 227
Owen, Frank 239
Oxford 38-40, 87-94; 95-7, 109-16, 117-26, 127, 148-9, 153; university clubs 96-7, 112-13, 117-18, 148

Pakenham, Frank 39
Panton, Selkirk 241
Papen, Franz von 65, 72, 245, 246, 271
Paris *see* France
Paul, Prince 256
Pettifer, Julian 282
Philby, Kim 128
Phillips, Morgan 182
Price, G. Ward 161, 274
Prouvost, Jean 263

Raynor, John 238
Read, Ronnie 152
Reed, Douglas 249-51
Rees, Goronwy 90
Riefenstahl, Leni 140, 141
Reimer, Charlotte 131-3, 151
Rendel, Jane 43
Renn, Ludwig 218, 226
Rhineland 187, 193
Rhodes, Cecil 12, 89
Ribbentrop, Joachim von 191, 200
Richtofen, Colonel 226
Roberts, Fifi 235
Robertson, Donald 264
Roehm, Ernst 130, 245
Rojo, Col. Vicente 217
Rokossovsky, Colonel 207
Romilly, Esmond 226-7, 228, 273
Romilly, Giles 226, 227-8
Roosevelt, Franklin 92, 109
Rothermere, Lord 182, 194
Russia 41-63, 149, 234; mid-30s attitudes to 148-51; treament of kulaks 56-8, 59, 150; Camel (state farm) 58-9; Kiev 60; Leningrad 44-8, 60-1, 62; Moscow 49-54; Nizhni Novgorod 55-6; Rostov 58, 60; Stalingrad 58, 62; Cold War 278-9, 281-3

Sagan, Leontine 114
Salter, Sir Arthur 122
Sargeant, Sir Patrick 177
Scherbatoff, Mara 264

Schirach, Baldur 141
Schleicher, Kurt von 72, 128, 245
Schuschnigg, Kurt von 252, 253, 265, 267
Scott, C.P. 183
Seagrue, John 251-2
Seddon, Richard John 17, 23
Sendall, Wilfred 191
Sevareid, Eric 267, 268
Shaw, G.B. 149
Sheffield, Emily (GC's great-grandmother) 15
Simons, Sir John 97
Small, Alan 169
Southland Boys High School 18-19
Soviet Union *see* Russia
Spanish Civil War 182, 188, 193-5, 197-201, 203-10, 211-16, 217-19, 221-9, 257, 261; Guernica 235
Sperle, General von 226
Stalin, Josef 50, 149, 186, 187, 218
Starhemberg, Prince 105, 106
Steinbeck, John 61
Stekel, Dr Wilhelm 99, 102-5
Stephenson, Ralph 27
Stern, Lazar *see* Kleber, Emilio
Stonehaven, Lord 121-2
Stout, Robert 17
Strachey, John 149
Strathclyde, Lord 152
Streicher, Julius 140
Summerhill 77-83, 123
Sutton, Charles 235, 241, 264, 267, 235, 270

Tabouis, Genevieve 198-90
Thatcher, Margaret 280
Thompson, Edmund 30
Trollope, Anthony 17-18
Tukhachevsky, M.N. 186-7
Turner, Cecily *see* Cox, Cecily

Ulbricht, Walter 218

Vallance, Alymer 156-7, 163, 165, 177-9, 184
Varela, General 197, 217, 219, 222
Vicky (Victor Weisz) 184
Vienna 99-108, 245-8; riot 105-6; socialist 99, 100-2, 128, 193
Vietnam 282-3
von Bose 245

Walker, Patrick Gordon 39
Watene (Maori chief) 13-14
Weaver, Denis 203, 213, 233
Webb, Beatrice 17, 149
Webb, Sidney 17, 97, 149
Weimar Republic 67-8, 71-2, 105, 112
Wells, H.G. 96, 223
Whitaker, John 267
Wilhelm II, Kaiser 47, 67, 102
Wilkie, Sir David 15
Williams, Sir Edgar (Bill) 115-16
Wilson, Sir Arnold 151-2
Windsor, Duke of *see* Edward VIII
Winterton, Paul 191
Wood, Alan 238
Wyatt, Woodrow 92, 283

Yindrich, Jan 205
Ypres 73, 74

Zalka, Mata 218
Zimmern, Prof. 119-20